The Political Economy of Emerging Markets

Rapid and sustained growth in the twenty-first-century global economy of large developing economies including Brazil, Russia, India, China, and South Africa, has captivated policy-makers and popular business press pundits alike. The coining of the new acronym BRICS and widespread adoption in international economics discourse of the designation "emerging markets" is symptomatic of that interest.

The Political Economy of Emerging Markets situates the BRICS phenomena in the global economic context of advanced economies continuing to languish in recession and hovering over a deflationary abyss several years after the meltdown. A key question this volume seeks to answer is whether the BRICS and so-called "emerging market" phenomenon is really the new miracle it is presented as, offering new or modified varieties of reloaded capitalist development to the world, or yet another mirage. Written by ten leading global experts, this book answers the tough questions over BRICS and emerging markets potentially realizing new varieties of reloaded capitalism. It is not only international and interdisciplinary but uniquely multiperspectival. Theories framing chapters are not of one genre, but generate theoretical debate at the frontier of knowledge in political economy along with nuanced empirical analysis which flows from it.

This book is of great importance to those who study political economy, development economics and international political economy.

Richard Westra is Designated Professor in the Graduate School of Law, Nagoya University, Japan. He is author or editor of 14 books. His work has been published in numerous international peer reviewed journals.

Routledge Frontiers of Political Economy

For a full list of titles in this series please visit www.routledge.com/books/series/SE0345

217. Creative Research in Economics
Arnold Wentzel

218. The Economic Ideas of Marx's Capital
Steps towards post-Keynesian economics
Ludo Cuyvers

219. A New Economics for Modern Dynamic Economies
Innovation, uncertainty and entrepreneurship
Angelo Fusari

220. Income Distribution and Environmental Sustainability
A Sraffian approach
Robin Hahnel

221. The Creation of Wealth and Poverty
Means and ways
Hassan Bougrine

222. Labour Managed Firms and Post-Capitalism
Bruno Jossa

223. New Financial Ethics
A Normative Approach
Aloy Soppe

224. The Political Economy of Trade Finance
Export Credit Agencies, the Paris Club and the IMF
Pamela Blackmon

225. The Global Free Trade Error
The Infeasibility of Ricardo's Comparative Advantage Theory
Rom Baiman

226. Inequality in Financial Capitalism
Pasquale Tridico

227. The Political Economy of Emerging Markets
Varieties of BRICS in the Age of Global Crises and Austerity
Edited by Richard Westra

The Political Economy of Emerging Markets

Varieties of BRICS in the Age of Global Crises and Austerity

Edited by Richard Westra

Routledge
Taylor & Francis Group
LONDON AND NEW YORK

First published 2017 by Routledge

2 Park Square, Milton Park, Abingdon, Oxfordshire OX14 4RN
52 Vanderbilt Avenue, New York, NY 10017

Routledge is an imprint of the Taylor & Francis Group, an informa business

First issued in paperback 2019

British Library Cataloguing in Publication Data
A catalogue record for this book is available from the British Library

Library of Congress Cataloging in Publication Data
A catalog record for this book has been requested

ISBN: 978-1-138-12122-5 (hbk)
ISBN: 978-0-367-25100-0 (pbk)

Typeset in Times New Roman
by HWA Text and Data Management, London

Contents

Figures

Tables

Contributors

Patrick Bond is Professor of Political Economy at the University of the Witwatersrand in Johannesburg, South Africa. His books include *Elite Transition* (3rd edn, 2014), *Politics of Climate Justice* (2012), *Talk Left, Walk Right* (2006), *Against Global Apartheid* (2003) and *Uneven Development* (1998). His (1993) PhD at Johns Hopkins University was supervised by David Harvey, following which he worked as a policy drafter in the South African government, including the president's office. From 2004–16 he directed the Centre for Civil Society at the University of KwaZulu-Natal in Durban.

Toby Carroll is Associate Professor in the Department of Asian and International Studies at City University of Hong Kong. His research concentrates on the political economy of development, with a particular geographical focus upon Asia. Toby has published in journals such as *Journal of Contemporary Asia, Globalizations, Development and Change, Pacific Review, Asian Studies Review* and *Antipode*. He is the author of *Delusions of Development: the World Bank and the post-Washington Consensus in Southeast Asia* (Palgrave 2010) and is co-editor (with Darryl Jarvis) of *The Politics of Marketising Asia* (Palgrave 2014), *Financialisation and Development in Asia* (Routledge 2015) and *Markets and Development in Asia: Citizens, Civil Society and the Politics of Neoliberalism* (Routledge 2016). He co-edits the Palgrave book series, *Studies in the Political Economy of Public Policy* and is a co-editor of *Journal of Contemporary Asia* and a thematic editor for *Asian Studies Review*.

Radhika Desai is Professor at the Department of Political Studies, University of Manitoba, Winnipeg, Canada. She is the author of *Geopolitical Economy: After US Hegemony, Globalization and Empire* (2013), *Slouching Towards Ayodhya: From Congress to Hindutva in Indian Politics* (2nd rev. edn, 2004) and *Intellectuals and Socialism: 'Social Democrats' and the Labour Party* (1994), a *New Statesman and Society* Book of the Month, and editor of *Revitalizing Marxist Theory for Today's Capitalism* (2010) and *Developmental and Cultural Nationalisms* (2009). She is also the author of numerous articles in *Economic and Political Weekly, New Left Review, Third World Quarterly* and other journals and in edited collections on parties, political economy, culture and nationalism. She is now writing on another book, *The Making of the Indian Capitalist Class* and editing a two-part special issue of *Research in Political Economy* on Geopolitical Economy as a new approach to the study of the capitalist world order. She co-edits the Future of Capitalism book series at Pluto Press with Alan Freeman and serves on the Editorial Boards of *Canadian Political Science Review*, *Critique of Political Economy*, *E-Social Sciences*, *Pacific Affairs*, *Global Faultlines*, *Research in Political Economy*, the *World Review of Political Economy* and *International Critical Thought*.

Angela Joya is Assistant Professor of Global Political Economy in International Studies at the University of Oregon. Her research focuses on the impact of economic globalization on the Middle East and North Africa with a particular focus on Egypt and Syria. She is the author of several articles in journals such as: *Review of African Political Economy*, *Research in Political Economy*, and *Middle Eastern Studies*. She has contributed chapters to *Empire's Ally: Canada and the War in Afghanistan* (edited by Jerome Klassen and Greg Albo, University of Toronto Press, 2013) and *Confronting Global Neoliberalism: Third World Resistance and Development Strategies* (edited by Richard Westra, Clarity Press, 2010). She is currently preparing a book manuscript tentatively titled *The Political Economy of Egypt under Mubarak: Accumulation by Dispossession and Land Relations, 1991–2010*. In other research, Dr. Joya is examining the role of Islamist opposition parties and their struggle for power in Egypt and Syria. She has conducted fieldwork research in Egypt, Palestine, Jordan and Turkey.

Minqi Li studied in Beijing University between 1987 and 1990 and participated in the 1989 student democratic movement. Between 1990 and 1992 he was a political prisoner. He received PhD in economics from University of Massachusetts Amherst in 2002. He taught political science at York University, Canada from 2003 to 2006 and since July 2006 he has taught economics at University of Utah. His recent books include *The Rise of China and the Demise of the Capitalist World Economy* (Pluto Press / Monthly Review Press, 2009) and *Peak Oil, Climate Change, and the Limits to China's Economic Growth* (Routledge, 2014). His new book *China and the 21st Century Crisis* will be published by Pluto Press in 2015.

Yonca Özdemir is an Assistant Professor at the Political Science and International Relations Program of the Middle East Technical University, Northern Cyprus Campus. She specializes in international political economy and comparative political economy. Her research examines politics of economic reform, role of the IMF and Washington Consensus, financial liberalization and instability, economic globalization, and the causes and effects of the economic crises. Her works include both cross-national studies and also comparative case studies of Turkey and some Latin American countries. She has had works published in *Middle Eastern Studies* and *Revista Brasileira de Política Internacional*, as well as some Turkish publications.

Paul Cooney Seisdedos is a political economist, who received his PhD. from the New School for Social Research in 1990, after obtaining his MS in Chemical Engineering from the State University of Buffalo in 1982. From 2006–2014 he was an associate professor at the *Universidade Federal do Pará* in the Brazilian Amazon. Since 2014 he has been professor at the *Universidad Nacional de General Sarmiento* in Buenos Aires, Argentina. He is currently writing a book comparing the processes of deindustrialization and reprimarization in Argentina and Brazil during recent decades. Other areas of his research include the current world crisis, neoliberal globalization in Latin America, and environmental impacts of reprimarization. In addition to being a member of the URPE Steering Committee and its current Treasurer, he is also on the editorial board of the following journals: *Research in Political Economy, Capitalism, Nature, Socialism,* and *Revista Ensayos de Economía.*

Sompong Sirisoponsilp is Associate Professor at the School of Agricultural Resources, Chulalongkorn University, Thailand. He was formerly a member of the Faculty of Engineering for more than 20 years and served as the Director of the Transportation Institute for eight years. His specialization is in the areas of logistics and supply chain management, transportation planning, and transportation engineering.

Ake Tangsupvattana is Dean of the Faculty of Political Science, Chulalongkorn University, Bangkok, Thailand. He received his PhD in Sociology from the University of Essex, UK. He was a Research Fellow at Nagoya University, Japan, and a Research Associate at Singapore Institute of International Affairs (SIIA). Among his publications are: "Driving the Juggernaut: From Economic Crisis to Global Governance in Pacific Asia" in Simon S.C. Tay, ed.,_*Pacific Asia 2022: Sketching Futures of a Region* Tokyo: Japan Center for International Exchange (JCIE) and the Brookings Institute 2005; "Thailand Election 2005: Authoritarian Populism or Participatory Democratic Governance" in Simon Tay and Yeo Lay Hwee, eds., *Elections in Asia: Making Democracy Work?*, Singapore: Marshal Cavendish, 2006; with Ora-orn Poocharoen, "National Integrity Systems: Transparency International Country Study Report – Thailand 2006", funded by Transparency International (see on-line publication at http://www.transparency.org/news_room/in_ focus/ 2007/nis_in_ east_ and_southeast_asia) 2007; "Consequences of Neoliberal Globalization in Thailand', in Richard Westra, ed., *Confronting Global Neoliberalism: Third World Resistance and Development Strategies*, Clarity Press, 2010; with Rob Stones "Social Theory, Current Affairs, and Thailand's Political Turmoil: Seeing beyond Reds vs. Yellows", *Journal of Political Power*, 5, 2, 2012.

Richard Westra is Designated Professor in the Graduate School of Law, Nagoya University, Japan. He is author or editor of 14 books. Among his most recent single-authored books are *Unleashing Usury: How Finance Opened the Door* *to Capitalism Then Swallowed It Whole* (Clarity Press, 2016) and *Exit from Globalization* (Routledge, 2014). His work has been published in numerous international peer reviewed journals. He is co-editor of *Journal of Contemporary Asia.* He received his PhD from Queen's University, Canada in 2001.

Preface and acknowledgements

This volume is number two in a three-volume set. The conceptual starting point of its predecessor – *The Future of Capitalism After the Financial Crisis: The Varieties of Capitalism Debate in the Age of Austerity*, published in Routledge Frontiers of Political Economy series in 2015 – was the "Varieties of Capitalism" debate which evolved from the 1990s in critical political economy and heterodox economics circles. The book situated that debate in the context of the post 2008–2009 global meltdown period which saw all advanced economy "varieties" mired in austerity and stagnation. It questioned whether persisting austerity and stagnating growth meant capitalist economies of whatever variety were becoming endangered species lurching toward extinction.

The starting point of the current volume is the rapid and sustained growth rates experienced in the early years of the twenty-first century by a group of potential global economic contenders including Brazil, Russia, India, certainly China, and South Africa. So captivated were policy-makers and business press pundits by the growth trend of these economies that the acronym BRICS bestowed upon them was soon widely adopted across international economics and development discourse. This volume situates the BRICS phenomenon in the global economic context of advanced economies continuing to languish in recession and hovering over a deflationary abyss several years after the meltdown. A key question the present volume seeks to answer is whether the BRICS and so-called "emerging market" phenomenon is really the new miracle it is presented as, offering new or modified varieties of reloaded capitalist development to the world, or yet another mirage.

Power, originality and scope of this volume derives from its recruiting ten leading global experts, writing from eight countries around the world, to answer the tough questions over BRICS and emerging markets potentially realizing new varieties of reloaded capitalism. Contributors to the book have not only mastered the empirics of regions and cases they write on but have each made significant, original advances in theorizing the global political economy. Therefore the chapters treating individual/groups of BRICS/emerging markets are rigorously theory informed and not simple "case studies". In this regard, the volume is not only international and interdisciplinary but uniquely multiperspectival. Theories framing chapters are not of one genre as is often the case with edited volumes.

Rather, the book generates theoretical debate at the frontier of knowledge in political economy along with nuanced empirical analysis which flows from it.

As editor of this volume I very much wish to acknowledge the support and efforts of Andy Humphries, Senior Editor of Economics and Finance at Routledge in bringing this book, as well as its predecessor, to press. His superintending of Routledge Frontiers of Political Economy series has made it the top political economy peer-reviewed, research and theory development book publishing outlet in the world. I would also like to thank the contributors to this volume for placing their cutting edge work in it. Readers will quickly see that the writing contained in this book is at least at the high level of quality and sophistication that is found in the world's top academic journals in the field of political economy.

Richard Westra
Nagoya, Japan
September 2016

Part I

Development theory from capital to capitalist development and the twenty-first-century global economy in crisis

1 From development to BRICS

The policy magical mystery tour

Richard Westra

It is certainly instructive that the coining of the acronym BRICs, referring initially to Brazil, Russia, India and China, as emblematic of the purported twenty-first-century wave of "emerging market" economies, would spring from the research department of an investment bank – Goldman Sachs, no less (O'Neill 2001). The prediction that the mantle of "development" was being newly donned by a group of countries from the erstwhile Third World captivated not only the investment community but politicians and pundits around the globe. BRICs, soon to become BRICS with South Africa added in, was being marketed as a capitalist investment nirvana where the sweeping world economic prosperity, initially promised by architects of the "free world" in the aftermath of World War II (WWII), was on the cusp of consummation (Wilson and Purushothaman 2003). However, from the perspective of this introductory chapter to a book collection on the emerging market phenomenon, there exists in the BRICS story a massive dose of déjà-vu.

To make its argument, the chapter procedure is as follows. First, the very question and meaning of *development* will be interrogated. After all, in its most basic dictionary level definition, development implies movement or change from one state or condition to another. Further, development as such necessarily calls forth some metric for assessing both the kind of change that is expected and whether it is realized in the particular state or condition that is arrived at; or, at least, that is taking imminent shape on the horizon. It is argued that in the world economic context in which the concept of development is used, as a term set out to capture a specific type of economic change, producing a metric for assessing change requires the problematization of capitalism. Problematizing capitalism, in turn, demands that we take up questions of capitalism and its development raised by Marx in *Capital* and the field of Marxian political economy which is constructed around that work.

Second, related to questions of economic change and the metric for adequately measuring such is the question of potential human "actions" that purportedly bring development about. Development, from roughly the period following WWII, in an academic field of that name, has been largely treated in terms of "policies" and the sort of agency to best operationalize these (Currie-Adler 2016). Yet, it is argued that to the extent such development "policy" analysis proceeds in the absence of the critical understanding of capitalism and grasp of the current global political economy presented here, it is destined to offer little more than an exercise in bourgeois ideological enchantment.

As captured in this chapter, mainstream conceptualization of development, which predominates in major academic institutions and intergovernmental organizations, guiding the "practitioners" of development, has remained rooted in neoclassical economics theorizing of "the market" as the ultimate "rational" means for organizing human material life. From the 1950s "formalist revolution", however, neoclassical economics has modeled "the market" less in terms of "really existing" economies and more in rarefied terms of high calculus as a "virtual economy" (Blaug 2003, 147–148). Leaps are then made from such "virtual" market economic models into the rough and tumble capitalist world with little account made for capitalist diversity, the historical transmutations of capitalism across its world historic phases of development or the perverse current structure of accumulation in major economies.

What Marxian political economy spotlights, as we shall see, is the irony that the whole development project came into being carrying with it all the confidence of "formalist" neoclassical economics at an historical point where the economies it upheld as embodying the particular condition advanced as "developed" operated at the greatest distance in capitalist history from "pure" market principles modeled in neoclassical theory. Such dissonance has plagued development thinking from its inception and continues to play out to this day in so-called emerging market and BRICS discourse.

Capital and the development of capitalism

Notions of development as applied to human society are rooted in Enlightenment thinking about progress. Progress, in turn, as maintained by Gilbert Rist, was given a naturalist gloss, as the necessary, indubitable, "order of things", by the late eighteenth century. This was topped off by social evolutionism in the nineteenth century which read into development social law driven change akin to that experienced by biological organisms (Rist 2014, 37ff.). Finally, naturalist renderings of both human progress and social evolution which factored into the defining of development were displaced onto capitalism and capitalist "growth". Rist advances a definition of development that he sees as best capturing the foregoing, and which renders development a condition that all humanity across the world may be perceived as being driven toward (Rist 2014, 13):

> 'Development' consists of a set of practices, sometimes appearing to conflict with one another, which require – for the reproduction of society – the general transformation and destruction of the natural environment and of social relations. Its aim is to increase the production of commodities (goods and services) geared, by way of exchange, to effective demand.

For Rist, the belief that development in the foregoing vein would become universal rather than something which select parts of the world exemplify was imbibed with religious fervor by academics and practitioners alike within the fields feeding into development thinking. So mesmerizing is the belief, Rist declares, that "more than sixty years after the international community officially set its sights on extending 'development'...this has still not come to pass". Yet, thinkers and practitioners routinely inculcated with all the accepted development incantations soldier on notwithstanding the abject failures of the total enterprise (Rist 2014, 23).

Though it is clear that in attempting to define development Rist has capitalism in mind as the central conditioning factor of development, the components of his definition do not adequately reflect the historical specificity of capitalism in a way that allows us to properly navigate the impact of the development of capitalism upon modern history. In dealing with the historical specificity of capitalism the most important point to be made is that it is not possible to define capital or capitalism is any simple fashion. Marx, who devoted his life to the study of capital, never attempted such. Rather, in his major economic writing, *Capital*, Marx theorized *capital* as the deep inner logical structuring mechanism operating in all capitalist societies. In this fashion Marx produced a "synthetic" definition of capital across the three volumes of *Capital* as a "totality" of logically interconnected commodity economic categories (Westra 2009, 19–42).

Let us explore the ramifications of Marx's theorizing of capital for development thinking through the prism of Rist's definition of development. It should be noted at the outset of this exercise that from Marx's "defining" of capital in terms of its deep, inner logical categories, it is only possible to sketch out the most general features of capitalism. These are features which hold across time and space in that all capitalist societies will manifest such. What follows is hardly intended to be exhaustive or a substitute for either Marx's synthetic definition or even a summary of propensities of capital in general. Nevertheless, for purposes of this chapter, these features serve to distinguish capitalism as an historical society from other "kinds" of historical societies and foreground later discussion.

First, while classical economists, followed by neoclassical economics, approached capitalism as a natural order, Marx saw this as the centerpiece of ruling class ideology of conformism. Capitalism, for Marx, as all human societies is socially and historically constituted and like all human societies is historically delimited and destined to pass from history as the material conditions of its existence are outpaced by historical change.

Second, capital operates to reproduce the material lives of human beings in capitalist societies but it does this only as a *byproduct* of its fundamental chrematistic of value augmentation or profit making. Put differently, production of goods in capitalist economies does not occur primarily to meet consumption (even conceptualized as monetary or "effective" demand) but for profit measured in terms of accumulated abstract mercantile wealth. Both classical and neoclassical theories begin with consumption or the "consumer". Consumption, however, is a transhistorical category and constitutes part of every existing human society. Marx, on the other hand, well understood that to produce knowledge of capitalism theory necessarily had to start with its most fundamental activity. That is, value augmentation or profit making. Marx's economic theory therefore starts with the "seller" or capitalist. Even in the simple act of "exchange" in capitalist society Marx shows that the seller only brings a good to market because they are not interested in its concrete, useful qualities as an object of consumption. This *indifference* to concrete, qualitative characteristics of goods, which distinguishes capital from precapitalist economies where community use (within the context of their social class relations) was the paramount consideration in production and distribution, pervades capitalism at every turn.

Marx treats the cardinal issue here with his elaboration upon the most fundamental contradiction of capital – that between *value* and *use value*. Succinctly put, use value is the substantive foundation of human material reproduction. No human society could survive without the metabolic interchange between human beings and nature through which the labor and production process furnishes the useful goods necessary for human material reproduction. Value, on the other hand, is the historically specific abstract, homogenizing, quantitative principle of capital. Looking back at our initial point on the historical delimitation of capitalism, it is precisely this: the existence of capitalist societies in human history is predicated upon the amenability of use value life to management according to the dictates of value augmentation. Capitalist economies thus arise in human history at the point where human wants and technologies available to satisfy them turn upon a relatively narrow range of standardized mass produced material goods. Production of such material goods lends itself to the suppression of qualitative, heterogeneous considerations in reproduction of human economic life in favor of abstract, homogenizing, quantitative ones. Of course, to state that a constellation of use values and forms of use value production are amenable to value augmentation does not mean that they offer no resistance to value or do not generate contradictions for capital. It is simply the case that capital is able to temporarily surmount the contradictions posed by particular forms of use value production in its chrematistic of value augmentation, at points deploying extra-capitalist practices and considerable extra-capitalist support, such as that of the state, to do so.

Third, it is through the grasp of the most fundamental contradiction of capital – that between value and use value – that the antithesis to nature, the environment and biosphere manifested by capital is best exposed. In the broadest sense, use value embodies not only the useful goods human beings refashion nature to produce, but nature itself in all its concrete, sensuous, qualitative terrestrial, geospatial and biospheric heterogeneity. Yet, as alluded to above, the wielding of human material life by capital for its quantitative, homogenizing social goal of augmenting abstract mercantile wealth renders it indifferent to all the foregoing except to the extent capital seeks to neutralize obstacles the sensuous, qualitative heterogeneity of nature might pose for profit making. It is this indifference to use value at the heart of capital which sees it regularly produce the most noxious goods (for nature and human beings) as vehicles of value augmentation. Ultimately, as capitalist production centered societies spread their tentacles across the globe, the technologies, production systems and energy sources which power capital in service of abstract, value augmentation wreak such murderous devastation upon nature and the biosphere as to call into question human existence itself.

Fourth, in the process of capitalist development the integrated self-regulating market operations of capital tend to destroy precapitalist interpersonal social relations of production. Capital, as Marx famously put it converts these into reified "relations among things". Market participants communicate through abstract, quantitative price signals attached to the "things" or commodities they impersonally buy or sell. But the emergence of capitalism and its extirpating of precapitalist social relations is never a fait accompli. That capital spawned initially only in select parts of the globe manifesting precapitalist social relations of a discrete kind is testament to its "alien" character vis-à-vis the socio-material conditions of the world's diverse humanity antedating it. Indeed, the "parcelization" of ruling social class power within "feudal" property relations provided the necessary "spaces" in precapitalist Britain, Western Europe and Japan for new bourgeois social class relations to germinate (Anderson 1979). It was on the basis of these that, in the case of Britain principally though in Western Europe as well, advances in navigational techniques, naval and war technology, and expansion of colonial commerce undergirded by the foregoing, concatenated to ensure the agglomerating of wealth destined for capital accumulation and spur the production centered activities of industrial revolution which cemented the capitalist era.

Without becoming ensnared in arcane debate swirling around transitions to capitalism, the "destruction" of social relations which led to successful crystallizing of capitalist social relations of production had two paradigmatic elements that have been reproduced in all societies where capitalism fully developed, including in the latest late twentieth-century capitalist developers (Kay 2002). One is the removal through either cooptation or forcible elimination of precapitalist landed classes leading to the constitution of private property and owner operated agriculture in land. Two, which followed upon the heels of this, is the massive release of surplus populations from agriculture in tandem with rapid growth of industry. Only with sustained productivity rises made by owner operated market oriented farming was mass commodification of labor power made possible. Food costs had necessarily to be kept low to check industrial wages during the nascent period of capitalist industrialization. Resultant profit fed capital accumulation which sustained the virtuous circle of industrialization and capitalist development even as wages ultimately began to rise with absorption of populations jettisoned from agriculture.

The sine qua non of the capitalist era is, therefore, the conversion of human labor power into a commodity. Through its commodification, labor power is rendered indifferent to the production of specific goods. Rather, capital purchases labor power on the market and sets it in motion in producing *any* good according to changing patterns of demand and opportunities for profit making. Looked at from another angle, all factors of production contribute to production of use values. But the historical possibility of capitalism is predicated upon a factor with the dual property of being use value and *value* productive. Commodified labor power is the only factor of production which lends itself to simultaneous application in a concrete specific fashion (as furnishing concrete use values of human sustenance necessarily remains the byproduct of value augmentation) and in an abstract general way (producing *any* good for capital) in the service of augmenting abstract mercantile wealth. Therefore, that the condition for labor power to be value augmenting is the same as that by which capital allocates social resources to reproduce human material life (as the byproduct of value augmentation) constitutes the *differentia specifica* of capitalism as an historical society (Westra 2014, 39–40).

It is reproduction of human material life by capital for its abstract, quantitative, "extra human" purpose of value augmentation that drives the accelerated "progress" of capitalist economies in expanding production of standardized material goods along with the material infrastructure of their provision. Referring back to Rist's definition of development, to "increase the production of commodities" is a capitalist goal only to the extent this fuels profit making. Yet, capitalist growth, the metric of capitalist profit making, was initially coupled with both industrialization and development as the building of production centered full-scale industrialized societies fostered growing prosperity in living and health standards.

As industrial revolution played out in Britain, the world's first definitively capitalist economy, the historical structure of capitalism as a production centered society rapidly materialized. By 1881, 44 percent of the labor force in Britain was employed in industry or occupations related to it with agriculture then employing only 13 percent of the working population. The remaining working population found employment in the service sector; particularly in varying facets of the transportation industry which directly underlabored for manufacturing and trade (Bayly 2004, 173).

Industrial revolution in Britain further set off what the best economic history to-date maintains is that global disjuncture or "great divergence" in wealth and living standards between advancing Western economies and the rest of the world (Osterhammel, 2014, 650–51). This was the case notwithstanding the expropriation and pillage Western Europe subjected the rest of the world to from the fifteenth century. Following Britain, Belgium was the second capitalist economy to experience industrial revolution. Industrial revolution then spread from the 1850s to France and later Germany, Austria and Northern Italy across the following decades. Britain, however, maintained a role as "workshop of the world" and center of international trade into the late nineteenth century, despite having only 2 percent of the world's population. This was due in part to the waves of emigration from it to the "white settler colonies" of the United States, Australia, Canada and New Zealand. Its transplantation of colonialists with common language and culture and imbued with ideologies of laissez faire government and capitalist market economy led to formation of what has been dubbed a "Lockean heartland" at the core of the increasingly integrated emergent global political economy (van der Pijl 2001, 5).

While capitalism in each of the above nation-state containers developed with its own idiosyncrasies as a relatively discrete "variety" of capitalism, the basic contours of capitalist development wherever it took hold in the nineteenth century were necessarily constant. "Follower" states blazed a similar trail as Britain with capital accumulation beginning in textile industries that were entrepreneurial and competitive (Bayly 2004, 175–176). As well, when marketization spread across nascent capitalist economies the new rhythms of material life it imposed on subsumed economies – its cyclical prosperity and crisis oscillations – were fatalistically accepted by all social classes (Gallarotti 2000). Further, during the initial period of industrial capitalism the extra-economic role of the state was also minimal, leaving economies largely managed according to abstract market principles. State activity in Britain, for example, as late as 1906, contributed a miniscule 7.5 percent of GNP (van Crevald 1999, 235). Even in France and the Netherlands, on the cusp of World War I (WWI), state expenditure as a percent of GDP remained a scant 8.9 and 8.2 percent respectively (Maddison 2001, 135).

If there ever did exist a point in capitalist history where the door for capitalist development was opened wide to the world, the nineteenth-century post industrial revolution period was it. After all, the technologies and light use value complex of mass produced textiles and other light industrial manufactures are easily governed according to the abstract commodity economic principles of value augmentation and capitalist market operations. The start-up costs of business were relatively low such that early capitalist firms were owned, financed and managed either by a single entrepreneur or family partnership. In 1838 the average British textile factory employed 137 workers, increasing in size to 171 by 1871 (Albritton 1991, 130). Rapidly generalized scientific inventions in production and steam power generation suggest that free-riding on technological innovation was rampant. And with the last vestiges of protectionism shed by 1850, interlinked global trade and the making of global transportation networks to facilitate it saw trade of early capitalist developers grow two to three times faster than their economies to ensure that by the close of the nineteenth century the share of trade in the world economy as a whole was seven or eight times greater than it had been in 1800 (Frieden 2006, 4–5).

In terms of theorizing capital Marx, of course, was procedurally correct to treat capital as an ontologically unique object of study in the social world. Mainstream economics never poses the question of the historical condition of possibility for economic theory or why economics as a field of study arises in the capitalist era. Economic historian Karl Polanyi provides what has been a widely accepted explanation in terms of the way capitalist market activities tend to "disembed" human economic life from other social practices (Polanyi 1957). However, Polanyi's metaphor of the economic "levitating" from politics, religion, ideology, culture, and so forth with which it was always enmeshed is, in terms of Marx's writing in the previous century, a rather imprecise rendering of what Marx understood as reification. That is, the economic appears "transparently" for theory to explore for the first time in human history in the age of capital because while capital is historically constituted its market operations tend to objectify the very subjects whose individual purposive actions set it in motion. It distills their actions into outcomes that no one intended but which satisfy its chrematistic of value augmentation. This is what the concept of capitalist reproduction of human material life as a byproduct of value augmentation ultimately means and why Marx referred to capitalism as an "upside down" society. In sum, why we even need economic *science* or theory in the first place is because it is *not* possible to study human economic life directly as it *only* appears "transparently" in its reified form in the capitalist era. Hence the task of economic theory as initially set out in Marx's unfinished *Capital* is threefold: to unfold all the categories of the capitalist commodity economy to show how it is possible for capital to wield economic life of a human society as a byproduct of value augmentation in the first place; to shed light on the basic constituents or "general norms" of economic life disentangled from their capitalist form to understand organization of material life in past historical societies as well how it may be organized in socialist societies of the future; and to offer a critique of bourgeois political economy and economic theories.

Marx was further methodologically correct to construct the theory of capital by tracking the very process by which capital abstracted from the concrete, qualitative, heterogeneous characteristics of use value life to wield human economic life for its abstract purpose of value augmentation. Marx generated the categories of capital by studying the way capital surmounts the contradictions posed by use value obstacles. While his theory of capital captures capital in its most fundamental abstract general incarnation, it constitutes a *materialist* theory because the process of abstraction through which it was constructed is "reality assisted" by *real* contradictions use value poses for value augmentation. In this sense, the abstractions made in *Capital* are different from subjective abstractions made by scientists as is the case with "ideal types" or "models" as deployed in mainstream economics. Rather, they are real or "objective" abstractions as even the basic act of buying and selling on the capitalist market abstracts from the qualitative heterogeneity of goods to bring the most diverse objects into relation with each other according to homogenizing, quantitative price criteria. It is in following the real (read material) processes of abstraction in the capitalist economy that disciplined thought (why the term transparent is placed in quotation marks) is able to unfold a complete set of basic economic categories of capital shorn of this or that ideological prejudice.

On the questions of the development of capitalism, at his mid-nineteenth-century historical vista Marx was further methodologically correct to theorize capital as if its inner logical tendency to "purify" material life of non-capitalist encumbrances across the globe would consummate itself as an historical fact. From his early 1848 *Communist Manifesto* through to *Capital*, Marx left numerous passages which lent credence to that view. In the *Manifesto* Marx said this about capital (Marx and Engels [1848] 2016): "All fixed, fast-frozen relations … are swept away… All that is solid melts into air…[N]ew industries…are the heavy artillery with which it batters down all Chinese walls… It compels all nations… to adopt the bourgeois mode of production". In 1867, in his Preface to the first German Edition of *Capital*, Marx sent a message to the European continent: "De te fabula narrator", which translates, roughly from Latin, "of you the tale is told" (Marx [1867] 2016). Of course, Marx also believed that working classes in the capitalist heartlands of Britain and Western Europe would be impelled by the sheer horror of this specter toward revolution long before a "pure" global capitalist economy ever materialized.

However, Marx's aforementioned statements most emphatically do *not* mean that he intended *Capital* as a genetic theory of capitalism where the development of categories purportedly follows their historical origination. The so-called "logico-historical method" attributed to Marx, which this wrongheaded view spawned, is one of the most debilitating impositions upon Marx's political economy. Indeed, Marx commences the theoretical elaboration of capital with the first fully formed really existing historical manifestation of capitalism and opens the theoretical process with the most fundamental category of capital appearing therein, the commodity, in which its central contradiction, that between value use value, is uncovered in its simplest form. Further, Marx well recognized during his lifetime that economic phenomena in actually existing capitalist history, even in Britain, the first capitalist economy, appeared with predictable distortions at the time of his writing and could not be addressed solely in terms of theoretical logic (Albritton 2007, 114–126).

In this historical context, the mixing by Marx, in *Capital*, of a theory of logical inner tendencies of capital with the structure of capital accumulation in mid-nineteenth-century Britain and empirical illustrative material on numerous facets of historical conditions in Britain and elsewhere in the world was of no great consequence. But with the great transmutations of capitalism that occurred at the close of the nineteenth century following Marx's passing, momentous consequences did arise, particularly for application of Marx's analysis of capital to theorizing capitalist development that, to the extent these were left unaddressed, would impoverish Marxian political economy and development thinking in perpetuity.

Stages of capitalism and capitalist development

As explored at length elsewhere, if there is one thing that binds together theorists of *imperialism* like V. I. Lenin and Rudolf Hilferding it is recognition that the seismic changes capitalism experienced following Marx's passing could not be adequately grasped in terms of empirical variations in the structure and trajectory of mid-nineteenth-century accumulation captured by Marx (Westra 2015). First, the very system of capital accumulation morphed from small entrepreneurial firms to giant monopoly and oligopoly companies which "concentrated" (expanded the amount of capital applied to production) and "centralized" (consolidated smaller firms in a single unit) capital. Second, the commanding heights monopoly enterprises were no longer textile firms selling to consumers but producers of steel and heavy chemicals geared toward infrastructure and transportation. Third, commanding heights businesses eschewed market outcomes where possible, preferring to set prices amongst themselves. Fourth, the financing needs of the monopoly sector outstripped the resources of single entrepreneurs and family operators leading to the generalizing of joint-stock companies and, often concurrent with this trend, the investment and management of shareholder interests by large banks. These changes dispersed ownership of capital away from entrepreneurs and family associations in a fashion that enabled the largest shareholders to control massive swaths of capital of far greater magnitude than their own capital investment. Fifth, as capital in its monopoly form eschewed market pricing it further recruited the state to deploy protectionist practices to ensure respective domestic economies remained the preserve of "national" monopolies. Russian tariffs on imported manufactures were 84 percent, for example, with the United States (US) coming in second, in this period, with tariffs of 44 percent (Frieden 2006, 65).

Fifth, monopoly capital and *its* state hatched the signature state policy of the era – imperialism. Imperialist policies of major advanced industrial states responded to the way protectionism and monopoly price fixing attenuated business cycles, blocking the "cleansing" effects in devaluations of capital the cycles brought on during crisis downturns. With giant monopolies deemed "too big to fail" economies were saddled with gluts of commodities and overaccumulation of capital. This drove imperialist states to frenetically accelerate colonial adventures to covet foreign territories which could then be sealed off from access by imperialist rivals and set up to exploit for benefit of the "home" imperialist economy. Imperialism involved the dumping of commodities such as excess steel products at fire sale prices in captured territories. It also entailed export of capital in the form of portfolio investment. Groups of expat investors from imperialist countries invested these funds in building transportation networks that both created demand for the heavy commodities produced by imperialist monopolies and rendered captive economies efficient suppliers of raw materials and foodstuffs for imperialist state businesses and consumers.

Importantly, imperialism altered the historical dynamic of capitalism. First, as per the inner logic of capital exposed in *Capital*, and as Marx captured in his analysis of the structure of mid-nineteenth-century British capitalism, marketization was increasingly purging economic life of its non-capitalist encumbrances. In social class terms, this meant that capitalist economies evinced tendencies toward the shaping of an entrepreneurial ruling capitalist class, deskilling and commodification of all labor power in industry and agriculture, and the establishment of bourgeois private property in land along with capitalist farming. Again, that nineteenth-century Britain was certainly a great distance from realizing such a "pure" capitalist economy did not detract from the fact that, for Marx, given the specific structural tendencies of accumulation, no foreseeable impediments beyond working-class revolution seemed to exist for "purifying" of capitalism in history.

Under imperialist accumulation all changed. Protectionism, monopoly price manipulation, the organization of giant monopoly combines and benefits of captive imperialist territories furnishing a welter of exotic commodities coalesced to divide the working class. A semi-skilled "aristocracy" of labor that arose during the imperialist era increasingly identified with the bourgeoisie as it displayed a life style that clearly diverged from that of the mass of deskilled labor power. Exigencies of managing giant monopolistic business systems along with the growing size and complex tasks of the state spawned a class of bureaucratic and administrative "salaried" functionaries that also identified with the bourgeoisie instead of the working class. Further, the displacing of small capitalists by monopoly businesses combined with opportunities created by generalizing of the joint-stock form of enterprise combined to engender a class of petit-bourgeois "rentiers". Last, the enlarging role of finance and bigger banks in industry generated a new capitalist fraction at the apex of the capitalist ruling class.

Second, there is room for debate over the extent to which, in the post industrial revolution world of markets and ostensibly free trade, opportunities to free ride on relatively inexpensive manufacturing technologies, low costs of business entry, entrepreneurial form of capital and so forth, colonialism in itself rather than resistant precapitalist social class systems beyond Western Europe served to retard the spread of capitalist relations of production across the globe. However, as policies of imperialism became internationally entrenched by the early twentieth century, and much of the world outside capitalist heartlands ensnared in an unwilling imperialist embrace, the possibility of the international thrust of capital "compelling all nations to adopt the bourgeois mode of production", to paraphrase Marx, was extinguished. It is not simply a question here of the exorbitant costs of entry in frontier monopoly sectors, economic protectionism, curtailed technology free-riding opportunities and military force of imperialist territorial occupation. In constructing the world's initial international interconnected transportation and communication networks, imperialist states configured global flows of capital and goods in ways that crystallized an infrastructure of predatory resource extraction, exploitation of indigenous peoples, and wholesale "extroverting" of economies the effects of which across what became the Third World persist to this day.

It is true that in sparsely populated territories of the "Lockean Heartland", where lands belonging to indigenous peoples' could easily be wiped clean of inhabitants, and among select territories in Latin America, imperialist export of capital, European emigration, building of transportation edifices, all to develop primary production for export, manifested itself in rapid capitalist economic development, urbanization, and genuine prosperity (Frieden 2006, 68–71). However, across most of the expansive soon to be Third World, imperialist and colonial policies had anything but such effects. The villains of the piece were often the settler colonialists who conspired with imperialist administrations to seize economic opportunities in land, resource and trade access from native populations, excluding the latter through both informal and formal "apartheid" like practices from what benefits imperialist global interconnections brought. As well, imperialist administrations often tended to ally themselves with local forms of rule by precapitalist classes whose power and interests were predicated upon maintaining social class relations rooted in the past but which inhibited capitalist development and germinating of capitalist social relations of production, including commodification of labor power. The modes of such inhibition were myriad, ranging from frustration of property rights maintenance to outright neglect of potential opportunities for industrialization, as occurred in China, and land practices that ensured floods of low paid laborers to work large plantation economy sectors that were often foreign owned and geared to servicing foreign markets (Frieden 2006, 87ff.).

Mainstream economics in the throes of its "marginalist" revolution, a significant mutative step on the road from classical political economy to neoclassical economics of today, was inherently impotent with respect to making any sense of imperialist transformations. On the one hand, marginalism as a discipline changed the name of its field to "economics". Economics was then hived off from classical political economy concerns over the conditions under which social wealth is produced to settle upon building a theory of market price movements based on the yoga of individual "rational" consumption choices. Questions relating to the wider social system were passed along to the new field of "sociology". The vulgar ideological intent of all this is glaringly evidenced in the fact that just as capitalist economic change was reconfiguring material life away from markets and individual entrepreneurship toward big collectivities of monopoly firms, bureaucratic states and organized labor movements, a spurious "methodological individualism" was being formalized in social thought (Albritton 1991, 199ff.). Such formalism, of course, bode ill for development thinking given the necessity for the latter to grapple with the momentous socioeconomic forces that were driving global transformations. It is precisely during the imperialist era that the sort of sterile biological, evolutionary perspectives, remarked upon by Rist, came into their own with the notion of "civilization" registering as a key trope in "humanitarian" justification of colonial practices (Rist 2014, 61–62).

Marxian political economic theorists of imperialism, as alluded to at the beginning of this section of the chapter, certainly attempted to meet head on the explanatory and theoretical challenges posed by the era's changes. The notion of a "stage" of capitalism was importantly entered into the Marxist lexicon in an effort to conceptualize nuances of imperialist capitalist development. Unfortunately, as argued at length elsewhere, given the overall state of Marxist studies the promise inhering in theorizing a stage of capitalist development was never fulfilled by theorists of imperialism (Westra 2015).

The central problem resided in the sway Second International doyen Karl Kautsky's construction of Marx's research program had on the political economic theorizing of imperialism. For Kautsky, Marxism, the name he is responsible for giving to the body of thought originating with Marx, was conceived as an overarching or master theory of historical directionality dubbed historical materialism. Its purported central claim, not too different from mainstream evolutionary sociology in Kautsky's hands, was that history is impelled forward by economic laws toward a socialist historical outcome. Kautsky is the original architect of the hackneyed "logico-historical method" which pegged Marx's *Capital* as a sub-theory of historical materialism. Rather than the genuine economic theory of inner logical categories which expose how capital wields material life of a human society as a byproduct of value augmentation, Kautsky read *Capital* (only Volume I was initially available to Kautsky when he formulated his approach) as simply an empirical verification in the capitalist context of the general economic laws driving history toward socialism.

Saddled with this problematic, and all theorists of imperialism operated with Kautsky's basic framework and assumptions about the course of history, Marx's *Capital* was essentially relegated to the position of a theory of the historical trajectory and "contradictions" of nineteenth-century capitalism (Gronow 1986).

Theorists of imperialism, notwithstanding their careful analysis of key features and accumulation tendencies of early twentieth-century capitalism, set their work to the task of attempting to explain what the signal changes in capitalism were which blocked the road preordained by historical materialism toward socialism. Strengths of the formative theorizing of imperialism then devolved from work on specifying the new "type" of capital characteristic of the major advanced economies of the era. But little work looked specifically at questions of capitalist economic development in the world beyond the capitalist heartlands.

Only in the intellectual milieu that existed in turn-of-the-century Japan, was a clear and compelling escape from the straightjacket of Kautsky's imposition upon Marxism formulated (Barshay 2007). As Japan imbibed intellectual traditions from the West during its modernization drive following Meiji tumults a concerted effort was made to place social thought on a scientific footing. In Anglo-US academies, though on the European continent as well, the positivist approach to natural scientific knowledge was quickly drafted into social science service with marginalist neoclassical economics set out as its social scientific benchmark. For the Japanese critical intellectual palate, in the early part of the twentieth century, in any case, the marginalist yoga of individual rational choice was viewed as heavily ideologically tinged. Similarly, the then increasingly hegemonic interpretation of Marxism in the West as a master theory of historical directionality forecasting a socialist historical outcome, this based predominantly on Marx's pithy historical commentary in the famous *Preface* and scattered remarks in *Capital*, Volume I, was seen as the ideological component of Marx's research agenda. On the other hand, Marx's *Capital* as a whole was apprehended as the basis of social scientific understanding of human material life.

Ultimately, the breakthrough came at the hands of University of Tokyo professor, Kozo Uno (Uno 1980; Sekine 1975). The primary task, as Uno grasped it, but which Marx, given his historical vantage point did not see as pressing, was to consummate study of the logical inner workings of capital in a self-contained theory or "totality" of immanent categories. By extrapolating the logic of capital to conclusion *Capital*, reconstructed as a theory of a purely capitalist society, would stand as a timeless, synthetic definition or referent of what capital *is* in its most fundamental incarnation. Secondarily, Uno picked up on the way *Capital* as left by Marx mixed a theory of capital's inner logic with analysis of the specific structure of mid-nineteenth-century accumulation in Britain, and empirical illustrative material on capitalist history. With the basic theory of capital consummated, Uno argued for reformulating Marxian political economy as a whole in terms of three "levels of analysis" – *Capital* reconstructed as the theory of a purely capitalist society, a "mid-range" stage theory of capitalist development, and historical empirical analysis of capitalism.

Writings of the main theorists of imperialism manifested a telling ambivalence in the proposed fashion their conceptualizing of a stage of capitalism connected to *Capital*. If one trend stands out it is the attempt to extrapolate a particular tendency or prime mover, such as the profit rate, from *Capital*. For Uno, however, the connector had to be the central contradiction of capital, that between value and use value. In elaborating the logical inner structure of capital in his *Capital*, Marx shifts between holding use value implicit (simply assuming for purposes of discussion that in a given context a use value is producible according to capitalist market principles) and referring to the light use value complex of cotton textile production central to capitalist industrialization in Britain. Indeed, Marx, here, was not far off the mark as in all capitalist history it is precisely the capitalist management of light technologies and use values typified by cotton textile production which conform most closely to the fundamental market logic of capital. Uno, then, theorized three world historic stages of capitalism predicated upon the paradigmatic form of use value production at the center of capitalist value augmentation in a stage. *Mercantilism* characterized by wool production and merchant capital was the formative stage, *liberalism* marked by cotton textiles produced by industrial capital, the second, and *imperialism* characterized by steel production and finance capital, the third. In naming stages according to the state policies which supported capital, Uno was influenced by Hilferding as he was by Hilferding's insight into how the form assumed by capital morphed from industrial to finance capital in the stage of imperialism.

Where the ultimate originality and intellectual power of Uno's approach is felt is in the way each "level" of analysis keeps its "logic" to itself such that the levels of analysis work in concert to produce complete knowledge of capitalism. The theory of a purely capitalist society captures the abstract logical interrelations among all the categories of capital. Stage theory grasps the way in which paradigmatic modes of use value production *refract* or *concretize* the abstract logic of capital in a stage specific type of capital accumulation. Stage theory is thus structural or synchronic and acts as a mediating bridge between the theory of capital's inner logic and study of capitalist history. As a level of analysis of capitalism, historical empirical analysis is diachronic and focuses upon capitalist diversity and change, the coming into being and passing of capital, and transitions between capitalist stages. Historical empirical analysis ultimately connects the study of capitalism with the study of other social forces or "histories" (patriarchy, race, etc.) impacting upon modern history as a whole (Albritton 1991).

Sadly, outside Japan, until the mid-1970s, the approach to Marxian political economy initially engineered by Kozo Uno was little known due to language barriers and thus there was no critical engagement with it among the raft of radical approaches which met the dawning of the new post World War II (WWII) capitalist era. To be sure, there was never any certainty that capitalism of some sort would emerge from the ashes of two world wars, a decade long Great Depression, and the world's first socialist revolution, but it did. Capitalism in its newest stage was in many ways unrecognizable among advanced economies, even from the perspective of imperialist capital.

First, capital accumulation congealed around a new use value complex of consumer durables with automobiles as the paradigmatic use value of the period. Second, monopoly combines of imperialism were superseded by oligopolistic transnational corporations (TNCs) which dominated not only automobile production but other commanding heights sectors such as petroleum, agricultural machinery, transportation equipment, electronics and electrical appliances. Production of consumer durables such as the automobile required coordinating the supply and distribution of thousands of standardized parts and components. TNCs integrated these along with research and design, advertising, marketing and so forth in multidivisional, multi-plant behemoths which functioned not unlike a centrally planned socialist economy. TNCs eschewed market pricing to a greater extent than imperialist monopolies. They largely "internalized" transactions for goods among their corporate divisions relying on the device of "transfer pricing" rather than markets. Even global trade became less market oriented as a result of TNC activity of internationalizing production. From the 1960s, hence, global trade was increasingly dominated by *intra-industry* and *intra-firm* flows.

Third, the state came to play a Herculean role in capital accumulation. Ubiquitous across advanced economies were the generous social wage and welfare benefits states doled out. As put by Frieden (2006, 242): "Modern societies may simply have required social democratic welfare states to survive". For post WWII capital the signature state policy was the support of ever-expanding mass consumption of consumer durables or *consumerism*, making the latter a fitting name for the stage in line with imperialism as the signal policy of its predecessor. With regard to ever-expanding mass consumption the state and capital brought mass labor movements into a tripartite "class accord". Uniquely in capitalist history labor unions were empowered to bargain with capital for significant wage and benefit packages commensurate with productivity increases. States' policy armature further included macroeconomic fiscal policy of countercyclical demand management to maintain the economy in a state of quasi boom. The idea was for government spending on a range of projects to kick in as signs of recession appeared in business cycles. Deficits would then clear during business cycle upswings.

Fourth, "national" projects of state policy making for prosperity were cocooned by the new international monetary system agreed upon by victorious WWII allies. The commodity money based gold standard was replaced within major economies by regimes of "fiat money". Internationally the Bretton Woods monetary system (BWMS) fixed exchange rates of national currencies to the US dollar which became world money. It then fixed the exchange rate of the US dollar to gold and contracted the US to exchange dollars for gold should states find themselves holding excess dollars. Currency controls on speculative capital movements were part of the cocooning as were the establishment of two new supranational macro management institutions – the international monetary fund (IMF) and World Bank (WB) – instating a modicum of political management of international economic affairs for the first time in the history of capitalism.

Instructively, the mainstream neoclassical economics profession buried its collective head deeper in the sand in the face of these changes by elevating its phantasmagoric high calculus of a virtual market, as noted at the outset of this chapter, to a status amounting to a secular religion. It is true testament to the power of "ideological state apparatuses" in modern society that such a condition could come to pass. Critical and Marxist scholarship bifurcated into two major strands. On the one hand scholarship sought to capture the sheer weight of institutional structuring of economic life, largely in advanced economies, by building theories of a new post WWII stage of capitalism. Probably the most internationally recognized theory of this genre germinated in France – the Marxist *Regulation Theory* which, in theorizing "Fordism" at a mid-range "level" as the given structure of accumulation post WWII capital assumed, came closest to the scientific advancement in Marxian political economy of the Uno approach. Where it miscarries is in failing to clarify the constituents of the "abstract" and "concrete" theory its mid-range theory purportedly mediates between and how the mid-range theory of Fordism relates to these "levels". This resurrected the problematic left unresolved by theorists of imperialism where one "level" of theory, such as that of capital's logic, ended up lording over historical analysis, for example, saddling the latter with an untenable determinism and impoverishing the whole Marxian political economic research agenda. With Fordism tending to produce a like functionalism of history as a reflex of its theorized structures the whole mid-range agenda degenerated into an institutional literature on "varieties of capitalism" shorn of the very theoretical touchstone – Marxian political economy – upon which the case can be made for the extent to which these "varieties" are even *capitalist* in the first place (Westra 2009, 55ff.).

On the other hand, and for purposes of this chapter and this book as a whole, much of the action in the development field followed a barrage of critical and Marxist scholarship which burst on the intellectual scene seeking to explain the socioeconomic condition of what had emerged as the Third World. Indeed it is precisely during the post WWII era of mass decolonization and eradicating of vestiges of direct imperialist domination that the question of development or, should we say, "underdevelopment" of a vast area of the globe was first posed. It is true, as Rist notes, that a notion of "stages of development" as a hierarchy of nations on the road to "civilization", where many a people had to be imperialistically "cajoled" up the road to development, was floated during the interwar period. But the contraposition of development as an end state and underdevelopment as the non-fulfillment of that end is a creature of the post WWII period (Rist 2014, 61, 74). There was, of course, a heady "optimism" in the air. Germany and Japan had been reconstructed through "plans" bolstered by significant financial and technological "aid" packages notwithstanding their role as war belligerents. So it was conceived that the newly liberated Third World might similarly have their development fostered by advanced states which at one time were their imperialist masters. Thus came "development practice as comprehensive and sustained efforts to improve poor places abroad: to grow their economy, reduce poverty, (re)build infrastructure, foster trade and strengthen local governance" (Currie-Adler 2016, 7).

Development practice, so the expectation was in the beginning, would be guided by development theory which, in turn, could be accessed in academic programs where career practitioners expected to be inculcated in the state of the art. The earliest salvo in development theory was fired from within US elite academia in the heat of the Cold War. It classified the end state as the modern mass consumption society and defined development as the modernization process that moved from a starting line of "backwardness" through "stages" of economic growth. "Modernization theory" held implicit all the assumptions of mainstream neoclassical economics and theories of trade based upon the position of the optimality of "the market" both in "national" and international economic intercourse allocating resources and distributing incomes. Its central policy exhortation was for the Third World to open borders and economies to global flows of goods and capital and nurture market workings at home.

The bourgeois ideological enchantment in all this soon began to hit home. With decolonization largely completed the world over and Third World elites spreading the modernization message they had received from their US "Ivy League" professors into domestic policy circles, it nevertheless became crisply clear that development characteristic of the dominant capitalist states was not occurring in the world beyond the capitalist heartland. Taking up the explanatory challenge of this condition was a new strain of radical theory. Interestingly, one theoretical trend merging into the radical critique germinated in an internal critique of mainstream economics and modernization theory. Scholars from Latin America argued from their empirical vantage point that configuring of global trade according to dictates of mainstream economic textbooks conferred advantages upon the already industrialized economies. The mainstream argument over "factor specialization", which led Latin America to specialize in raw material production for export, became a road to serfdom rather than one of economic progress. Globally, following bourgeois trade theory manifested itself in an international economic structure of wealthy "center" economies exporting industrial goods, the prices of which tended to rise, and impoverished "peripheral" economies of the Third World exporting raw materials and foodstuffs subject to falling prices, and to a process of "unequal exchange" with the center. The policy implication for this was that Third World states seek to deploy foreign investment in efforts to diversify their economies through import substitution industrialization (ISI) supported by the state.

Melding with this initial critique of modernization theory was a confluence of more radical scholarship from both Third and "First" world Marxists. TNCs that were to be recruited in foreign investment development strategies of the Third World had, to be sure, played an initial positive role in the internationalization of production characteristic of international capital in the post WWII era. Nascent foreign direct investment (FDI) entailed "tariff jumping" where TNCs captured economies of both scale and scope by building advanced technology production facilities – such as US production of automobiles in Western Europe – which satisfied domestic market demand in the countries invested in and employed local labor under similar regimes of high wage class accords as existed in their "home" markets. But by the early 1970s, under gathering storm clouds of economic crisis in the US and European Union (EU), TNCs connived to unleash a new mode of FDI which replaced components of their own domestic production in the lowest value added tasks with international production from "export platforms" in the low wage Third World. These were intended to service TNCs' own global production networks and sell in global markets. Radical theories, therefore, rightly questioned claims that TNCs might become a benign force for transferring technologies. Third World countries soon discovered sprouting industrial sectors of their economies usurped by TNCs. In resources and mining the usurpations were even more total. Further, technology transfers came at exorbitant costs. The whole ISI dream soon foundered on shoals of burgeoning debt at the precise point at which the process of substituting domestic production for imports turned from that devoted to production of light consumer goods toward capital goods and the goal of full-scale industrialization.

Noteworthy was the contribution to this radical current by economist Paul Baran. He followed up on work by theorists of imperialism to maintain that the monopoly structure of capital in its post WWII "phase" carried an inbred tendency to stagnate. To this Baran added the insight that so-called "backwardness" of the Third World followed from the international thrust of capitalist development itself. The argument built on a novel "defining" of capitalism as a "world system" with a hierarchical structure in which more developed countries exploited less developed ones by siphoning off part of what is referred to by Baran as their "economic surplus". The loss of that "surplus" then imparts to Third World states all the economic features modernization theory interpreted as backwardness. Baran's work led to formulation of one of the major enduring approaches to development studies – *world systems/dependency theories*.

Bracketing debate over variations among all the perspectives feeding into world systems/dependency theory, this much can be said about their family resemblance. First, all seek to anchor the study of development within understandings of a world systemic economic logic of capitalism which purportedly took hold in the fifteenth- and sixteenth-century spread of trade and colonialism by the advanced European "center" of the world economy. Dependency theories claim this logic not only engenders class division and significant social inequalities in "national" capitalist contexts but, in world economic interaction between advanced economies and the Third World, yields economic outcomes in the latter qualitatively different from what capitalism produces in the former. In effect, the interaction spawns a "world system" marked by glaring and persistent social division and inequality. Second, world systems/dependency theory characterize Third World capitalism in terms that reflect what they perceive as its peculiar economic orientation vis-à-vis the world economy and developed states ("dependent", "extroverted", "peripheral", "semi-peripheral" and so on). World systems/dependency theory contends this particular orientation is at the root of persisting Third World underdevelopment. Third, all dismiss outright neoclassical economics' theory of "comparative advantage" and free trade. The latter provides ideological cover for the "unequal exchange" occurring in international economic intercourse between dominant producers and exporters of industrial goods and the economies of the world based on primary production. Fourth, the policy implications of dependency theory involve some measure of "delinking" from the world economy to build an "introverted" capitalism or preferably socialism. This placed a spotlight upon the *state* – its economic or class character, international position in the world systemic scheme, and so forth – as the organized force of development policy direction.

Strengths of world systems/dependency theory reside in part in the large canvas their theories worked with in painting a picture of a world marked by glaring asymmetries. The easily understood theories with their global ranking map of countries resonated at a basic level with the lived experience of Third World populations and their educated critical elite intellectuals, as well as with a significant radical element across advanced economy campuses. Further, mainstream theories occluded the thorny question of whether international relationships between so-called sovereign states or groups of states might culminate in extremely negative development outcomes. World systems/dependency theories brought this question to the fore. It may be recalled in our earlier discussion of colonialism and imperialism that the main villains of the capitalist development piece in a world of ostensibly free trade were settler colonialists and sycophantic ruling classes of various ilk, precapitalist, "comprador", and so forth, that worked to thwart the emergence of capitalist social relations of production with their broad social wealth effects. World systems/dependency theories further showed that history matters. Though on the temporal origins of what fixity the structure of global economic intercourse of the 1970s inherited from the past they were wrong. After all, there was nothing very "systemic" about global trade even into the early nineteenth century, certainly not in the fifteenth or sixteenth (Bayly 2004, 92–94, 135). But as touched on above, the specific patterning of global transportation networks of the imperialist era along with ways various parts of the Third World were connected and the reasons for a particular connection to this or that imperialist state most definitely carried enduring, empirically traceable insidious legacies into the post WWII era.

Yet problems of world systems/dependency theories are legion. First, their attempt to "define" capitalism as a "world system" around a few simple axioms made nonsense of Marx's ontological and epistemological breakthrough's in social science and subsequent unraveling of the inner logic of capital to expose what capital is in all its cunning. Most of the economic forms world systems/dependency theory fixated on as fifteenth- and sixteenth-century (or before) indicators of capitalism – markets, trade, wages, money, profits, and so forth – existed in some measure in virtually every human society in history in the "interstices" of those worlds as Marx put it. Their existence, however, was always external to the specific principles by which these precapitalist societies reproduced their material lives. The dawn of the capitalist era is marked by the "internalizing" of all those forms which operated as "externalities" in precapitalist societies and the drawing of the forms into a unique symbiosis predicated upon the commodification of labor power such that the use value foundation of human societies was subsumed by the market principle of value. The concrete implications of this relate to the fact that through all the asymmetric wealth distributions, exploitation, purported "unequal exchanges", capitalism must organize an allocation of social resources and production of basic goods in a particular way to ensure the material reproducibility of the human society as a byproduct of value augmentation notwithstanding its ills. Only by painstakingly elaborating upon all the categories of capital in their logical immanence is it possible to define capital in a fashion that will allow us to grasp the possibility of the aforementioned and to distinguish between the capitalist and non-capitalist in the most complex humming and buzzing historical environments, an issue that emerges writ large today, as we shall see below.

Second, world systems/dependency theory appeared to obviate the foregoing by shifting the "unit of analysis" from capital and its initial substantive formation within particular nation-state containers to the "world system", yet this only compounded the problems of specification. To begin with the notion of capitalism as a "world system" elides from the outset questions of the extent to which capital is even international at this or that major historical conjuncture and the differing forms the international dimension of capital has assumed across capitalist history. Indeed, the systematization capitalism was imbued with internationally in the mid-nineteenth-century stage of liberalism derived from the international projection of the institutional structure of British capital. British law brought into being a system where the Bank of England and commercial banks connected to it were mandated to change banknotes into gold with no restrictions placed upon imports or exports of gold the price of which was then fixed in pounds. This creature of British industrial, commercial and financial interests became the foundation for over a half century of "systemic" world trade as the Bank of England, Britain's central bank, effectively emerged as the world's first central bank underwriting the seamless integration of all international, national and local monetary relations for all states tied into the global trading network of the gold standard (Westra 2016, 119–120). Each stage of capitalist development entails precisely such a projection of the paradigmatic form of "national" capital in the period, rendering it imperative that analysis move from the logic of capital to its paradigmatic structure as materialized geospatially by the dominant accumulator(s) of a period to the international dimension of capital and its historical impact, not vice versa.

Third, related to the above, scant if any cross-fertilization occurred between world systems/dependency theories and Marxist theorizations of post WWII capitalism such as Regulation Theory and its US counterpart, Social Structures of Accumulation Theory. What these latter theories captured, as alluded to above, was the way the seismic transmutation of capital in the US and other major economies of the post WWII era spawned capitalist economies supported by extensive arrays of non-economic, non-capitalist practices. The leaning of capital accumulation upon complementarities of market governing institutions was integral to capitalist management of the use value complex of automobiles and consumer durables. Capitalist economic growth in advanced economies was based upon ever-expanding mass consumption of consumer durables. All the institutional armature of extra-economic support was marshaled to realize that end. Rebuilding war torn economies in the post WWII period revolved around "national" accumulation projects of state supported capital which were cocooned by an increasingly politically organized international monetary and trading order. In fact, under the General Agreement on Tariffs and Trade (GATT), the US had slashed its tariffs for high technology imports (believing itself immune to competition on that front, much to its chagrin) as GATT offered the Third World as a whole relatively favored treatment compared to its neoliberal successor, the World Trade Organization (WTO). States in Latin America, which as a region was the part of the Third World decolonized earliest, simply lacked requisite levels of domestic capital to play in the advanced economy game (Westra 2012, 68 –69).

World systems/dependency theory never came to grips with the exigencies of capital accumulation in advanced economies during the so-called post WWII "golden age". What such investigation would have revealed is an engine of capitalist development turning upon enormous *surplus value* extracted from commodified labor power operating semiautomatic assembly line mass production technologies in consumer durable industries which fueled TNC reinvestment of profits from internal resources. It was that dynamic with its imposing state support system rather than siphoning of an "economic surplus" from the Third World which characterized capital accumulation in advanced economies during the post WWII period. For that matter "economic surplus" is a hugely imprecise and deficient concept which Marx himself never used in his analysis of capitalism. Surplus value is the valorizing of surplus labor under capital. We have to remember that profit, rent and interest constitute divisions of surplus value. TNC profit (measured as profit rate) during the "golden age" years of the capitalist stage of consumerism was extraordinarily high as were rates of investment/reinvestment and the productivity increases in commanding heights industries this all drove. As we shall see, much of what has changed in global production systems and the ways these link economies around the world at the turn of the twenty-first century reside in the peculiar re-division of surplus value in the face of which notions of "economic surplus" lay impotent.

Fourth, world systems/dependency theories had held out "delinking" from the capitalist "world system" and potential of socialist development as the policy implication of their research agenda, yet they never produced a clear model of what the new socialist model of development would look like and how it would reproduce the material lives of people in the delinked societies.

The final stage of capitalism and the disintegration of capital

Placed on the defensive by radical theories of development and the stark reality of development disappointments across the Third World, mainstream neoclassical economics in its neoliberal guise fought back in the 1980s. It did so grasping the coat-tails of a rising clutch of "tiger", newly industrializing economies (NIEs) in East Asia. In what amounted to one of its signal policy documents, the WB codified its interpretation of the NIE phenomenon and commenced the fervent peddling of the documents' policy prescriptions across the Third World (World Bank 1993). Quite simply the WB argued that at the root of East Asia's dash to the forefront of world market competition was its dedication to market economic principles. In its interrelations with the world economy this meant "getting prices right". That is, rather than the distortions in price structure purportedly fostered by ISI in the Latin American experience, East Asia allegedly commenced its development drive by exporting light consumer goods and somehow managed to "compress" a century of development from this through heavy steel industry and then automobiles and consumer durables by export oriented industrialization (EOI). To be sure, the decade of the document's publication had not even run its course when East Asia suffered a devastating financial crisis forcing WB wizards to add caveats about "good governance" and "prudential regulation" to their market story (Stiglitz and Shashid 2001). But essentially they remained unperturbed and continued to foist their neoliberal policy message onto the world.

Probing of East Asian development by Marxist and other critical scholarship, however, resulted in several revealing findings. First, the reference here to East Asia excludes the trading entrepôts' phenomenon represented by "city states" such as Singapore and Hong Kong. Neither can be upheld as general development models given how they never faced the daunting hurdle of transforming agricultural societies with a sizeable rural populace and semi-feudal ruling class into a modern capitalist society with independent farmers a proletariat jettisoned from the land, and an indigenous industrial bourgeoisie. On the other hand, from the entire Third World, South Korea (largely) and Taiwan are the only states to attain full-scale capitalist industrialization along with living standards approximating Britain and Western Europe, Japan and the "white settler colonies" of the US, Australia, Canada and New Zealand.

Second, both South Korea and Taiwan were recipients of gargantuan civilian and military aid packages. In Taiwan these amounted on a per capita basis to over three times its per capita income between 1953 and 1967. In 1946–1976, South Korea was the recipient of total aid from US taxpayers, Japan and international institutions amounting to around $600 per capita and equal to total aid received by Africa and half received by all Latin America during the same period. This booty, of course, along with similar largesse in the form of technological patents and military procurements for Japan came courtesy of US Cold War anticommunist policies (Westra 2012, 59–60). The sheer amount of funds here carried Marshall Plan like impacts for South Korea and Taiwan that, as Eichengreen puts it, "solved the catch-22 of having to export in order to pay for imports but being unable to produce for export without first importing materials and machinery" (Eichengreen 2007, 65). Nothing, to be sure, along these lines, appears in the WB policy manual.

Third, as alluded to above, just prior to their industrialization drive, both South Korea and Taiwan experienced radical land reform which eviscerated landlords as a political and economic force and redistributed land holdings to peasant farmers (Kay 2002). Fourth, the state, in the hands of disciplined authoritarian rulers dedicated to capitalist development utilized a variety of instruments from control of finance to outright ownership of key sectors to ensure capital accumulation reached its maximum impact. In South Korea an indigenous big bourgeoisie was engendered by state policy as it supported growth of capitalist "champions" among the largest corporations that would prove their worth as "tiger" companies prowling global markets. This was accomplished without repression of rural wages (the so-called scissors effect deployed by socialist states in their force march to modernity) and resulted in a rapidly evolving society of mass production and mass consumption of consumer durables as per the capitalist stage structure of consumerism/Fordism. Though all the glory in WB policy exhortations is given to export prowess the true East Asian story is more about rising domestic incomes, expanding domestic demand and mass consumption.

Fifth, the rise of East Asia in the global economy occurred at precisely that historical juncture where capital accumulation of the stage of consumerism in its initial advanced economy heartland found itself in the midst of death throes as a concatenation of market saturation, international competition, renewed class strife, faltering productivity, declining rates of investment and diminution in the profit rate sent waves of funds sloshing across the globe seeking profitable investment outlets. East Asian economies such as South Korea and Taiwan along with a supporting cast of trading entrepôts and "tiger" wannabes in South East Asia were the main beneficiaries of this initial international thrust of increasingly global footloose capital. But make no mistake about it. While South Korea and Taiwan "compressed" development from light consumer goods to automobiles and consumer durable economies to attain economic structures of the capitalist stage of consumerism the inevitable capitalist reckoning was never far off. Webber and Rigby put it thus: "As capital sought to unbind itself from constraints of labour and demand in industrial capitalist countries so it has brought additional economies into the bounds of those constraints" (Webber and Rigby 2001, 261).

Capitalism, however, never recovered from the tendencies driving the disintegration of the structure of accumulation it assumed in the stage of consumerism. Beginning in the US, yet generalizing rapidly among advanced economies, commanding heights industries disinternalized their production centered activities as manufacturing sectors which had powered whole economies were disintegrated and disarticulated across the globe. Major pieces of disintegrated and disarticulated global manufacturing were emplaced in our "tiger" economies as statistically it appeared that finally manufacturing was exploding in the Third World. Manufacturing activity, however, was endowed with a neoliberal look where its disarticulation devolved into "global value chains" (GVCs). These substantively reconfigured patterns of global trade away from trade in goods to "trade in tasks". To the extent material things do move through GVCs it is largely as intermediate goods or sub-products. The Third World experience of increased FDI in manufacturing turned upon the rising share of intermediate goods in their trade in manufactures. Such trade in manufacturing intermediaries is part and parcel of their expanded export orientation as a proportion of GDP, but had little to do with attaining full-scale industrialization (Milberg and Winkler 2013, 35–39). The lopsided export orientation of the Third World followed their subjection to the dictates of neoliberal policy exhortations foisted upon them by the WB and other neoliberal policy organs. Exhortations compelled things like currency devaluation, privatization of public enterprises, closing of government development banks, slashing wages, "deregulation" to remove impedances to global flows of funds, and so on; all leaving these economies easy TNC prey.

TNCs retained command and control power over the new fragmented production systems and GVC networks through advances in information and computer technologies (ICTs) which revolutionized global communication, coordination and logistics. Hence, a shrinking proportion of any particular good is made in a single country. TNCs morphed into "brands", largely divesting themselves of the business of making things, running factories, or maintaining pesky, and expensive, mass commodified labor forces. TNCs headquartered in advanced economies retained their "core competencies", including design, research and development (R&D), finance, marketing. However, production under TNC auspices is "outsourced" to low wage countries where much is managed by a new generation of contract suppliers.

TNC governing of international production networks of contract suppliers operates with "non-equity modes" (NEM) of control. More often than not, Third World economies host TNCs and their NEM suppliers in special economic zones (SEZs) that offer low tax environments, infrastructure subsidization and "liberalized" rules on profit repatriation. By 2006, 130 countries hosted SEZs (Milberg and Winkler 2013, 33, 42, 53). In 2010, NEM arrangements alone employed 20 million workers globally and generated $2 trillion in sales. NEM control by TNCs is responsible for 90 percent of production costs in toys and sporting goods, 80 percent of production costs in consumer electronics, 60 to 70 percent of production costs in the automotive component sector (Hart-Landsberg 2013, 18–19). Of the 100 largest TNCs in the world their global operations accounted for 60 percent of assets, 65 percent of sales and 58 percent of the employment by these TNCs. It is estimated that in 2012, GVCs under TNC suzerainty accounted for 80 percent of global trade. By 2009–2010, 51 percent of total world manufacturing exports flowed through TNC global production networks. Between 1990–1991 and 2009–2010 the share of the Third World in this "trade" grew from 18.5 percent to 47.3 percent (Hart-Landsberg 2015, 3–4).

But this brings us to the crux of the argument in this chapter and proves the utility of commencing the study of capitalist development from the ground level anchored in the theorizing of capital in its most fundamental incarnation. Commodification of labor power, as elaborated above, is the specific means by which capital manages the metabolic interchange between human beings and nature in capitalist economies. This management entails the simultaneous augmentation of value and the reproduction of human material existence in capitalist societies as its byproduct. Part and parcel of this reproduction under auspices of capital is the necessity for social resources, most importantly human labor power, to be allocated in ways that produce those goods which people in society, particularly workers, need and want while ensuring minimal chronic waste. Capitalist economies operate "optimally" in this regard when it is *direct costs* of commodified material inputs and labor power which factor into the abstract, quantitative calculus of business profit making according to market principles. And the foregoing hinges on the existence of a production centered economy the historical possibility of which is predicated upon a delimited range of standardized mass producible use values and technologies appropriate to their production.

During the capitalist stage of consumerism of the post WWII era contradictions to accumulation posed by the complex of consumer durables, particularly the key use value – the automobile – forced capital to recruit a welter of extra-economic, extra-capitalist supports to manage the labor and production process of society as a process of value augmentation. Automobiles and heavy electric goods such as refrigerators or electronic use values like the television were amenable to standardized mass production. These use values also initially brought to bear a significant proportion of direct costs into capitalist production calculus. As well, the de/semiskilled proletariat in the advanced economies constituted a proportionately large percentage of the total labor force. Feinstein shows by 1950 the average percent of working populations employed in agriculture drops to below 30 percent across 25 economies of the Organization for Economic Cooperation and Development (OECD) while that in industry rises to near 35 percent, though during the 1950s in Britain and Belgium employment in industry is 49.9 and 49 percent of working population respectively. While during the 1960s industry employment in the Netherlands and United States is at 41.1 and 36 percent respectively. By 1971 the OECD average in agriculture is just over 10 percent, industry near 40 percent (Germany comes in here at almost 50 percent) and services average around 50 percent. However, at this juncture, growth in services is closely correlated with their support for industry as per the employment profile for capital in history set by Britain in the nineteenth century. This configuration of commodified labor power infused into the advanced economies their modicum of capitalist market rationality despite the oligopoly structure of capitalist business. Yet by 1998 the employment landscape alters qualitatively with service sector employment among the OECD 25 hypertrophied at near 70 percent of total employment while industry average plummets to a level below that in 1900 and agriculture settles in around 6 percent (Feinstein 1999).

While mainstream neoclassical economists and their neoliberal acolytes were shrilly spreading the word of a reloaded *capitalist* market at the turn of the century, nothing could be further from the truth. With the production centered economy disintegrated and the manufacturing labor force eviscerated, the virtuous connection between capitalist surplus value production and meeting of general norms of economic life through maintenance of labor power as a commodity is severed. One of the most instructive indicators of the neoliberal masquerade is that after decades of its policies in advanced economies by 2014 no major OECD economy evidenced state spending as a percent of GDP below 34 percent. For the US the figure is 38 percent, Britain comes in near 44 percent and France hovering toward 60 percent (OECD 2016). Such massive state spending tends to exclude fiscal, macroeconomic policy outlays of the sort which supported the production centered edifice of TNC capital in the stage of consumerism. Moreover advanced economies currently find themselves trapped in near deflationary states and have resorted to vicious austerity measures in social spending. In short, what is clear is that it is not for want of trying but without state financed life support of such large magnitudes economies would simply collapse.

ICTs further corrupt possibilities of societies with eviscerated manufacturing employment and bloating service sector employment allocating resources according to market principles. Remember, the condition for human labor power in capitalist economies to be value augmenting is its abstract general aspect. Capital renders commodified labor power indifferent to production of particular goods. Rather, capital applies commodified labor power to production of *any* good according to shifting opportunities for profit making. The condition for human labor power to be value augmenting is therefore the same as that by which capital allocates social resources to guarantee the material economic reproducibility of capitalism as an historical society.

Services, of course, are found in every form of society in history. They even have an important place in capitalist economies. Many services are essential to operations of capitalist businesses. And services ranging from management to retail contribute to the efficiency of the capitalist circuit of value augmentation. Unlike commodified labor power, however, services are traded in the capitalist market for their *concrete specific* attributes. They do not *directly* produce surplus value. More importantly for us here, not only is a "service economy" an oxymoron in the sense that no human society could survive without a labor and production process. But no human society can allocate resources in a way that guarantees its economic "viability" on market principles with workers bound to specific tasks as is the case with services.

Prices for services are also largely set according to *subjective* criteria. The arbitrary allocation of resources in an economy attempting to deploy the market principle which follows from the impact of a swollen service sector on pricing is exacerbated by ICT. To the extent ICTs factor into remaining production centered activities they saddle material use value production with an increasing proportion of *indirect costs* and subjective determinations in pricing entailed by the latter. Indirect costs, or "intangible assets", such as ICT patents, are estimated for the US economy to account for between a third to one-half of its TNC sector. The sheer extent of indirect costs across commanding heights industries of advanced economies has proved vexing not only to TNC allocations but systems of national accounts generally (Seabrooke and Wigan 2014, 259).

Further, the evidence shows that while enormous surplus value is extracted from remaining production centered activities TNCs have disarticulated across the globe, precious little is actually reinvested as profits in the specific sense of the term (Westra 2016, 169–170). Rather, the flow of the division of surplus value is toward rent – particularly technological, design, patent rent, and so forth – and interest and dividends. In the latter regard TNC revenues derive increasingly from their transformation into arch arbitrages buying and selling their own stocks. TNCs garnering revenues in this fashion tend to be the same companies that have most extensively outsourced production and sourcing to low cost NEM and like contract suppliers (Milberg and Winkler 2013, 214ff.). The foregoing is at the root of the burgeoning inequalities now sweeping across advanced economies.

Intimations surrounding the purported shift in world economic gravity to BRICS and emerging markets are that these economies will dawn the mantle of global development as they move toward full-scale industrialization along the development sequence of advanced economies including the last capitalist developers to join the advanced economy club, South Korea and Taiwan. But this will never come to pass. In the world as a whole, including across the Third World, the shift of populations from agriculture to industry which characterized the capitalist era has come to an end. Rather, according to the International Labor Organization (ILO), from 2006 populations have been shifting directly from agriculture to services (ILO 2008). BRICS and so-called emerging markets find themselves entrapped in a peculiar economic twilight zone where, on the one hand, the diminution of peasant populations in agriculture has fed the creation of a "planet of slums" that sees urban agglomerations ringed by displaced rural dwellers who will never be absorbed into the kind of capitalist dynamic from which modern societies germinated (Davis 2007). On the other hand, populations across the Third World continue to require "footholds" in peasant subsistence agriculture to survive. They swarm in and out of slum ridden cities to meet demand from GVCs for contingent and precarious work. Labor power is not commodified as wages fall far below the product of what is required to reproduce these workers as a class. China is the poster economy for such destitute existence where over 400 million peasants or 40 percent of China's total labor force languish with no hope of ever experiencing the wealth effects of capitalism (Standing 2011, 106–107). It is the height of hypocrisy to see the WB advocate this twilight zone existence for Third World humanity as a component of "development" policy (World Bank 2008).

Remember, of the BRICS, China is the largest economy, larger in fact than that of Russia, India, Brazil and South Africa combined. Russia, as a BRIC, is a post-communist state that within the bigger scheme of global development is seen as a developed state in decline, not an "emerging" economy (Stuenkel 2015, 158). BRICS, as well, along with other so-called middle-income countries are the current global site of burgeoning inequalities *within* states. This fact vitiates development policy assumptions held to from the outset of the post WWII development enterprise that as capitalist development and growth infolded wealth effects would spread throughout society (McMichael 2012, 287–288). The perverse conclusion here is that today growth has been decoupled from development as development has been decoupled from industrialization as the foregoing had marked capitalist development from its inception. Indeed, even the meteoric growth that did occur in China, for example, did not follow upon mainstream neoclassical policy exhortations but from varied resistances to them (Westra 2017).

Finally, ICTs and the technological advancements they drive in remaining capitalist production centered activities around the world will only exacerbate the growing mismatch between the forces of production, as Marx put it and existing social production relations (Brynjolfsson and McAfee 2014). Thus humanity has reached the condition where the capitalist mode of production through which it reproduced its economic life has been outpaced by history and the rise of BRICS and emerging markets offers nothing that will turn this dire reality into a happy ending.

References

Albritton, R. 1991. *A Japanese Approach to Stages of Capitalist Development* (Basingstoke: Macmillan).

Albritton, R. 2007. *Economics Transformed: Discovering the Brilliance of Marx* (London: Pluto).

Anderson, P. 1979. *Lineages of the Absolutist State* (London: Verso).

Barshay, A. 2007. *The Social Sciences in Modern Japan: The Marxian and Modernist Traditions* (Berkeley, CA: University of California Press).

Bayly, C. A. 2004. *The Birth of the Modern World 1780–1914* (Malden, MA: Blackwell).
Blaug, M. 2003. "The Formalist Revolution of the 1950s", *Journal of the History of Economic Thought*", 25, 2: 145–156.
Brynjolfsson, E. and McAfee, A. 2014. *The Second Machine Age: Work, Progress, and Prosperity in a Time of Brilliant Technologies* (New York: W. W. Norton & Co.).
Currie-Adler, B. 2016. "The State of Development Studies: Origins, Evolution and Prospects", *Canadian Journal of Development Studies*, 37, 1.
Davis, M. 2007. *Planet of Slums* (London: Verso).
Eichengreen, B. 2007. *The European Economy since 1945: Coordinated Capitalism and Beyond* (Cambridge, MA: MIT).
Feinstein, C. 1999. "Structural Change in the Developed Countries during the Twentieth Century", *Oxford Review of Economic Policy*, 15, 4.
Frieden, J. 2006. *Global Capitalism: Its Rise and Fall in the Twentieth Century* (New York: W. W. Norton).
Gallarotti, G. M. 2000. "The Advent of the Prosperous Society: The Rise of the Guardian State and Structural Change in the World Economy", *Review of International Political Economy*, 7, 1.
Gronow, J. 1986. *On the Formation of Marxism* (Helsinki: Finnish Society of Letters).
Hart-Landsberg, M. 2013. *Capitalist Globalization: Consequences, Resistance, and Alternatives* (New York: Monthly Review).
Hart-Landsberg, M. 2015. "From the Claw to the Lion: A Critical Look at Capitalist Globalization", *Critical Asian Studies*, 47, 1.
ILO. 2008. *Global Employment Trends*. International Labor Office: Geneva.
Kay, C. 2002. "Why East Asia Overtook Latin America: Agrarian Reform, Industrialization and Development", *Third World Quarterly*, 23, 6.
Maddison, A. 2001. *The World Economy: A Millennial Perspective* (Paris: OECD).
Marx, K. 1867. *Capital* Volume I, Accessed September 21 2016, https://www.marxists.org/archive/marx/works/1867-c1/p1.htm
Marx, K. and Engels, F. 1848. *Manifesto of the Communist Party*, Accessed September 20, 2016. https://www.marxists.org/archive/marx/works/download/pdf/Manifesto.pdf
McMichael, P. 2012. *Social Change and Development: A Global Perspective* (Thousand Oaks, CA: Sage).
Milberg, W. and Winkler, D. 2013. *Outsourcing Economics: Global Value Chains in Capitalist Development* (Cambridge: Cambridge University Press).
OECD 2016. OECD Data: General Government Spending, https://data.oecd.org/gga/general-government-spending.htm, accessed September 14 2016.
O'Neill, J. 2001. "Building Better Global Economic BRICs", Global Economics.Paper No: 66, Goldman Sachs Global Economic Research, http://www.goldmansachs.com/our-thinking/archive/archive-pdfs/build-better-brics.pdf.
Osterhammel, J. 2014. *The Transformation of the World: A Global History of the Nineteenth Century* (Princeton, NJ: Princeton University Press).
Polanyi, K. 1957. *The Great Transformation* (Boston, MA: Beacon Press).
Rist, G. 2014. *The History of Development: From Western Origins to Global Faith*, 4th edition (London: Zed).
Seabrooke, L and Wigan, D. 2014. "Global Wealth Chains in the International Political Economy", *Review of International Political Economy*, 21, 1.
Sekine, T. 1975. "Uno-Riron: A Japanese Contribution to Marxian Political Economy", *Journal of Economic Literature*, 13, 3.

Standing, G. 2011. *The Precariat: The New Dangerous Class* (New York: Bloomsbury Academic).

Stiglitz, J. and Shashid, Y. (eds.) 2001. *Rethinking the East Asian Miracle* (Oxford University Press).

Stuenkel, O. 2015. *The BRICS and the Future of Global Order* (Lanham, MD: Lexington).

Uno, K. 1980. *Principles of Political Economy: Theory of a Purely Capitalist Society*, translation by T. Sekine (Sussex: Harvester).

Van Crevald, M. 1999. *The Rise and Decline of the State* (Cambridge, MA: Cambridge University Press).

Van der Pijl, K. 2001. "International Relations and Capitalist Discipline", in R. Albritton, M. Itoh, R. Westra and A. Zuege (eds.), *Phases of Capitalist Development: Booms, Crises and Globalizations* (Basingstoke: Palgrave).

Webber, M. J. and Rigby, D. L. 2001. "Growth and Change in the World Economy Since 1950", in R. Albritton, M. Itoh, R. Westra and A. Zuege (eds.), *Phases of Capitalist Development: Booms, Crises and Globalizations* (Basingstoke: Palgrave).

Westra, R. 2009. *Political Economy and Globalization* (London: Routledge).

Westra, R. 2012. *The Evil Axis of Finance: The US-Japan-China Stranglehold on the Global Future* (Atlanta, GA: Clarity).

Westra, R. 2014. *Exit from Globalization* (London: Routledge).

Westra, R. 2015. "In the Tracks of Imperialism", *Journal of Contemporary Asia*, 45, 4.

Westra, R. 2016. *Unleashing Usury: How Finance Opened the Door for Capitalism then Swallowed it Whole* (Atlanta, GA: Clarity).

Westra, R. 2017. "China Down", *World Financial Review* (forthcoming).

Wilson, D. and Purushothaman, R. 2003. "Dreaming With BRICs: The Path to 2050", Global Economics Paper No: 99, Goldman Sachs Global Economic Research, http://www.goldmansachs.com/our-thinking/archive/archive-pdfs/brics-dream.pdf.

The World Bank. 1993. *The East Asian Miracle: Economic Growth and Public Policy* (World Bank Policy Research Report) (New York: Oxford University Press).

The World Bank. 2008. *World Development Report 2008*. Accessed on line March 20 2013, http://siteresources.worldbank.org/INTWDR2008/Resources/WDR_00_book.pdf.

Part II

BRICS up close

2 Current paths of development in the Southern Cone

Deindustrialization and a return to the agro-export model

Paul Cooney Seisdedos

Introduction

This chapter seeks to understand the current development paths that have been pursued in the two most industrialized countries of the Southern Cone, namely Brazil and Argentina. It has been argued that both countries have been pursuing new developmentalism[1] and yet that which has dominated in reality are the processes of deindustrialization and reprimarization. In order to understand these tendencies, the specifics of each country are examined. In addition, the impact of neoliberal globalization is assessed, including the role of the IMF and WTO, as well as transnational corporations. The chapter begins with a summary of the historical experiences of industrialization in both Argentina and Brazil, which began in the 1930s. This is followed by an evaluation of the processes of deindustrialization for both countries. In the case of Argentina, this process began with the arrival of the dictatorship in 1976. In contrast, Brazil actually experienced a third stage of import substitution industrialization while the military was still in power during the 1970s, and only began a process of deindustrialization under democratic conditions in 1985.

Through the 1990s, both countries experienced a strengthening of neoliberal policies and were increasingly integrated with a globalized world economy. As a result of the expansion of and hegemony of transnational corporations, and based upon a number of polices pursued over several decades, the shift toward a greater dependency on primary production, namely, reprimarization, came to be evident in both countries. Since the turn of the century, given the rise of China and the necessity to adhere to the rules of the WTO, industry has continued to decline in general, at the expense of the expansion of primary production, be it soy, cattle, mining or petroleum.

This chapter then examines the development paths being pursued in both Argentina and Brazil and the nature of the changes just described and identifies the principal factors involved. There is increased concern that the shift toward reprimarization is not in the best interest of the working populations of either country over the medium to long run, though it may be very propitious for an increasingly transnational elite in both Argentina and Brazil at present. Key issues to be examined include the socio-environmental impacts of primary activities, namely large scale mining, transgenic soy production and cattle expansion among others.

In addition, the final sections of this chapter will seek to provide an assessment of the current development path, often referred to as "new developmentalism" in both countries. With the arrival of the PT in Brazil with Lula, and the Kirchners in Argentina, the expectations on the part of the working classes and poorer sectors of society were optimistic. However, in spite of progressive governments being elected since the early 2000s, there came to be a number of structural problems that continued, if not worsened in the last 15 years, in spite of an allegedly new development model. Of greatest concern besides economic growth and social programs, seeking to reduce social exclusion, are the problems of real wages, employment, precarization and the informal economy. The chapter concludes with a discussion of the general consequences and implications for these new paths of development, assessing their advances and also the troubling prospects for the near future given the recent shift to the right with Macri being elected in Argentina and the technical coup ousting Dilma Rousseff in Brazil.

Processes of industrialization in Argentina and Brazil

During the period of the Great Depression in the 1930s, many countries pursued import substitution industrialization (ISI): a combination of tariff policies, incentives and subsidies to foment nascent industry. Many have argued that industrialization advanced as a result of the impact of external shocks, caused by WWI and the Great Depression. The main impetus was the lack of availability of imports from Europe and the US. A critical aspect in the advances of industry during the process of ISI was the formation of an industrial bourgeoisie, and the shifts in class alliances in subsequent decades.[2] One aspect in common was the emergence of industrialists from the landed oligarchy: for Argentina, it was the Pampean oligarchy, while for Brazil it was the coffee producers, principally from São Paulo, that constituted the main base for the formation of an industrial bourgeoisie. An important aspect for the expansion of industry was the growth of available wage laborers and in this sense, the flow of immigrants was extremely important for both countries. The expansion in urban centers or cities was also critical for the development of an internal market, increasing the demand for manufacturing goods. The industries with most success tended to be those linked to agro-exports and this aspect is once again relevant today in the twenty-first century, as will be seen in the section on reprimarization below.

Argentine industry

Although there had been earlier advances, there was a new push for industry as a result of the beginning of WWII. The industrial park in Argentina was able to grow significantly during the 1940s, especially in the sector of non-durable consumer goods, primarily for local consumption. Nevertheless Argentine industry had still been very dependent on inputs from heavy industry, in particular capital goods and fuel. The implementation of policies fomenting industrialization during the government of Perón faced significant resistance from the landed oligarchy but still achieved notable success, even in heavy industry, such as the automobile, steel, and machinery sectors. The main policies pursued were a combination of tariff and non-tariff barriers to protect nascent industry and the state also provided credit at lower rates of interest. As a result of the redistribution of agrarian rent towards industry, the push to expand the internal market, and thus a battle over income distribution, a noticeable increase in real wages for the Argentine working class became feasible. A source of much debate was the role of foreign capital, which had been resisted in part during the first period of Perón, but subsequently foreign investment was sought in order to overcome the economic crisis. The dependence on foreign capital grew even more with the government of Frondizi from 1958–1962. However, as a result there were significant advances for the automobile, petrochemical, metallurgy, electrical and non-electrical machinery sectors, reflecting this second stage of ISI. The downside was the growing dependency on foreign TNCs operating within the Argentine economy.

Brazilian industry[3]

Industry grew significantly during the 1930s, beginning with the Vargas government in 1930. In this first stage of industrialization there was support for light industry and at a later stage for heavy industry. There were several advances for industry during the Vargas period, though one concern was the degree of industrial concentration in the province of São Paulo. The second stage of ISI advanced significantly with Kubitschek and his famous Plan of Goals[4] during the years 1956–1960. This period is characterized by the state reformulating economic strategy through the mechanisms of economic policy and planning. In this sense, direct and indirect incentives were key for strategic industries such motor vehicles and auto parts. As a whole, the manufacturing sector grew at an annual rate of 6.3 percent between 1928 and 1955, with the percentage of GNP growing from 12.5 percent to 20 percent during this period. The areas which achieved more success during the government of Kubitschek were hydroelectric dams, naval construction, the automobile sector, electrical and heavy machinery, constituting a base for production and capital goods in the country.

The role of the state with respect to credit was critical, and here the establishment of state banks was a clear advantage for Brazil in its ISI period. Besides an Agricultural Line of Credit (Carteira de Crédito Agrícola), and the Industrial Bank of Brazil, which had been established in 1937, another important bank is the National Bank of Economic and Social Development (BNDES), originally formed as BNDE en 1952, and which continues to play a major role up through to the present-day, and in fact, during the crisis of 2008–2010.

During the end of the 1960s and then during the 1970s, the military government accelerated industrialization, employing high tariff barriers and the government of Geisel (1974–1879) instituted an ambitious program for heavy industry, known as the Second National Development Plan (2° Plano de Desenvolvimento Nacional PND II). In spite of many problems during the dictatorship, especially the repression against the working classes and poor, with particularly low wages, Brazil had experienced a strengthening of their industry, evidenced by the expansion of the production of consumer durables, capital goods and other industrial inputs; effectively a third stage of ISI. Unfortunately, at the end of the 1970s, after the Volcker shock, the IMF forced Brazil to pay back its debt, and thus their programs of industrialization had to be put on hold or scaled back.

Neoliberal globalization

During the 1970s the IMF encouraged the expansion of debt for countries such as Argentina, Brazil and Mexico. This led to increased industrialization for Brazil and Mexico, but unfortunately to deindustrialization for Argentina. From the middle of the 1970s, the IMF and other international financial institutions encouraged the expansion of debt for countries such as Argentina, Brazil and Mexico, as a scheme for the recycling of petrodollars on the world market.[5] In the case of Argentina debt grew from US$ 9.7 billion in 1976 to US$ 45 billion in 1983, thus resulting in an increase of 363 percent of their foreign debt for the period of the military dictatorship. In Brazil from 1971 till the end of their dictatorship, the debt grew from US$ 14.8 billion in 1973 to US$ 111 billion in 1985, an increase of 650 percent. At least the debt contributed to the expansion of the manufacturing sector in Brazil and Mexico but, unfortunately, Argentina experienced its first wave of deindustrialization.

This increased debt became problematic, especially after the Volcker interest rate shock of 1979. In fact, it was seen as the principal catalyst for the debt crisis in Latin America during the 1980s. As a result, the IMF and creditors of the first world used the debt crisis as leverage for forcing countries to adopt neoliberal policies, often undermining national industry.

The historical changes which took place in countries such as Argentina and Brazil with the end of ISI, and the shift toward neoliberalism, though with distinct trajectories, resulted in major steps backward for the processes of industrialization and development for the populations in both countries. The transition towards neoliberal globalization complicated the conditions for manufacturing industry and industrial workers. For example, the process of trade liberalization strongly impacted the processes of ISI, eliminating or reducing protection and subsidies for national industry and thus exacerbating competition without achieving major productivity gains, or improvements for workers. Another aspect which impacted the manufacturing sector was financial deregulation, resulting in the conversion of much productive investment into speculative activities and thus impacting both manufacturing production and employment. Lastly, the push toward privatizations led to major layoffs of public employees, and the selling off of many productive state enterprises to transnational capital.

A key aspect of the process of neoliberal globalization has been the role of transnational corporations and the manner in which they have transformed the processes of production for the whole planet. Associated with the increasing domination of TNCs, there has been the emergence of a transnational capitalist class (TCC), as argued by Robinson (2004) and Sklair (2001).[6] This has been concomitant with the expansion of transnational commodity chains across the globe. Given the imperative to accommodate the interests of TNCs and the new TCC, there has been a decline in terms of the importance or relevance of national industrial policies. Between transnationalization and the implementation of neoliberal policies, there was a clear end to the alternative represented by ISI.

The transformations achieved by TNCs are quite significant when considering the growth of outsourcing, whether in industry or in agriculture. Although outsourcing initially sounds positive for industrial expansion, it implies an increasingly precarious situation, whether for the firms of the periphery or the industrial workers, in free trade zones such as in Manaus or Tierra del Fuego. Therefore, the acceleration of technological change facilitated the shifting of production towards countries in the periphery where labor costs and benefits as well as tax burdens were much lower or cheaper. The shifting of production also reflected locations where environmental restrictions and regulations were lax or minimally enforced.

The first implementation of neoliberal policies began in the Southern Cone with military coups in 1973 in Chile and Uruguay and then in 1976 in Argentina. These were seen as neoliberal experiments reflecting a shift toward the laissez-faire perspective associated with the Chicago Boys, led by Milton Friedman and also Robert Lucas. The majority of Latin America experienced the shift toward neoliberal policies during the 1980s, especially after the debt crisis in Mexico in 1982–1983. For Latin America, as a whole, the 1980s became known as the "lost decade". The IMF used the debt as leverage, forcing countries to adopt austerity policies.

In contrast, Brazil is really a case of "late neoliberalism", given that it only adopted neoliberal policies at the beginning of the 1990s.[7] The government of Collor de Mello began with trade liberalization, significantly reducing tariffs: the average import tariff was reduced from more than 40 percent in 1988 to approximately 13 percent in 1994. It was during his tenure when the Brazilian economy experienced its worst recession in its modern history, during the years 1990 a 1992 (a −6 percent drop in GNP). Indiscriminate trade liberalization took place without sufficient protection or precautions for small and medium sized firms and given the absence of an industrial policy, resulted in a recession with serious negative impacts for both industry and the working class.

Although Collor was the first Brazilian President to begin the transition to neoliberalism, it was really Cardoso, first as Economics Minister, charged with implementing the Real Plan in 1994, and then, as President, from 1996–2002, when a full set of neoliberal policies were implemented. The most notable changes made by Cardoso were the indiscriminate deregulation of finance and trade, and the overvalued currency. The latter combined with the highest interest rates in the world, seeking to attract foreign investors, implied a major step backward for Brazilian industry, trying to compete in global markets. The policy of an overvalued currency reflected the monetarist perspective of controlling inflation and thus wages, in addition to the advantages for the strengthening presence in Brazil of an emerging transnational capitalist class. The rate of exchange came to play a key role in the processes of deindustrialization and reprimarization of the Brazilian economy during the decades of the 1990s and 2000s, as will be seen below.

The experiences of deindustrialization in Argentina and Brazil

Argentina's deindustrialization[8]

As seen above, Argentina pursued ISI from the 1930s through to the 1970s and in spite of several coups and military governments achieved some serious advances. For example, from the middle of the 1960s manufacturing goods grew such that they came to occupy two-thirds of exports in 1973 (Kosacoff and Azpiazu 1989, 109). However, when the junta came to power in March, 1976, the new government had other plans and the importance of Argentine industry would never be the same. This was evident in the neoliberal economic policies implemented by the junta with the new Economics Minister, Martínez de Hoz. A major goal of the military government was to shift their support away from manufacturing industry and towards agro-industry. It was argued that the rent from agriculture, principally from cattle and grains, would be used for the development of agro-industry instead of subsidizing the less efficient manufacturing industry.

There were three principle factors which can be identified as key in this transition. One represents the change in alliances, away from the industrial bourgeoisie and a shift back to the landowning oligarchy, but now more modernized and fused with transnational agro-industry and finance, the latter often referred to as the *patria financiera.*[9] At an institutional level, this reflected the government allying itself with the key institution representing agro-business since the nineteenth century, namely the Argentine Rural Society (*Sociedad Rural Argentina*) instead of with the weaker industrialist institution, the Industrial Union of Argentina (*Unión Industrial de Argentina*). The second factor reflects the obsession on the part of the junta in eliminating the worker's resistance in general, but especially where there were concentrated organized workers and unions. Most notable was the memory of the strikes and popular uprisings, such as the confrontations in Córdoba, Rosario, Tucumán, etc., at the end of the 1960s and the beginning of the 1970s, especially the *Cordobazo* in 1969. The junta was committed to eliminate the industrial park in Argentina because it was associated with the promotion of labor organizing, subversive workers, communists, Peronists, etc. The third factor was accommodating TNCs, who stood to benefit if Argentina concentrated on agriculture and primary goods production and leaving industrial activities, such as automobiles, steel, and heavy industry to TNCs operating locally.

The economic and social policies pursued by the military dictatorship had a very negative impact on Argentine industry, especially the manufacturing sector. Between 1975 and 1981, the percentage of GNP which represented the manufacturing sector declined from 29 to 22 percent. Industrial employment also experienced a drop of more than 36 percent, and industrial production as a whole dropped 17 percent (Smith 1989, 251–253). The result of neoliberal policies of the junta began the first wave of deindustrialization in Argentina. As can be observed in Figure 2.1, deindustrialization began in Argentina from the early 1970s, with the second wave during the government of Menem, when industry declined from roughly 22 to 15 percent in terms of GNP, and manufacturing jobs declined by 32.6 percent, from 1,132,499 to 762,992 between 1991 and 2001. The factors contributing to this decline were the overvalued peso during the period of convertibility, high rates of interest, implying greater costs for industrial firms and the pursuit of free trade policies instead of a national industrial policy. After the depression of 2001–2003, between destroyed capital and extremely low wages, during the government of Nestor Kirchner, industry recovered, gaining 2 percent from 2003–2008. Nevertheless, this percentage dropped 1 percent over the next five years, as the economy slowed down.

Brazil's deindustrialization

During the second half of the 1980s there was a slow process by which industry became disarticulated given the debt crisis and eventually there was an intense process of neoliberal restructuring for the majority of Brazilian firms; the alleged aim to push them to be more competitive internationally, but ultimately many simply went bankrupt. Much of the industrial restructuring was simply defensive, adjusting productive processes through changes in labor management and increasing the role of outsourcing. Through most of the 1990s, the elimination of jobs led to a notable increase in productivity, though not necessarily employing technological change.

Another factor was the growing presence of foreign TNCs, often connected to privatizations and mining concessions. For example foreign direct investment

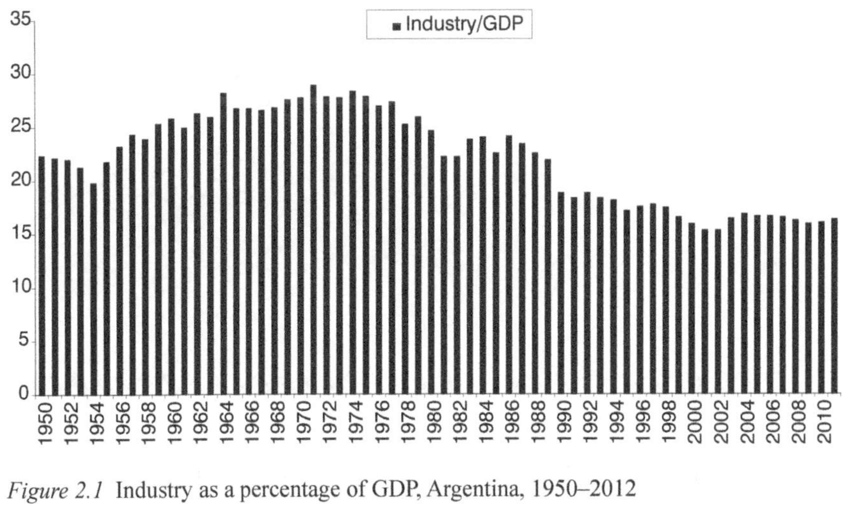

Figure 2.1 Industry as a percentage of GDP, Argentina, 1950–2012

grew from US$ 2.1 billion in 1994 to US$ 10.8 billion in 1996 – a five-fold increase in just two years – and then reaching US$ 34 billion in 2007. The result of accommodating TNCs seeking state assets was often merely the transfer of ownership, not a reflection of expansion of productive activities.

It is possible to argue that the process of deindustrialization began in 1985, when the manufacturing[10] value added as a percentage of GNP, reached its high point of almost 36 percent, as can be seen in Figure 2.2 below.[11] Afterwards, it dropped almost continuously until 1998 when it fell below 16 percent. Since then it has varied, reaching 19 percent en 2004, but dropping to under 13 percent in 2012. In addition to this decline in manufacturing, the sectors which have shown growth have been those associated with less advanced technology, while the high tech sectors have shown greater decline (Carneiro 2008, 21–22).

A major problem for manufacturing in Brazil has been the continuation of a number of neoliberal policies. For example, even during the government of Lula, the rates of interest continued to be the highest in the world and also with an overvalued currency. Both policies worsened the situation for Brazilian firms trying to compete in international markets, given the higher costs of capital and thus undermining any attempt to expand. In recent years there has been some effort or shifting in both the interest rate and exchange rate, primarily as a result of the global crisis and increased external vulnerability. The tendencies of deindustrialization witnessed for both Argentina and Brazil, though for distinct time periods, have contributed toward an overall tendency of reprimarization. The next section elaborates on the specifics of these shifts for both countries and identifies the factors that have been crucial, from the amazing growth of China and their demand for raw materials to the roles played by TNCs and the WTO.

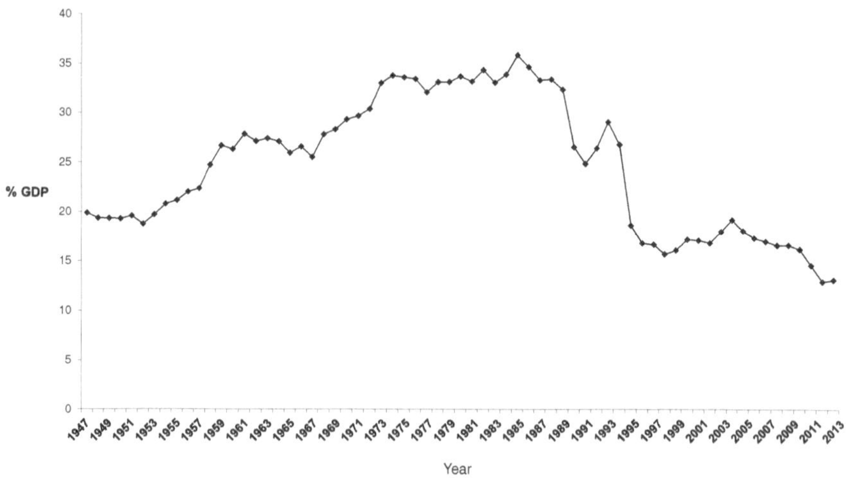

Figure 2.2 Value added by Brazilian manufacturing industry, % GNP, 1947–2013

The current tendency toward reprimarization in Argentina and Brazil[12]

During the first decade of the twenty-first century, the *commodities* boom could be seen as a great advantage in terms of capacity for countries to export agricultural products, minerals and other raw materials. The dynamic of growth of both the agro-industrial sector and other primary good sectors, such as minerals and oil, constitute the reprimarization of both these economies. On the one hand, Argentina actually began this process at the end of the 1970s, while Brazil made structural changes starting at the end of the 1980s. In any case, since the beginning of the 1990s, the economic policies being implemented in the two countries clearly reflect the framework of neoliberal globalization. These processes are also strongly influenced by the options, or lack of options, that come as a result of the rules regarding protection and subsidies to which they must adhere as members of the WTO, which have been in effect as of 1996, when both countries entered. The upshot is that in general, independent industrial policies fomenting local industry in a serious way are no longer feasible for countries of the periphery. The possibilities of competing in manufacturing at a global level have changed significantly, between major advances in productivity, but also given the role of an institution, such as the WTO, severely limiting the autonomy of most countries in the periphery.[13]

Very much related to the WTO control is the need to accommodate transnational capital and thus fit into the global value chains of TNCs. The latter dominate the industrial and development policies of both countries, in part, as a result of the increasing role of the transnational capitalist class, whether that involves foreign investors, Argentines or Brazilians. Given the transnational dimension of the economic interests of local politicians, it can be argued that the interests reflected in current governments correspond more with transnational interests, which tend to get better deals than national companies, as opposed to the traditional national interests associated with the ISI period (Robinson, 2004).

For both countries a major concern is the increased degree of dependence of the economy with respect to agribusiness, mining and other extractive sectors, and at the expense of the manufacturing sector. In this sense, the rates of growth for the primary sectors have been higher as a result of the commodities boom on world markets in the last decade or so, primarily as a result of the growth in China. For many countries, their relation with China was the most notable change of trade relations since the beginning of the twenty-first century, especially for the continents of Africa and Latin America. The two examples of Argentina and Brazil experienced a very strong growth of trade with China during the last decade.[14]

China is interested in securing the supply of a range of raw materials and in order to achieve this they are insuring solid trading partners, such as Brazil and Argentina. Moreover, China is providing loans and expertise for infrastructure projects in addition to purchasing lands and brokering development projects, reflected in deals and treaties with Brazil and Argentina, in July 2014. Their main interest is obtaining control over primary products: soy and related products, beef, and other food products, oil, natural gas and several minerals, etc. The concern of this development is that the two countries are orienting themselves so as to concentrate growth in the raw materials sector more and more, and second in the industrial sectors with low technological content and based on natural products, such as the food and beverage sector.

In the case of both Argentina and Brazil, the industrial sector with the most growth and dynamism in recent decades is the food and beverages sector, similar to the early days of ISI in the 1930s. In the case of Brazil, this sector grew almost 280 percent during the period 1996–2007, in absolute terms, and generated more manufacturing employment: reaching almost 21 percent of all industrial employment in 2006. In the case of Argentina, the food and beverage sector has had the largest levels of total investment for the period 2003–2010, reaching 23.62 percent of all industrial investment in Argentina. There has been less consistent growth since the crisis of 2008–2010 and the current recessions in both countries, but given the reprimarization tendency it is expected that the food and beverage sector will continue to be the most dynamic industrial sector going forward.

Solid evidence of the reprimarization tendency in the Brazilian economy is provided by Figure 2.3 below, which presents the ratio of primary exports in relation to the percentage of manufacturing exports. Since 1995, the ratio of primary to manufacturing exports grew from roughly one-third to one in 2014, the greatest acceleration taking place since 2007. It is most likely that since 2014 the primary exports have now surpassed manufacturing exports. Moreover, the changes in Brazil´s export profile is evident when considering that during the period of ten years (1999–2009), exports grew roughly 318 percent overall, while exports of primary goods grew at 525 percent.

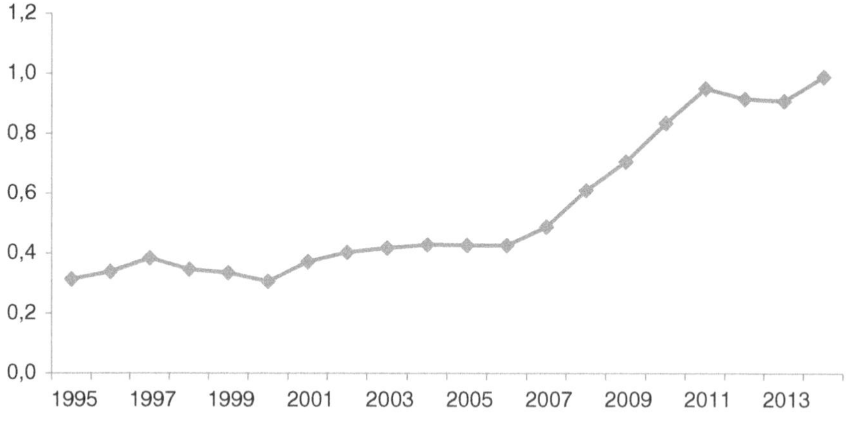

Figure 2.3 Ratio of primary to manufacturing exports, Brazil, 1995–2014

Reprimarization and the environment[15]

This section examines the implications for the environment, as a result of the reprimarization tendencies in Argentina and Brazil. There are a range of key impacts on the environment that deserve examination, the most notable being: (1) deforestation of the Amazon Rain Forest linked to the expansion of lumber, cattle and soy; (2) air, water, and soil pollution as a result of mining and the use of pesticides in agriculture, especially for soy; (3) soil erosion as a result of mining and soy. There are also major socio-environmental issues around the issue of hydroelectric dams, strongly tied to mining in Brazil.

Deforestation of the Amazon Rain Forest[16]

The Amazon currently constitutes a frontier for capital accumulation, with an ever growing presence of TNCs. In recent decades, the economic expansion in the Amazon has been increasingly integrated with world markets, primarily for soy, cattle, lumber, and minerals. A common trajectory is the removal of trees for the lumber industry in order to establish cattle ranching. This is often followed by the planting of an intermediate crop prior to the planting of soy, given the need for reestablishing the nutrients in the soil lost during livestock production. Although soy is heralded as a green and environmentally friendly alternative to cattle ranching, it is often the motor behind the process of deforestation in the Amazon, given its higher profitability. Moreover, the issue of deforestation is not just a Brazilian issue, but is relevant for concerns of climate change for the planet. From 1990–2007, the gross value of soybean production in the Amazon region grew by 21 percent per year, while cattle herds were growing at rates of 7 percent per year, compared to less than 1 percent for the rest of Brazil. Most of the growth in Brazilian cattle – an increase of more than 180 percent in 16 years – occurred in the Amazonian states of Mato Grosso, Pará, and Rondônia, where deforestation is greatest.

Soy, pesticides and GMOs[17]

The famous Green Revolution took place in the 1970s, introducing new varieties of grains, cereals and seed-oils, with biotechnology being the key to production of soy, among other crops. The recent shift toward a more intensive use of biotechnology reached a more mature stage in the 1990s. This was with the introduction of a technological package including genetically modified zero-tillage seeds (GMOs), more agro-toxins, such as fertilizers, pesticides and herbicides (Teubal 2006), especially glyphosate. In Argentina, this shift led to a significant replacement of cattle for soy and wheat, especially the former and the increasing role of the ever more dominant GMOs and toxic cocktails. At present, both Brazil and Argentina, are two of the main producers and exporters of soy with transgenic soy constituting almost 100 percent of Argentine production, and 93 percent of Brazilian production.

"Roundup Ready" (RR) is a variant of a soy seed particularity resistant to glyphosate. As a result, the intensive use of "zero tillage" combined with RR increased productivity and reduced the level of erosion initially. However, afterwards the opposite took place as the toxic cocktail ended up impoverishing the soil in terms of nutrients, particularly impacting the microbial mechanisms necessary for healthy subsoil. The soil eventually suffers erosion worse than the initial one and leads to the destruction of key aspects of the biosphere. The use of pesticides also affects workers and moreover, pesticides are transported through the air, impacting adjacent communities, causing general health problems as well as more serious illnesses, such as cancer or anencephaly.

The growing expansion of zero tillage, the transgenic seeds and pesticides increased land concentration in Argentina significantly: 82 percent of the producers occupy only 13 percent of the land, while 4 percent of the large producers occupy 65 percent. Currently, six major export companies dominate all the value chain production of soy and 50 percent of the lands are in the hands of 2 percent of the property owners (CIFRA 2011). A key factor is the transnationalization of inputs, in which a small clique of TNCs achieved consolidation as providers of seeds, fertilizers, and pesticides and thus capturing an increasing portion of the ground rent generated by such activities. The TNCs associated with agrochemicals include Monsanto, Syngenta, Nidera and Bayer, while those which dominate the grain business are referred to as ABCD: Archer-Daniel Midland, Bunge, Cargill and Dreyfus (Kejsefman 2014).

Environmental impacts and resistance in mining[18]

In Latin America, at least 14 countries made changes to accommodate TNC investment in mining in recent decades. Between 1991 and 1999, Latin America went from being the fourth to the first most common destination for investment in mineral exploration, as a result of a 500 percent increase in investment. The amazing growth of China then led to the surge in the prices of metals at the world level, quadrupling between 2002 and 2007. As a result, many Latin American countries experienced an increased role of the state in mining and associated infrastructure projects, whether for highways, waterways or hydroelectric dams. The importance of the latter is clearly related to the need for electricity for the processing of minerals. This has brought about a number of serious social and environmental conflicts during recent years.[19] Another environmental problem with mining involves the generation of toxic waste, the processing and chemical treatment of thousands of tons of rock, which lead to substantial quantities of both solid and liquid waste. There are diverse forms of chronic contamination and accidents which impact the air, soil and water, deforestation, and irreversible changes to the water table, etc. These are all issues generating negative effects for public health.

According to the Observatory of Conflicts in Latin America (OCMAL),[20] in 2014 there were around 180 social conflicts around the mining areas in Latin America; the region with greater indices of conflicts of this type, reflecting the negative impacts on peasant and indigenous communities. In the particular case of Argentina, OCMAL documented 26 social conflicts linked to large scale mining projects over the last two decades, from the provinces in the north, such as Jujuy through to Patagonia, such as Santa Cruz. There are numerous examples of communities becoming organized around environmental issues related to mining and soy among other issues, many involved with the Union of Citizen Assemblies (Unión de Asambleas Ciudadanas-UAC), composed of concerned communities all over Argentina.[21] There are many other relevant cases in Argentina and Brazil, but due to space limitations, they cannot be elaborated upon here. Beyond the environment, there are also major socio-economic concerns associated with the tendency toward reprimarization. There seems to be a contradiction between this tendency and the claims of a new developmentalism being pursued in both Argentina and Brazil. In the next section, an attempt to reconcile these aspects is presented as the current development paths are evaluated.

Current development paths

As referred to above, since the turn of the century, Latin America experienced a shift towards the left, and several Latin American countries broke from orthodox neoliberal policies. In the case of the two largest economies of South America, namely Argentina and Brazil, several authors describe these changes as constitutive of a new model of economic development, namely, new developmentalism.[22] Given space limitations, the different theoretical debates around this new model cannot be elaborated upon, but rather this section will concentrate on presenting the main results of the PT and Kirchner governments and assess to what extent they represent a new advance in terms of development.

In order to evaluate the changes that have taken place in Argentina and Brazil, several key socio-economic variables are considered, beginning with growth rates as shown in Figure 2.4 below. After a drop of almost 11 percent during the depression of 2001–2002, Argentina achieved high growth rates of roughly 8–9 percent from 2003 through 2008. However, since then, the results varied significantly, though with a downward trend in recent years. After an anemic 0.5 percent in 2014 and 2.1 percent in 2015, Argentina has officially entered a recession in 2016, with a forecasted −1 percent for the year 2016.

In the case of Brazil, during Lula's presidency from 2003–2010, GDP grew 4 percent and during the government of Dilma Rousseff from 2011–2014, it was slightly more than 2 percent. However, it was a mere 0.1 percent in 2014, and in 2015, Brazil entered a recession, with a decline of −3.8 percent, and an estimated drop of −3.4 percent for 2016.

Given the electoral promises of Lula and the PT, many Brazilians anticipated improvements, not only in terms of growth, but also in wages and employment. There was a clear political push to insure a steadily increasing minimum wage and this also translated into a general upward trend, though less pronounced, for the real wage. However, since 2014 there has been a worrisome decline, in part, the result of austerity measures implemented by Joaquim Levy, the former Economics

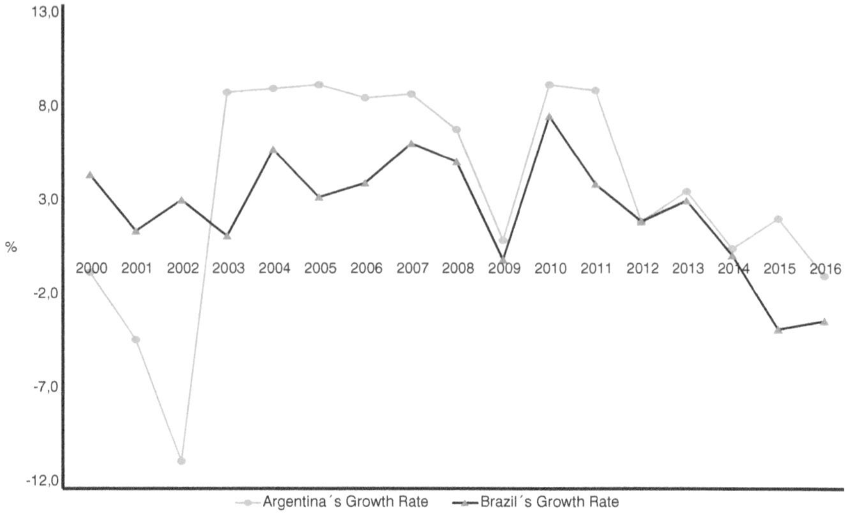

Figure 2.4 GDP growth rates, Argentina and Brazil, 2000–2016

Minister under Dilma and now further exacerbated with the new conservative government of Temer. In terms of unemployment the PT was successful for a decade, as there was a decline from 10.5 percent when Lula took office, down to 6.7 percent in 2012 under Dilma. However, as of 2013 it began to rise again and has reached 11.9 percent in the fourth quarter of 2016. In terms of employment, unfortunately, the percentage of informal employment had reached the level of 58 percent in 1999, but declined steadily reaching 46.4 percent in 2013, though increasing again as the recession worsened. With respect to redistribution and social programs, the most notable by the PT government was the *Bolsa Família*, a state welfare program aimed at the poorest and most vulnerable families. More than 13 million families benefited from this program and there was a significant reduction in poverty as a result. Nevertheless, these policy changes did not address in a lasting way, the structural problems of unemployment, low wages, and the informal economy, associated with peripheral capitalist economies.

As Nestor Kirchner came into office at the nadir of Argentina's depression, there really was no alternative but improvement. Fortunately, the growth experienced for the first five years was historical, including the expansion of industry. Besides breaking from neoliberal policies, investment surged as a result of extremely low wages and the competitive exchange rate. At the height of the crisis in 2002, unemployment and underemployment combined reached 40 percent, but afterwards this declined to 15 percent in 2013. However, given the worsening economic situation it has been around 16 to 17 percent during the last few years.[23] Unfortunately, the national statistics office, INDEC, is considered less and less reliable, both during the last years of Cristina Kirchner´s government, and since Macri came to power. After being so low in 2003, real wages ended up increasing very significantly through 2008, but as the economy slowed down, so did wages. Since inflation has come to be a problem in recent years, reaching between 25 and 30 percent, if not higher, the situation for wage earners is far from ideal and real wages are decreasing. Similar to Brazil and the Bolsa Família program, the Kirchners implemented several welfare programs in Argentina,[24] in order to assist the poor and most vulnerable families. Both sets of programs in Brazil and Argentina were significant in reducing inequality and providing a safety net for the most vulnerable.

In contrast to the Cardoso government, the role played by the Brazilian state for infrastructure projects increased significantly, and is associated with the Program for the Acceleration of Growth (PAC) begun in 2007 under Lula.[25] Nevertheless, most of these infrastructural projects were associated with projects linked to reprimarization, such as hydroelectric dams, transport systems and energy. In the case of Argentina, a recent agreement with China reflects the latter's increased role supporting infrastructure in Latin America, where it facilitates the production and transport of principally primary goods.

If "new developmentalism" has been pursued and the dominant result is reprimarization, with its negative consequences for the environment and limited social gains, one must ask what is meant by developmentalism, and what are the goals that progressive governments are seeking to achieve. A shift in strategy toward primary exports, because it is a period of high commodity prices, is by no means a serious strategy to achieve development. The tendency of deindustrialization followed by reprimarization is not suggestive of a favorable development path for the majority of the populations of either country. If there were at least a tradeoff in terms of greater employment perhaps it could be encouraging but the activities such as soy and mining are capital intensive and not major generators of employment. Instead it is more consistent with a strategy to maximize the gains for the TNCs and elites of a given country. The strategies pursued suggest the need for accommodating the working class and poor, through social inclusion programs like Bolsa Família, and improvement in labor markets, thus strengthening a social base to insure reelection. Evidently the commodity boom has not continued and thus the capacity economically and politically to continue pursuing this model of "new developmentalism" seems to have reached a limit.

Returning to the issue of GDP growth in Brazil, although there were years of reasonable growth with the PT, the average annual rate was under 3 percent for the period 2000–2015, which remains far from the average annual rate of 7.3 percent registered for the period 1960–1980. This clearly demonstrates that the Brazilian economy had a much improved growth performance during the ISI period compared to this period of new developmentalism. In assessing the current development paths pursued by both Argentina and Brazil, the harsh reality is that in spite of some advances over a decade or so, the structural problems of unemployment, stable growth of GDP and wages, remain elusive. This is part of the reality of being a peripheral country with limited industry, dependence on foreign transnationals and insuring the proper functioning of capitalism, with the priority of accommodating both local and transnational elites.

The domination of industrial policy and even trade policy between two major members of Mercosur is strongly influenced by, if not dictated by, the transnational corporations operating in these countries; just consider the automobile industry, and the soy and mining sectors. Lastly, in spite of many solid efforts and discussion for advancing Mercosur, the problem of the agenda and strength of TNCs clearly limits what a genuine progressive government would seek to accomplish, such as a serious regional industrial policy. The scenario of greater regional integration of Mercosur, in spite of many problems, seemed to provide a more optimistic possibility for strengthening industrialization and redistribution in South America, and thus achieving greater results in terms of development. Unfortunately, the current economic and political conjuncture suggests that this is very unlikely at present and may not be feasible for some time to come, if at all.

It is necessary to recognize that the elite base of economic power is often the same for progressive governments, needing to accommodate increasingly transnationalized elites, which have placed their bets on the processes of reprimarization and global financial markets. Neither in Brazil nor Argentina, is there a popular push to break from capitalism, in spite of some sectors, parties or social movements that advocate for it, and thus these peripheral countries need to maintain a functioning capitalist economy, where the interest of capital take precedence, in spite of much progressive rhetoric or even good intentions.

Final considerations

It is not clear what the development trajectories for both Argentina and Brazil will be in coming years given the return to conservative neoliberal orthodoxy with Macri in Argentina and Temer/Cunha[26] in power at present in Brazil, though the continuity of reprimarization seems to be a certainty. Although such a strategy could have success in the short run, depending on trends in the global economy, historically, the prices of primary goods tend to be more volatile and with declining terms of trade. If the tendency toward global recession continues, even China may very well end up experiencing a recession. In such a case, the possibility of another financial crisis in the not-so-distant future is probable, especially given the fact that the underlying problems of the global economy have not been resolved. There is still the political hegemony of neoliberal views, and the willingness to continue with speculative finance as the modus operandi. Therefore, in spite of economic failure, the neoliberal politicians are still in power, whether in the US, Europe or China, or the recent return of neoliberals in Latin America.

In the case of Argentina and Brazil, it is expected that a recessionary trend will continue if not worsen, with a push for more neoliberal austerity programs all but certain, suggesting a rather discouraging scenario in the short to medium run. This is consistent with the rest of South America, considering the prediction by ECLAC of a contraction of roughly 1 percent for all of 2016, caused by the decline in commodity prices and the recessionary trend globally.

In spite of efforts by recent progressive governments to strengthen Mercosur and develop progressive autonomous institutions such as Bancosur or Unasur,[27] the present governments are seeking to dismantle what little advances had been achieved. Instead, they are pushing to seek trade pacts with either Europe, or with the Trans-Pacific Partnership, and are also pushing for greater accommodation with foreign transnational capital.

The implications of reprimarization for the environment were examined above for Argentina and Brazil. In the case of the Brazilian Amazon, it was shown that the problems of deforestation, pollution and social disruption were clearly linked to the expansion of lumber, cattle, soy and mining. Moreover, the expansion of soy along with the use of pesticides was seen as causing a number of public health issues. In addition, there are concerns of soil erosion and pollution, given the intensive use of toxic chemicals in agriculture, not to mention concerns for food production for local populations, not just exports. Lastly, there is the range of socio-environmental problems associated with mining. The major concerns here are with respect to air, water and soil pollution, in addition to the socio-environmental impacts of hydroelectric dams, promoted primarily for mining, and often leading to major displacement of local and indigenous populations.

In the last section, the results of the recent development paths pursued in Argentina and Brazil were evaluated. On the one hand, there was a clear shift away from the orthodox neoliberal model, however, the push by both the government and the elites for a "neo-extractivist" model, emphasizing primary goods production, implied the continuity of the tendency of reprimarization. The pursuit of a strategy of reprimarization can be criticized but it is necessary to seriously evaluate, what options, politically and economically, are currently available for a country of the periphery in the present world, given the domination of TNCs and the necessity to adhere to WTO rules. The reality is that any country that is a member of the WTO has by necessity a neoliberal trade policy, and thus a reduced possibility of independent industrial policies. This has resulted in the loss of autonomy for countries to pursue policies aimed at fomenting national development.

It is evident that the current trajectory of reprimarization reflects an economy dominated by increasingly transnationally-oriented elites. Therefore, the idea that an industrial bourgeoisie can either be reconstituted (as in Argentina) or persuaded to establish an alliance with the working classes, as many a kirchnerista or petista has suggested, namely a return to a class alliance associated with industrialization and ISI, is more and more an illusion, and does not reflect the current reality. In summary, although a number of the changes in Argentina and Brazil, which broke from neoliberal orthodoxy, were able to achieve improvements regarding social inclusion, they did not result in structural changes necessary for pursuing a new model of development capable of sustained improvements in the standard of living for the majority.

Notes

1 In Spanish the term is *neodesarrollismo* and in Portuguese *novo desenvolvimentismo*.
2 Although this development was much clearer in Brazil, there are some Argentine scholars who argue that there never was an Argentine industrial bourgeoisie. I would point to authors that have provided evidence and analysis to the effect that there was: see Dorfman (1983) or Schvarzer (2001).
3 For early Brazilian industrialization, see Suzigan (2000).

4 Plan of Goals (*Plano de Metas*), was a plan by Kubitschek to achieve the advancement of 50 years of progress in just five years.
5 The combination of the crisis of accumulation of the 1970s, where much of First World capital sought to escape declining profitability, especially in manufacturing, and the huge increase in the price of oil, led to the necessity of recycling petrodollars.
6 Due to space limitations, a proper elaboration upon the concept of a TCC and transnational State cannot be presented here. In summary, Robinson argues that there is evidence of an emerging transnational capitalist class, and provides solid empirical analysis for the case of Latin America (Robinson 2004).
7 See Cooney (2010) for the discussion of Brazil corresponding to late neoliberalism.
8 For an analysis of deindustrialization in Argentina see Cooney (2007).
9 Reference to *patria financiera,* as a concentration of financiers, though over time with increasing links to agro-industrialists.
10 The term *Indústria de Transformação* translates into manufacturing industry in English.
11 In spite of the fact that the IBGE simply presents one series, it is important to know that there was a change in the methodology in the Brazilian National Accounts as of 2008 for data starting in 1995. Therefore, for the period 1995–2013 there is a lack of consistency with the earlier series for the period 1947–1995, which is reflected in the notable drop in the series between 1994 and 1995. Ideally the two series should be presented separately, to reflect the two methodologies.
12 For a discussion of reprimarization in Brazil, see Trindade *et al.* (2016) or Cooney (2016).
13 In fact, if the WTO rules were in effect in the nineteenth century, it is unlikely that either the US. or Germany would have had the success they had in competing against Great Britain (Chang 2002).
14 By 2012, China became the primary trading partner for Brazil for both imports and exports and is the second most important trading partner for Argentina for exports, and third for imports (Slipak 2014, 49).
15 Parts of the text in this section are derived from a forthcoming article (Cooney 2016).
16 For further discussion on the Amazon and deforestation see Rivero and Cooney (2010).
17 The analysis of soy in Argentina has benefited from discussions with and the text by Mariano Treacy (2014).
18 For more on reprimarization in Latin America, especially for mining, see Cooney and Sacher (2015).
19 There have been major conflicts, such as Rio São Francisco in the northeast of Brazil and Belo Monte, in the state of Pará, with the projected displacement of 24,000 people, many of whom are indigenous communities.
20 See http://basedatos.conflictosmineros.net/ocmal_db/, accessed on May 9th, 2014.
21 See the newspaper article by Dario Aranda in Página 12, December 18th, 2015. "Por el crecimiento pero verde."
22 Authors associated with new developmentalism include Bresser-Pereira, Aldo Ferrer, Davidson, Palley, Chang, among others (Sicsu *et. al.*, 2005).
23 One should also bear in mind that the shift of methodology to no longer include people who were unemployed and who give up because of desperation, produces an underestimate of unemployment for most countries, and this includes both Argentina and Brazil.
24 Two major programs are *Asignación Universal por Hijo*, support for low income or poor parents and *Jefes y Jefas de Hogares Desocupados,* a program of support for unemployed heads of households.
25 PAC stands for *Programa de Aceleração do Crescimento* which began in 2007 under Lula, with a budget of R$ 504 billion, and PAC2 began in 2010 under Rousseff, with a budget of R$ 1.6 trillion.

26 Although Temer is officially the president in mid-2016, many regard Eduardo Cunha as the power broker, having been the equivalent of the Speaker of the House in Brazil's Parliament and the main force in the conspiracy to oust Dilma Rousseff.

27 *Bancosur* is a monetary fund and lending organization established in 2009 by Argentina, Brazil, Paraguay, Uruguay, Ecuador, Bolivia and Venezuela and *Unasur* is an intergovernmental regional organization comprising 12 South American countries, since 2008, and both had a progressive orientation up until now.

References

Bresser-Pereira, Luiz Carlos. 2011. "An Account of New Developmentalism and its Structuralist Macroeconomics", *Brazilian Journal of Political Economy*, 31, 123, pp. 493–502.

Carneiro, R. 2008. *Impasses do desenvolvimento brasileiro: a questão produtiva.* Texto para Discussão, n. 153. (Campinas, SP: Unicamp).

Chang, Ha-Joon. 2002. *Rethinking Development Economics* (London: Anthem Press).

CIFRA. 2011. *Rentabilidad, empleo y condiciones de trabajo en el sector agropecuario*, Documento de Trabajo No. 8. (Caba, Argentina: CIFRA).

Cooney, P. 2007: "Argentina's Quarter Century Experiment with Neoliberalism: From Dictatorship to Depression", *Revista de Economia Contemporânea*, 11, 1, pp. 7–37.

Cooney, P. 2010, "'Late Neoliberalism' in Brazil: Social and Economic Impacts of Trade and Financial Liberalization", in R. Westra (ed.), *Confronting Global Neoliberalism: Third World Resistance and Development Strategies* (Atlanta, GA: Clarity Press).

Cooney, P. 2015. "Evaluación de la validez de la caracterización de la economía Argentina como neodesarrollista para el período de pos-convertibilidad", presented at Jornadas de Enseñanza en Economía, UNGS, Buenos Aires, Argentina.

Cooney, P. 2016. "Reprimarization: Implications for the Environment and Development in Latin America: The Cases of Argentina and Brazil", *Review of Radical Political Economics*, 48, 4, pp. 1–9.

Cooney, P., and W. Sacher. 2015. "Reprimarización en Argentina y Brasil y la relevancia del concepto de 'acumulación por desposesión'" presented at the VIII JEC, Rio Cuarto, Argentina.

Dorfman, A. (1983). *Cincuenta años de industrialización en la argentina 1930–1980* (Buenos Aires: Ediciones Solar).

IBGE. 2016. www.sidra.ibge.gov.br/ (accessed July 2016).

INDEC. 2016. www.indec.gov.ar/ (accessed July 2016).

IPEA. 2016 www.ipeadata.gov.br/ (accessed July 2016).

Kejsefman, I. 2014. "El 'nuevo' agro argentino: transformaciones productivas en el sector y la inserción de la Argentina en el actual capitalismo mundial (1990–2012)", mimeo.

Kosacoff, B., and D. Azpiazu. 1989. *La industria argentina: desarrollo y cambios estructurales* (Buenos Aires: Centro Editor de América Latina).

MDIC. 2012–2015. http://www.mdic.gov.br/sitio/ (accessed December 2015).

Rivero, S., and P. Cooney. 2010. "The Amazon as a Frontier of Capital Accumulation: Looking Beyond the Trees", *Capitalism, Nature, Socialism*, 21, 4, pp. 50–71.

Robinson, William I. 2004. *A Theory of Global Capitalism: Production, Class and State in a Transnational World* (Baltimore, MD: Johns Hopkins University Press).

Robinson, William I. 2008. *Latin America and Global Capitalism: A Critical Globalization Perspective* (Baltimore, MD: Johns Hopkins University Press).

Schvarzer, J. 2001. "Terratenientes, industriales y clase dominante en el ya antiguo debate sobre el desarrollo argentino." *Desarrollo Económico,* 41, 161, pp.121–126.

Sicsú, João, Luiz Fernando de Paula and Renaut Michel (eds), 2005. *Novo-desenvolvimentismo: um projeto nacional de crescimento com equidade social* (Barueri, SP: Editora Manole and Konrad Adenauer Stiftung).

Sklair, Leslie 2001. *The Transnational Capitalist Class* (Oxford: Blackwell Publishers).

Slipak, Ariel M. 2014. "Un análisis del ascenso de China y sus vínculos con América Latina a la luz de la Teoría de la Dependencia." *Realidad Económica,* no 282, pp. 99–124.

Smith, W. C. 1989. *Authoritarianism and the Crisis of the Argentine Political Economy* (Stanford, CA: Stanford University Press).

Suzigan, Wilson. 2000. *Indústria brasileira: origem e desenvolvimento* (São Paulo: Editora Hucitec, Editora da Unicamp).

Teubal, M. 2006. "Expansión del modelo sojero en la Argentina. De la producción de alimentos a los commodities", *Realidad Económica*, no. 220, pp. 71–96.

Treacy, M. 2014. "Transformaciones en el agro argentino y conflictos socio-ambientales en el Siglo XXI" presented at COLCA, UNGS.

Trindade, J.R, P. Cooney, and W. de Oliveira. 2016. "Industrial Trajectory and Economic Development: Dilemma of the Reprimarization of the Brazilian Economy", *Review of Radical Political Economy*, 48, 3, pp. 269–286.

3 A BRIC despite itself

Sustained growth versus neoliberalism in India

Radhika Desai

In the summer of 2016 the Indian press was awash with a jubilant nostalgia. Exactly a quarter century before, Narasimha Rao's Congress minority government had had taken major steps to liberalize the Indian economy with former World Bank economist, Dr Manmohan Singh, at the helm as Finance Minister. Rao's government has been elected amid a concatenation of political and economic crises – the collapse of the previous coalition government of smaller regionally based parties, the assassination of former Congress Prime Minister, Rajiv Gandhi, on the campaign trail in the general election that ensued, the minority Congress government that was its verdict and a full-blown balance of payments crisis, complete with resort to an IMF loan with its attendant conditionalities.

The neoliberal consensus in India and the West is that these reforms transformed a *dirigiste* economy whose "license permit raj", confined it to a disappointing "Hindu rate of growth" of 3.5 percent per annum into a fast-growing dynamic BRIC and G20 economy, doubling the growth rate which even clocked in at about 9 percent per annum in the mid-2000s. That this transformation contributed to moving the world economy's center of gravity to the east and opening the doors of the inner sanctums of world power to India's leaders constituted much-awaited satisfaction to a ruling class long resentful of India not receiving its international due. The jubilation was all the more effervescent because just two years before the Indian electorate had not only given a parliamentary majority to a single party, the first since 1984, but given it to the most right-wing party, the Bharatiya Janata Party, under the leadership of the man most favored by India's corporate classes, Narendra Modi, to keep India on the neoliberal straight and narrow. And it got a further boost as the latest figures from the Central Statistical Office catapulted India to the top of the growth league tables for the world's larger economies, with 7.3 percent growth in the last quarter of 2015, higher than even China's even though this represented a deceleration over the previous quarter and many criticized the new method of calculating GDP for overstating it by as many as 2 percentage points (Mallett 2016).

The consensus view represents, however, a Nero-like fiddling while Rome burns, ignoring the many problems decades of economic liberalization have created for the Indian economy. It simply extends and adapts to India the western mainstream discourse on development which is, in turn, the replacement of the western discourse on imperialism and colonialism that had previously articulated the developed West's relationship to the less developed rest. Reduced to its essence, this discourse advocates free markets and free trade (FMFT) or, in contemporary parlance, "sound economic policies" and "openness" as the keys to development. This discourse has long been contested: intellectuals from Friedrich List and Alexander Hamilton to contemporary developmental state theorists have demonstrated that, on the contrary, the FMFT approach is a recipe for stagnation, poverty, low or de-industrialization and of colonial, semi-colonial and neo-colonial subordination to imperial/developed economies. The path to successful development lies, on the contrary, in state-directed industrialization including infant industry protection, import substitution industrialization, state investment in the social sector and last, but far from least, social and productive transformation of agriculture. Productive power has spread around the world only through these means: such was the industrialization that lay behind the first challenges to Britain's industrial and imperial supremacy from Germany, the US and Japan (and indeed, behind Britain's own industrialization) (Chang 2002) which first made the world multipolar. These means have also been critical to the growth of the emerging economies and BRICS which are making it more so (Amsden, 2001, 2007) and seeing the history of the world economy one in which it has been getting progressively more multipolar as productive capacity spreads to more countries, rather than one of "globalization" or a succession of "hegemonies" is far more informative and instructive (as I argue in Desai 2013).

In this view, what is today called multipolarity is, on the one hand, only the latest phase in its spread. On the other, it is distinctive in at least two rather contradictory senses. First, it is historic in challenging the structures of western domination and imperialism that have been in place for centuries. The countries that are today making the world multipolar are not only not imperial, as the first challengers to Britain's industrial supremacy were; not only did they not escape imperialism as most of the communist countries which also industrialized successfully had, they do not enjoy special protection and support of major powers, as the major newly industrializing countries of the1970s, South Korea and Taiwan. They were themselves colonies and semi-colonies and must industrialize in the face of attempts by the major power to preserve their absolute and relative positions in the world economy. Their development represents a qualitatively new type of development experience.

Second, other than Communist Party-ruled China, whose leadership is probably more aware than most of the role of neoliberalism as an imperial doctrine, the other BRIC and emerging economies are led by classes too invested in it and in the policies it advocates. They are, in a sense, BRICs despite themselves, growing along inherently volatile and unsustainable neoliberal growth paths whose success owes a great deal to the very dirigiste (and in Russia's case, Communist) past they would reject, its persisting effects and legacies and the political and economic compulsions that lead to key deviations from the neoliberal path.

To be sure, full-blown doctrinaire neoliberal policies have never been implemented anywhere quite simply because, as Polanyi argued long ago

(1944/1985), self-regulating market societies are an impossibility. FMFT is, in fact, little more than a figment of the most fevered capitalist imaginations which cannot be borne in reality even by the capitalist classes themselves, something which Marx and Engels also understood (Desai 2010a, 108). Certainly, neoliberalism in India, as elsewhere, has been about implementing liberal economic policies selectively to shore up the power and privileges of the capitalist class, expand opportunities for them, reduce the risks they undertake while imposing the very opposite on working people of all descriptions.

While the dangers and flaws of neoliberalism are not entirely lost on the current leaderships of Brazil, thanks to the disasters of Structural Adjustment in the 1980s and 1990s and Russia, thanks to those of Shock Therapy in the 1990s, and have even seen something of a reversal in state policy under the Lula-Rousseff and Putin governments respectively, India is still led by the most enthusiastically neoliberal ruling class of all the BRICs. This chapter explores why this is so, what the consequences are and what might change it.

I begin by briefly recounting what the Modi government represents in the decades-long trend toward increasingly liberal economic policies in India. I then discuss the dialectic between imperialism and development, i.e. between the forces of uneven development and those of combined development, arguing that it is the dynamic of capitalism's international politics much as the struggle between capital and labor that is at the core of domestic politics. In it, the opposition of FMFT and developmentalist discourses constitute the opposing "forms of consciousness in which [nations] become conscious of the conflict and fight it out". Against the background of this discussion, we can analyze the evolution of India's political economy, its abandonment developmentalism which occurred not, as most people, including most critical scholars, would have it, in 1991 but, as I have argued before (Desai 2010b, Desai forthcoming) in how the economic and fiscal crisis of the late 1960s was resolved. For it replaced the strategy of raising productivity in Indian agriculture through land reform with one which sought to do so through the market incentives of the green revolution. Placing the turn away from dirigisme at this juncture permits us to appreciate more clearly how the social basis of ever more liberal economic policies, always rather narrow in the predominantly poor country that is India, has narrowed even further over time, a process that culminates in the Modi government. The penultimate section surveys the results of over four decades of progressively more liberal economic policies and the conclusion reflects on what it would take to shunt India onto an economically more productive and egalitarian and politically more stable path.

What Modi represents

The Modi government, the power of the corporate capitalist class which, boosted by decades of increasing economic liberalism, has become great enough to determine political outcomes in the country. These corporate interests in India stand, moreover, opposed not just to the lower classes and castes but also to the provincial propertied classes and their parties which had constituted the wider social base for economic liberalism and powered India's "bourgeois revolution from the middle up" (Stern 2003). For, in India as elsewhere, what has really advanced under the covering free market and competition rhetoric is not some large capitalist class composed largely of smaller, competitive, firms, but the power of large monopoly corporations (Crouch 2011). As this development has matured, the social bases of the political parties that supported neoliberalism in each country has also narrowed (Mair 2011, Desai 2006), as small property is threatened by large and the low employment generation record of these corporations shrink the better-off sections of the working classes that might also be expected to support it. This is clear from the anti-establishment candidacies of Sanders and Trump in the US presidential primaries and from the vote in favor of Brexit despite the weight of the entire political establishment in favor of remaining in the European Union.

The Indian counterpart of these developments, the most consequential political fruit so far of the increasingly powerful Indian corporate sector, was the defeat of the Congress-led United Progressive Alliance (UPA) coalition government. It was the only government of recent neoliberal decades to have won re-election after a full term in office (in 2009) because during its first term, it was forced to dilute its neoliberalism and take greater account of the interests of the poor, the rural poor in particular, for electoral reasons. In its place, the corporate classes backed the election of the most narrowly based government in the country's history. In 2014 the "greatest corporate heist in history" (*Economic and Political Weekly* 2014) delivered an historically unprecedented parliamentary majority to the fascist Bharatiya Janata Party (BJP) on the strength of only 31 percent of the votes cast (which, accounting for the turnout, translated into only about a quarter of the electorate), composed disproportionately of the upper castes, the middle-caste propertied and men. This result has probably set a record of sorts for the imbalance between parties' popular vote and their representation in parliament that India's first past the post electoral system is capable of producing. The BJP's previous stint in office (1998–2004) was, by contrast, made possible only through the formation of the National Democratic Alliance coalition with parties of the "provincial propertied classes" (Balagopal 1987, these parties are hereinafter called PPPCs), the political vehicles of the regionally specific new capitalist classes that emerged out of middle-caste rich peasants and capitalist farmers in most major states to take power there and had fractured national politics in a long process that originated in the 1960s and matured in the 1980s and 1990s. The new majority BJP government was not only unencumbered by these representatives of smaller property, each also with their own populist compulsions for retaining power in their states, it was also under the leadership of its most hard-line leader hitherto because the corporate classes backed him most fulsomely.

In so backing the Modi-led BJP even though most other parties were broadly committed to the same neoliberal path, India's corporate classes were indicating that they no longer wished to tolerate compromising with the interests of small property, which the NDA coalition required, or with those of the lower castes and classes, including the overwhelming majority of Dalits, Adivasis (literally, the "original inhabitants", never integrated into India's caste order) and Muslims which Congress-led UPA represented. Such competing priorities countered their own interests. They backed Modi because he promised them more unrestricted control over the state apparatus, policies that would be more unreservedly in their favor and rapid economic growth that would expand their opportunities for lucrative contracts and big risk-free profits.

Indeed, during the election campaign a very specific diagnosis of, and prescription for, India's economic ills was articulated by two economists to promote corporate backing of Modi. Columbia University's Jagdish Bhagwati and Arvind Panagariya argued that growth has slowed down under the UPA because of corruption scandals created "gridlock" – "worried about the risk of being called out for corruption, officials prudentially put off making decisions", because environmental clearances for major projects were held up and because of coordination problems within the government induced a "policy paralysis" (Panagariya 2014). A Modi government would, they argued, be far more effective and efficient. Referring to Modi's allegedly excellent administration of Gujarat, where he had served as Chief Minister since late 2001, they argued that a Modi government would be far more effective and efficient: it would immediately cut subsidies. It would increase regressive taxes and "capital expenditures" – like setting up 100 "smart cities" – which, through public-private partnerships (PPPs) constitute the essential slop-trough for twenty-first-century large corporate capital. It would privatize more of the public sector, including the huge public sector banks that dominate the financial sector in India in an unprecedented bonanza for both domestic and foreign capital, and prepare Indian Railways (the largest state-owned enterprise in India which merits its own separate budget which is presented to parliament before the government's own budget). It would also prioritize reforming labor and bankruptcy laws and reform higher education in India. These immediate priorities would be followed up with "Track II" measures like "addressing the food security, employment, education, health, and wellness of the Indian public".

By justifying their backing in this fashion the Indian corporate capitalist class did not stop to consider, indeed even denied, the risk that a BJP government under Modi would embolden the BJP and the Sangh Parivar, its fascist fraternity of dozens of organizations, to engage in their oppressive, divisive and often violent activities targeting progressive and secular forces, women, lower castes, Adivasis, Muslims and other minority and marginalized groups (for the backstory of the Modi government, see Desai 2014).

While the promise, whether of growth or even simply a more corporate governed economy (How much more so could it get and with what consequences for India's working people and petty propertied, not to mention the environment?) is yet to materialize, the risks already have. Under the Modi government of the past two years, India's political stability and social cohesion are certainly being tested. Sangh Parivar organizations feel empowered in asserting caste and gender privilege and imposing vigilante punishment on those who resist whether in remote villages or in metropolitan university campuses and streets; the increasingly saffronized state apparatus looks the other way when it is not actively complicit in these actions; and women, Muslims, Dalits, and even the middle castes hitherto willing to cooperate with the BJP politically, agitate in the streets for causes which have no place in the BJP agenda narrow corporate agenda. Economic growth and the "development" the Modi campaign promised to all those willing to look away from the fascist character and record of the BJP in general and Modi's reign in Gujarat in particular, which included the 2002 genocide of Muslims just months after he took power in the state (on Modi and Hindutva in Gujarat see Desai 2011), is yet to materialize. The Modi government's economic performance has been, at best, lackluster with even the corporate classes far from satisfied with it (because, quite simply, the so-called "Gujarat Model" and its alleged success was always something of a fiction based on little more than corporate give-aways and the imposition of punishing discipline and repression on labor and the minorities, as Hensman 2014 argues) and the neoliberal bent of its policy is only taking India further away from the path of sustained growth and development.

The BRICs in capitalism's uneven and combined development

The FMFT view on development lies at the core of the mainstream discourse about the BRICs. While Goldman Sachs's Chief Economist, Jim O'Neill, did not discuss policies or causes of growth when he first alerted the world to the phenomenon and coined the term (O'Neill 2001), his paper was followed two years later with another one from that august development agency which did precisely that, attributing the BRICs success to the extent to which FMFT policies had been followed and arguing that perfecting them would lead the BRICs to even greater success (Wilson and Purushuthaman 2003).

As I have argued (Desai 2013), the contest between the FMFT approach advocated by the dominant economies of the world and the developmentalist approach of its contender economies hoping to challenge that dominance by expanding their own productive capacity is practically as old as capitalism. It is the ideological form in which the key international struggle of capitalism unfolds. This struggle, effectively the international counterpart of the class struggle within nations, was outlined by Trotsky (1934) in terms of the dialectic of uneven and combined development (UCD), though it is also present in classical Marxism more broadly and was introduced into mainstream thinking by Alexander Gershenkron (1962, on the Marxist derivation of his ideas, see van der Linden 2012).

UCD can be briefly outlined (see also Desai 2013 and 2015b). Capitalist development is inherently uneven, concentrated in certain countries and regions. The more advanced capitalist nations seek to maintain and extend this unevenness and inequality. After all, they must retain their capacity to externalize the problems created by capitalism's contradictions, chiefly its gluts of commodities and capital. Their power over other nations, productive as well as military and political, in effect imperialism, enables such externalization. The chief reason why imperial structures are not constant and unchanging, why, in fact, the frontiers of imperialism have been progressively pushed back, is that other nations do not suffer their subordination gladly. Those who can, seek to challenge it through combined or contender development, hothousing industrial development by protecting and planning their economies. This can take capitalist forms, as in the industrialization of the US, Germany and Japan in the late nineteenth century, or non-capitalist forms as in that of the USSR and China. While dominant states seek *complementarity* between their economies and those they dominate, for example by consigning them to be markets for industrial products, suppliers of cheap raw materials or labor, and venues for investments more lucrative than might be possible in their home economies, contender nations seek *similarity*, in terms of levels of industrial and technological development (Desai 2015b) and reject subordinate complementarity. While combined development does not always succeed, no catch-up development has been possible without it, whether in the West (Chang 2002) or elsewhere (Amsden 2007).

In this dialectic, the ideology of FMFT plays critical ideological functions. By assuming that the world economy is or should be a single unified economy whose division into a multitude of national economies is inconsequential or undesirable and in which states play or should play no significant role, FMFT economic cosmopolitanism has long dissimulated the activism of imperial states in securing the political and geopolitical conditions for their dominance, including through formal and informal imperialism and even disguised it as benevolently "hegemonic"; and "developmental". It has also discouraged, where possible (and the record of contender development shows that this is not always possible), subordinate states from undertaking the only sorts of projects – state-directed "protectionist" development – that can succeed.

The power behind the FMFT view is certainly formidable. Friedrich List, critic of the first version of this discourse, English Free Trade, complained that "No branch of Political Economy presents a greater diversity of views between men of theory and men of practice, than that which treats of international commerce and commercial policy" (List 1841/1856, 61). While the theory proclaimed the everlasting truth of FMFT, in practice all countries had industrialized through the opposite strategies. More recently, Erik Reinert constructed a veritable "other canon" of economic theory contesting the FMFT view (Reinert and Daastøl, 2004). However, this power has certainly not prevented the industrialization of contender nations in the long line that includes the industrialization of the first challengers of Britain's industrial supremacy – the US, Germany and Japan – through to that of the Soviet Union, the state-directed post-war recoveries of Western Europe and Japan, the rise of the NICS and now, that of the BRICs and other emerging economies. And such practical critique has a theoretical counterpart. The FMFT view and the twin Ricardian fictions on which it rests – Say's Law and Comparative Advantage – had only uncertain support in classical political economy. Not only did Marx criticize both, List greatly exaggerated the extent to which even Smith advocated them. And when they were installed at the core of the new discipline of neoclassical economics (Desai 2016), the Ricardian fictions were frontally criticized by Keynes and by those writing about developmental states after their resurgence in the form of neoliberalism in the 1980s and 1990s.

The power of the cosmopolitan FMFT comes from being the imperial discourse and just as within a society the ruling ideas are the ideas of the ruling class, ideas that articulate its interest as the national interest, so in the international sphere, the ruling ideas are those of the dominant nations, seeking to articulate their interests as the general interests of humanity and the role of the dominant nations as benevolently "hegemonic", and "developmental". If this was not enough, insofar and powerful interests in the subordinate economy benefit from such subordination, they add their voices to the already powerful chorus behind cosmopolitan free market and free trade policies. On the other hand, however, while this discourse has been openly contested – by Germany, Japan or the US in the late nineteenth century to the Third World's demand for a New International Economic Order in the 1970s, even when it is not and when ruling classes are inclined to some version of neoliberal policies, they are often driven to policies that negate it through bitter experience of the often disastrous results of FMFT policies and/or because of their political consequences.

We can now appreciate that mainstream discourse about the BRICs thesis is simply another in the long series of battles over Third World development. They began with the formation of the G77 group of Third World countries and UNCTAD in 1964 (Murphy 1983, Toye 2014) and continued in the contest between Modernization Theory and Dependency Theory in the 1970s. There was then the challenge to the increasingly dominant neoliberal orthodoxy by a small and determined band of developmental state theorists in the 1980s and 1990s in light of the emergence of the first newly industrializing countries (NICs) – South Korea, Taiwan, Hong Kong and Singapore – a contestation that continued in the aftermath of the 1997–8 East Asian financial crisis. During that phase, while Japan sought to back developmental state thinking by proposing to deal with the financial crisis in a way that would preserve something of the developmental states of north-east Asia, its proposal for an Asian Monetary Fund was successfully scuttled by the US (Wade and Veneroso 1998), that could not prevent the neoliberal orthodoxy from taking a considerable beating, leading the IMF to lose most of its clients in the decade thereafter. Today, with the rise of China in particular and other emerging economies in general, such views contesting the western FMFT views are increasingly heard in debates in international economic governance and the result is either to bring key multilateral bodies to a standstill or the emergence of new bodies created by the contender economies.

The slow-motion counterrevolution against planned industrialization

The Indian and western dominant view that India's economy grew slowly until the big bang reforms of 1991 and speeded up spectacularly thereafter has been contradicted on its own terms: the acceleration of growth had already begun in the 1980s. However, its very terms need questioning. It is important to recall that the biggest break in modern India's growth came even earlier: the 3.5 percent "Hindu rate of growth" represented the greatest break from stagnation so far. As Deepak Nayyar has pointed out, both the Sivasubramonian and Maddison estimates concur in indicating minimal (1 percent and 0.8 percent respectively) average annual growth in national income and negligible (0.2 and 0.04 percent respectively) growth in per capita national income between 1900–1 to 1946–7. These stand in sharp contrast with the average annual growth in the period 1950–1 to 2004–5 of 4.2 per cent per annum growth in GDP and 2.1 per cent per annum growth in per capita income. The average annual GDP growth for the period from independence to 1980, 3.5 percent, alone represents, arguably, the sharpest break in India's growth record. This was achieved precisely by overturning the "one way free trade" imposed by British colonial authorities and undertaking planned industrialization.

Neoliberal wisdom that state intervention is inherently inefficient and that the strategy of state-interventionist planned industrialization in India was bound to fail is so untenable in the case of India that few voiced it during the 1950s and 1960s, the heyday of planned industrialization (Ghosh 1998). After all, Indian nationalism had been based on a primarily economic critique of the effects of British colonialism – including poverty, deindustrialization, drain of surplus and lack of investment – and with the 1944 Bombay Plan, the bourgeoisie committed itself to planned industrialization. However, beginning with Bhagwati and Desai's opening salvo against Indian Planning (1970), the trend of critique of state intervention in Independent India – of its export pessimism, overvalued exchange rates, capital-intensive import substituting industrialization, neglect of agriculture, etc. – culminated in an endorsement of more generic "getting prices right" arguments against economic planning as such (Patnaik 1998).

In reality, the problem with planned development in India lay not in planning as such, nor in how it was adapted to the specificity of Indian conditions (Frankel 1978 remains the best account of how it was conceived and carried out) but, as I have long argued (Desai 2004a, 2004b, forthcoming) in the political shortcomings of the Congress as a nationalist movement and political party. Resting as it did on levels of political mobilization carefully calibrated to achieve national independence under bourgeois leadership without overshooting into something more radical, the independent Indian state's political capacity was considerably more limited than that, say, of the Chinese revolutionary state. This limitation was historically decisive.

For industrializing the Indian economy required more than mere industrial investment: it required effecting an agrarian transition, a transformation of agriculture in a way that would support, and not obstruct, industrialization. As was most clear in Soviet debates on industrialization, this essentially required some way of increasing agricultural production and productivity that could release surpluses for further investment, supply food and raw materials and be capable of absorbing industrial producers' and consumers' goods as they became available.

Seeking to conserve scarce funds and foreign exchange for industrial investment, the planners sought to achieve their agricultural goals in the initial phase chiefly through land reform. This was to be the keystone of the agrarian transition they wished to effect. The idea was that removing landlordism and achieving a more equal distribution of land among India's peasants and addressing landlessness would vastly increase agricultural productivity simply by correcting the distorted incentive structure, by giving peasants an incentive for greater effort and investment by ensuring that they and their families, rather than landlords or money-lenders would benefit from expanded production. The resulting surpluses, which were expected to suffice both for materially improving the peasants' lives as well as for industrial investment, were to be garnered by taxing agriculture and a state trading system for grain. To ensure that these surpluses did not just benefit industrialists privately, industry was to be highly regulated in the interests of balanced national development, featuring substantial state ownership in sectors where private initiative could not suffice and focusing in the first instance on creating and expanding basic industrialization rather than consumer goods. Trade policy would restrict the import of consumer goods to save foreign exchange for investment goods.

The problem with this strategy was not in its conception but in its political assumptions, specifically that land reform could be implemented thoroughly and agricultural and other property taxed to the levels necessary. Congress as a nationalist movement and later governing party was the party of the Indian bourgeoisie which, moreover, relied on the leading sections of the "dominant caste" peasantry – according to M. N. Srinivas's (1955) classic definition, the regionally specific middle-caste cultivating castes that controlled the most and best land in the villages – as the "link men" who would deliver the required votes for Congress in the countryside. This reliance determined the outcome of the land reform process and, eventually, of the strategy of development itself.

The power of the dominant castes, best represented in the state legislatures and governments, ensured that land reform, a state subject in India's federal system – did not go beyond making them owner cultivators where, as in most of the north Indian Gangetic plain, they were tenants of large landowners. It also left the latter with consolidated and more efficient, albeit less land.

Further redistribution was out of the question. These groups would not tolerate their holdings being nibbled away to provide more land to the land hungry and equip landless farmers with land. They typically ended any tenancy relationships where they had leased or sub-leased land out well before the long-announced legislation came into effect and ensured that the land ceiling legislation, which would limit the size of individual land-holdings, was riddled with loopholes to exploit. In sum, the power of the dominant castes ensured that land reform was simply the vehicle that took the north's dominant castes, who were tenants, to the status of being owner cultivators like their counterparts in the rest of the country.

By the 1960s, dominant castes' power within the Congress system was already compromising planning and its implementation, diverting more resources towards agriculture than had been intended, scuttling state trading in food grains that would have acted to tax them and thwarting plans to tax them in other ways. The resulting tensions were making them restive within Congress and this became shockingly manifest in the 1967 general elections in which Congress saw its majority at the center seriously diminished and lost eight states, including large and important ones like Uttar Pradesh and Tamil Nadu.

These developments ensured, first, that Indian agriculture was set on a marketist and increasingly capitalist path of development, accelerating the differentiation of the peasantry into large landowners and rich and some middle peasants becoming capitalist farmers and the rest being left with smaller, often marginal, parcels of land or none at all. Second, the power of the dominant caste cultivators in the countryside as well as the urban propertied was expressed in a great refusal to be taxed and otherwise controlled by the state, leading to the fiscal problems mounting to crisis (Patnaik 1985).

By the late 1960s, with little growth in agricultural productivity overall and a series of bad monsoons, India faced a major food, economic, fiscal and foreign exchange crisis which could only be resolved through an US loan whose conditions included the adoption of green revolution techniques for Indian agriculture to increase its productivity. Given their capital-intensive character, they were bound to increase peasant differentiation and the power of the richer farmers, shelving the planned agrarian transition and, given its centrality to the strategy of planned industrialization, constituted its effective abandonment. In the long run, the path of green revolution increased production and productivity enough to ensure India's food security as a nation, but not for the vast largely rural reserves of the poor (Patnaik 2007).

In these circumstances, the agrarian transition that eventually transferred agrarian surpluses to industrialization took an entirely different and more limited form than that envisaged by the planners. It was one devised and enforced by the dominant castes themselves. The former would have ensured a more egalitarian pattern of land-ownership, widely distributed productivity increases, vigorous industrial growth and a mutually reinforcing relationship between a developing agriculture and an emerging industrial sector, with the former coming to serve as a broad and deep market for industrial products and the latter helping to increase its productivity in a broad and more equal fashion. The agrarian transition that now began to be effected also transferred surpluses from agriculture into industry but under the control of the surplus producing dominant castes themselves, enriching them and transforming them from landlords and rich peasants into capitalist farmers and then, as they ceased expanding their agricultural operations and investing in industries and urban services, into capitalists plain and simple, with rural and urban investments. This agrarian transition would take place at a pace and in a pattern of the dominant castes' choosing, not as part of a plan for national industrialization.

The transformation of rich peasants and landlords into capitalist farmers and then capitalists has been variously recognized. K. Balagopal early on identified the capitalist class emerging from the countryside as the provincial propertied class (1987). Patnaik *et al.* referred to the "proliferation of the bourgeoisie" (1996), which began with the emergence of "landlord capitalism" and "rich peasant capitalism" and continued as these new capitalists "moved into a whole range of other activities, namely building cinema halls, setting up commercially run local hospitals, establishing small-scale industrial units, contracting for construction activity and so on" (1996, 67). Robert Stern spoke of India's bourgeois "revolution from the middle up" to be distinguished from both "revolution from above" and the more conventional revolution, from below. Given how they interrupted the planned, near-revolutionary, transformation of the Indian economy and society and enforced a much less productive and more inegalitarian one, I referred to this phenomenon as a "slow-motion counterrevolution" (Desai 2008 and forthcoming).

Initially, the class that enforced this turn, and supported the progressive liberalization of economic policy was a relatively wide, and widening, capitalist class that would soon stretch India's villages and bustling towns to its vast metros and beyond among the numerous "non-resident Indians" who exerted an influence far beyond their material ties to the country. Though never more than about 10 percent of the population, if that, they formed a relatively more popular base for right-wing policies. This relatively wide social base has narrowed and the Modi government represents a transition away from this more popular base for neoliberal policies in India.

The transformation of the Indian political system

While the first three general elections largely reinforced the Congress position as India's overwhelmingly dominant party (often compared with Mexico's PRI and Japan's LDP), enjoying cross-caste and class support and effectively marginalizing parties to both left (the Communists) and the right (Swatantra and various Hindu right parties), from the fourth general election in 1969, three major political trends accompanied liberalization of economic policy in agriculture and reinforced the trend toward further such liberalization. First, the long decline of Congress began. It would be drawn out over decades but, by the late 1990s at least, was unmistakable in historical perspective. Second, the regionally specific dominant castes began asserting themselves politically, either by forming their own parties, the parties of the provincial propertied classes (PPPCs) as in most Indian states or by joining Congress (usually in the economically less dynamic states) or BJP (typically in the more prosperous ones). Increasingly they would hold power at the state level, again either singly or in coalition with the BJP or Congress, and made single party government impossible at the union level. Finally, upper class and caste began defecting to the right and the party of Hindutva (the Bharatiya Jan Sangh before 1977 and BJP after 1980) soon occupied the entire right of the political spectrum, leading to the electoral rise of the BJP. The latter two developments were derived from the former. Congress declined because the upper and propertied middle castes were increasingly abandoning it. In some states both went over to the BJP while in most, the upper castes went over to the BJP while the middle castes formed their PPPCs who ruled their states on their own or in alliance with the Congress or, more usually, BJP. Congress's social base was increasingly confined to the poor, lower castes and classes, Adivasis and Muslims.

The upper and middle-caste propertied classes and their parties have formed the social basis for the liberalization of economic policy in agriculture in the late 1960s, the increasing decontrol of industry which began with the Janata government of 1977–80 and continued when Mrs Indira Gandhi returned to power after 1980, temporarily and partially reversing Congress decline by pandering to the propertied classes. This continued in 1984, with the electorate giving the Congress under the newly minted leader, Rajiv Gandhi the biggest share of the vote and parliamentary majority as "sympathy wave" swept across it after Mrs Indira Gandhi was assassinated. Thanks to the PPPCs that began to proliferate in the late 1980s, 1984 was also the last time until 2014, that a single party majority government was elected in New Delhi.

Continuing the pandering to the propertied that the electorally chastised Mrs Gandhi was forced into, Rajiv Gandhi initiated the most substantial decontrol of industry, including a limited opening to foreign investment, aimed chiefly to satisfy the increasingly clamorous middle-class demand for consumer durables. However, catering to a small elite was hardly the recipe for winning elections in a predominantly poor country and between 1989 and 1991, there was a short-lived and unstable coalition of the PPPCs under V.P Singh and I.K. Gujral which was followed by the Congress minority government under Narasimha Rao from 1991–6. Another short-lived coalition of parties of the provincial propertied classes followed only to be replaced in 1998 by a more stable formation: the National Democratic Alliance of the BJP and PPPCs of the more prosperous parts of the country.

Uniting as it did the upper and middle-caste propertied in the most stable expression of the caste-class polarization of the country in the decades of neoliberalism, the NDA was the coalition of the propertied par excellence (Desai 2004b, 56–7). After winning mid-term elections, during which it picked up a couple of more allies from among the PPPCs, the NDA government lasted until 2004 when it too fell victim to the rule that the predominantly poor Indian electorate had never re-elected a government after a full term during its neoliberal decades since the late 1960s. The Congress-led UPA government that followed did, however, manage to escape this fate, winning a second term in 2009. The underlying reason was simple: the caste-class polarization in the country which had made the NDA coalition the classic coalition of the propertied had left the Congress and its allies in the UPA with a predominantly poor and lower caste, Muslim, Dalit and tribal constituency. It already required that the Congress's neoliberalism be tempered with at least some pro-poor policies and programs. The UPA's reliance on the support of the Communist Party of India Marxist and other smaller left parties in 2004 meant that this tempering was more substantial, including the implementation of a major employment guarantee program, the National Rural Employment Guarantee Scheme, providing one member of all families living below the poverty line a minimum of 100 days of employment to address dire rural poverty in the country. Post-election polls showed that this had played a key role in the Congress's re-election in 2009 (Desai 2010b).

Increasingly liberal economic policies and the resulting caste-class polarization of Indian society have given the NDA and UPA coalitions distinctive electoral bases. At the same time, since the BJP has increasingly become the party of choice for the capitalist classes while the Congress has sought, increasingly desperately, to remain a party of capital, both electorally competing coalitions still seek to represent the interests of the capitalist and propertied classes, much as the Republicans and Democrats in the US.

So, notwithstanding the great variety of parties and coalitions that have been in power in New Delhi, the interests of the capitalist classes have advanced more or less without interruption. As they have advanced, they have also narrowed with the formation of a distinct and increasingly demanding corporate class whose interests do not necessarily coincide with the lesser propertied. Earlier demonstrations of their influence included the sheer rage with which they greeted the election of the UPA in 2004, the tantrums in the media and the stock market that ensured that Mrs Sonia Gandhi, suspected of harboring dangerous European social democratic ideas, would not be prime minister and forced the appointment of Manmohan Singh, the architect of the 1991 reforms, instead. Even so, the corporate classes could hardly undo the electoral verdict which required the Congress to rely on the support of the Left in parliament or change the ransom the Left demanded: a modicum of socially progressive policies, such as the National Rural Employment Guarantee Scheme (NREGS).

While they ensured the UPA re-election, the second UPA government was wracked by a series of contradictions. First was the long-standing one between the Congress leadership's desire to remain the party of capital and the policies which its electoral base among the poorest dictated. A second was that between the middle and professional middle classes' demands for measures against corruption and the Congress' inability to institute regularized decision making procedures, a problem which became all the more evident as the state's interface with the corporate sector widened through normal requirements of regulation and through increasing public-private partnership in infrastructure building. The result was that, despite presiding over the highest growth rates in the history of the country, the government was judged an economic failure and the corporate classes lined up behind the BJP as soon as Modi was chosen as its prime ministerial designate.

The balance sheet of Indian neoliberalism

The turn to marketist policies in Indian agriculture thus constituted a turn in India's political and economic evolution as dramatic as it is disregarded. Its growth path since then has been based on a narrow and progressively narrowing social base and market, which the rising political power of the propertied classes, unmatched by any corresponding organization of the ever widening circles of the losers from the process, has only exacerbated. This power ensured that the process gathered speed over the decades to come and while 1991 certainly marked a major step up in it, it would not have been possible without the earlier abandonment of planned development in the late 1960s and, given the far greater growth acceleration after 1947, not even the most important one.

Those who argue that the reforms of 1991 were conceived and implemented by a new breed of bureaucrats (one of whom, Prime Minister Manmohan Singh, became finance and then prime minister) who were educated in the West and had served in its key institutions such as the IMF and the World Bank are undoubtedly right. And, having argued at the time that IMF conditionalities made the unpopular measures necessary, these very people are now eager to take credit for having implemented a set of "home grown" reforms (Ahluwalia 2016). However, as will be clear by now, while neoliberal intellectuals with western ties were critical in the implementation of the reforms, they would not have been possible, nor have gone as far as they did, without considerable domestic support for them.

The economic effects have been a pattern of growth biased in favor of big corporate capital, compromising the interests of small and petty property in addition to those of workers, industrial and agricultural, exploding, largely informal, service sector, disappointing industrial and export growth and an agrarian crisis.

The GDP and industrial growth record

In the 1950s and 1960s, fairly robust industrial growth was led by public investment which rose from less than half of private investment to roughly equal from the late 1950s to the mid-1960s. State regulation and investment, particularly in heavy industry laid the basis for a diversified industrial structure and private investment tended to "crowd in" around public investment.

The fiscal crisis of the late 1960s broke this pattern and slowed industrial growth for the next decade. Though it is normally blamed on the dirigiste measures, it was rooted in the sabotage of planned industrialization by India's propertied classes. Indeed, some of the most extensive were taken after the late 1960s – including the nationalization of the major commercial banks, increased regulation of big industry through the Monopoly and Restrictive Trade Practices Act and increased control of capital flows through the Foreign Exchange Regulation Act – in order to outflank the rebellion of the propertied and to deal with the world-wide crisis and high prices of oil.

When growth picked up in the late 1970s it took place within a policy framework that would lean progressively towards economic liberalism and would adapt to, rather than overcome, fiscal constraints. While state investment picked up again, and remained roughly level with private investment, it was concentrated in the oil and energy sector in the wake of the oil shocks of the 1970. Meanwhile,

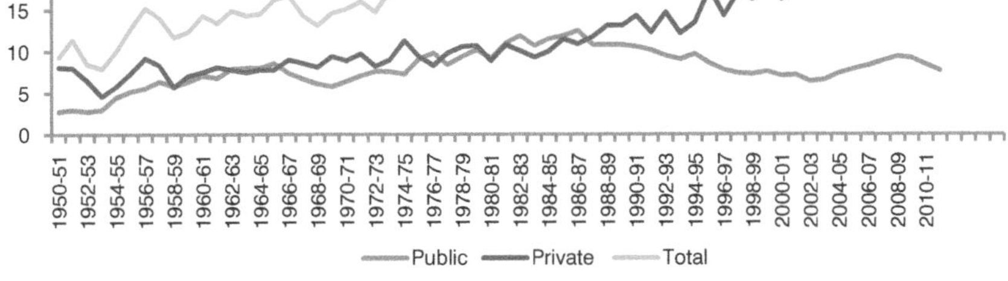

Figure 3.1 Gross fixed capital formation

state spending also began to support private sector growth in a new way. As the progressively decontrolled private sector of industry focused on providing what consumer goods India's absolutely large but relatively narrow middle-class market would demand, public spending was financing such industrial growth at the consumer end by expanding middle-class consumption capacity though tax cuts and increased public sector employment, wages and salaries.

Not having resolved its original fiscal crisis, this was financed through more state deficits and higher rates of borrowing from abroad. While the internal borrowing was based on the maturation of the Indian savings rate to over a fifth of GDP in that decade, a development in which state-owned banks had played a central role, the external borrowing was more problematic. It was made necessary thanks to the high import content, including oil, of middle-class consumption for which the growth pattern increasingly catered and because India's trade balance remained in deficit thanks to these imports. This was what led to the 1991 balance of payments crisis and the extension of economic liberalization, hitherto largely confined to deregulating the domestic economy, to lifting critical controls on trade, investment and capital flows (Patel 1993).

Private investment picked up in the 1980s and until the late 1980s both public and private investment accounted for the pick-up in growth. Thereafter public investment has ceded ground to private investment in quantitative terms, though, as we see below, it remains important in qualitative terms.

Such growth clocked in at 5.9 per cent from 1984–5 to 1994–5 and 7.1 per cent from 1994–5 to 2004–5 (Chandrashekhar 2016) and was decelerating at the end of that period. The period between 2000 and 2003, under the NDA government was, in fact, the weakest, with about 5 percent growth. The main reason for this was, of course, the reduced fiscal stimulus which could be directly attributed to the adoption of even more neoliberal policies. The credit financed consumption boom of the 1990s also meant stagnation in savings rates and, in turn, in investment

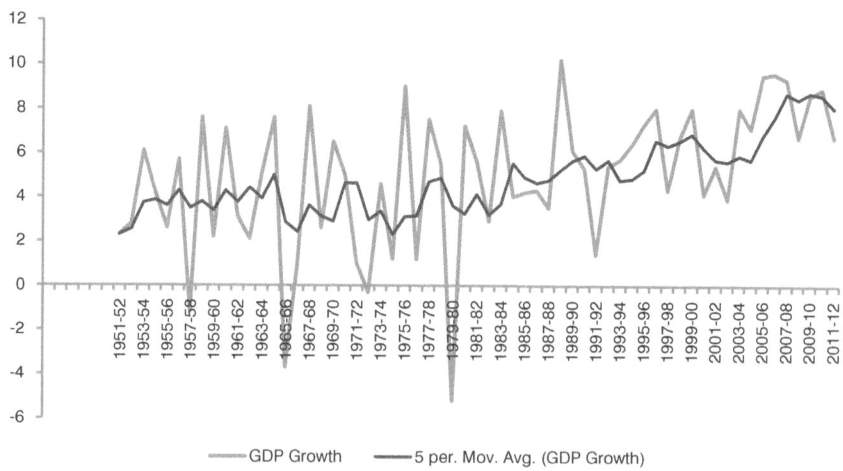

Figure 3.2 GDP growth

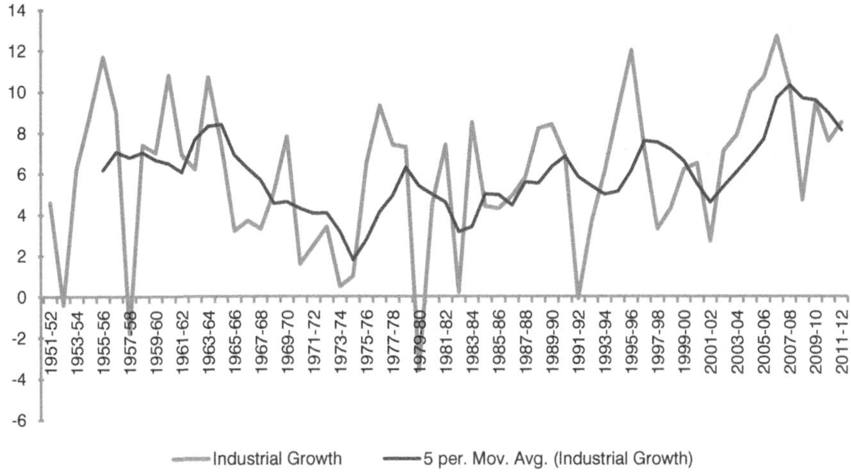

Figure 3.3 Industrial growth

rates. It might be added that despite all the measures undertaken to attract foreign investment, foreign investment did little to widen the gap between domestic savings and investment: the gap was in fact higher in the 1980s at 2.5 percent of GDP than in the 1990s at 1.3 percent of GDP (Chandrashekhar and Ghosh, 2002, 49). In general, India has not been favored with the rates of FDI seen in China and multinational corporations have tended to see India as their market rather than as a base for world market production. The pattern of industrial growth was shaped by its reliance on the narrow middle-class market.

If this less than spectacular growth and industrial growth performance was followed by a "Dream Run" (Nagraj 2013) of growth of an average of 9 percent that lasted about five years, from 2003–4 to 2007–8, effectively spanning the first UPA government, it was powered by

> (private) corporate debt-led growth that until the 2008 crisis tapped into an exceptional rise in world trade. Unlike the conventional consumption-led boom and-bust cycles, this one was led by investment financed by domestic savings, boosted by an unprecedented influx of foreign private capital … of nearly 10% of GDP by 2007–08. Apparently, easy global monetary conditions boosted capital inflows; credit supply at low interest rates encouraged risky investments, raised corporate debt sharply, and also perhaps contributed to a steep rise in stock and real estate (asset) prices.
>
> (Nagraj 2013, 40)

We may add here that, in addition to the factors adduced by Nagraj, the NREGS also boosted income, demand and growth in rural India in this period, as discussed below.

After 2008, however, growth slowed. It was not due to the largely western (Desai 2016) economic and financial crisis. Given that the investment boom was largely reliant on domestic economy, its shock may have been sharp, but India had seen worse and it was short. On the one hand, Indian exports had diversified away from western markets and come to rely more on Asian ones (Das Krishna 2015) and on the other, with credit conditions easing even more, capital inflows soon resumed. While India recovered from that shock relatively quickly, after 2011, slowing world growth did affect exports just as domestic engines of growth were also sputtering.

Analyzing the growth record

Domestically this growth was based on three key things. First, middle-class consumption expanded, critically undergirded by higher salaries in the state sector. Indian industry, usually in collaboration with western multinationals, began to supply an expanding range of consumer goods, including durables, of an international quality. Second, state investment, after growing during the 1970s and most of the 1980s and plateauing until the 1991 crisis, began to decline as a share of GDP for most of the 1990s and through the NDA years into the early 2000s. However, it still remained substantial, aiding higher private sector investment particularly through public-private partnerships (PPPs) in infrastructure development which not only adds to total factor productivity of the economy as a whole but also aids the private corporate sector by providing investment opportunities and risk-free high profits in one-of-a-kind contracts where market competition does not operate and returns are guaranteed. Third, after remaining stuck for very long at about 5 percent of GDP until the late 1980s and concentrated in low technology and low skill sectors such as leather goods, gems and jewelry and clothing, Indian exports began a steep rise, touching 20 percent in the mid-2000s, and experience a massive diversification such that manufacturing, including automobiles, began accounting for most Indian exports, reaching 87 percent of exports before yielding to another growth sector, refined petroleum products.

However, this growth pattern had several critical shortcomings. None of the three main drivers of growth contributed to major expansion of employment with one result of neoliberalism in India being that the overwhelming majority of the workforce remains confined to the informal sector, with its low wages, uncertain employment and complete lack of benefits or regulation of working conditions. While estimates vary depending on the definition of informality, one estimate, which defined informality as employment in enterprises outside the public and private corporate sectors which employed five or fewer workers, concluded that in 2004–0 84.7 percent of jobs in the economy were in the informal sector, 4.5 percent in the public sector, 2.5 percent in the private corporate sector and 8.4 percent in the "formal" household sector, consisting of enterprises employing more than five workers (Kolli and Sinharay 2011). Naturally, such a pattern of growth is unlikely to expand the domestic market which, for countries the size of India, is ultimately the only reliable growth stimulant.

Second, despite the growth and diversification of its exports, India runs persistent trade and current account deficits. There are two key reasons. The first is, quite simply, foreign competition in the form of import penetration consequent on trade liberalization, with Chinese manufactured goods in particular raising their share of the Indian market from 2.7 percent in 2000 to 10.7 percent in 2012, as well as stiff competition in international markets. In a sense, Indian exports can be said to be too diversified, with no one sector or set of products holding a commanding presence in the international market (Das Krishna 2015). Much was made in the early 2000s of India's software exports. However, they were, and remained, too reliant on English-speaking country markets. Their growth peaked in 2004 at over 38% percent, and the decline thereafter turned into a plunge in 2008. Though they recovered somewhat, growth remained in the low double digits and dropped to 6.9 percent in 2012 (Chandrashekhar 2013).

Third, growth in Indian manufacturing and manufacturing exports has been driven by high value and high-skill production which caters to the domestic middle class and international markets and which, thanks to the shallowness of the industrial base in these sectors, also requires high imports of intermediate products. This situation has led to a "hollowing out" of Indian manufacturing where "domestic value added represents a diminishing share of its total output" (Banga, 2014, 57).

Fourth, the resulting current account deficits have been closed by inflows. The most important are remittances from the millions of temporary workers that India sends aboard each year and which cover most of the current account deficit. The irony of the class biases of the Indian state is that the "non-resident Indians" (NRIs) it celebrates and favors with offers of attractive investment opportunities for their investments tend to the better-off émigrés who have emigrated with their families need not and do not send remittances home. The temporary migrants who needs must send home the remittances which constitute much larger inflows and are critical to closing the yawning current account deficit tend, instead, to not only remain uncelebrated but often suffer losses in their foreign exchange transactions.

Fifth, the smaller of the flows that help close the current account deficit are short-term capital flows, including those of the NRIs attracted by offering them exclusively high rates of interest. As has been clear at least since the 1997–8 East Asian Financial Crisis, such flows can be fickle and their reversal can lead to currency and even economic crises while the stock piling of reserves necessary to avoid them tends to draw capital away from more productive uses. Over the past decade or so, they have been prompted by lax monetary policy in the US and Europe and are prone to reversals at the slightest hint of tightening. Such inflows may have swelled India's reserves but they are completely unlike China's which are based on persistent and large trade surpluses.

Agrarian crisis

Perhaps the most important shortcoming of the pattern of growth seen in the neoliberal decades is that, after an initial spurt of growth in agriculture, that still critical sector of the Indian economy which employs nearly half its workforce, has entered an acute crisis. In the 1970s and 1980s, the green revolution was still accompanied by state efforts to ensure its wide diffusion through expenditure on agricultural extension, subsidized inputs, support prices and the provision of public and concessional credit and together, they increased the growth rate of Indian agriculture from 2 percent to 3 percent for a decade and a half. While, given the power of the propertied these measures were limited in their impact, they did ensure that the fruits of the green revolution were more widely diffused than they would otherwise have been.

By the late 1980s, however, growth rates declined as the technological potential was exhausted in the parts of the sector green revolution technologies had reached. What was needed was to increase public expenditure and state effort to ensure that it was now extended to farmers further down the socio-economic scale and to regions, typically those still confined to rain-fed agriculture, still untouched by it. The latter would have required large investment in irrigation. However, the 1991 reforms intervened to ensure that the opposite happened and public expenditure was scaled back.

Agricultural growth then slowed until 2004. With the partial restoration public expenditure going to the agricultural and rural sectors, agrarian growth recovered somewhat under the first UPA government before declining again. Both major phases of decline, from the late 1980s to 2004 and that since 2009 were results of cuts in public expenditure and credit while the latter was particularly affected by trade liberalization. By the early 2000s there was talk of "agrarian crisis". Effectively, increasing liberalism of economic policies was imposing an "income deflation" on rural India (Patnaik 2007). Public expenditure was reduced not only for ideological reasons but also because the partial liberalization of the capital account transmitted the prejudices of international investors to Indian policy-making. Second, farmers were squeezed from both sides by the agribusiness corporations that were suppliers of inputs as well as mono- or oligopsony buyers of marketed produce. Third, the 1991 reforms also liberalized trade in agricultural products spurred by international prices that were above Indian costs. However, in reality, these measures exposed Indian farmers to volatile international prices and competition from the heavily subsidized agricultural sectors of the developed

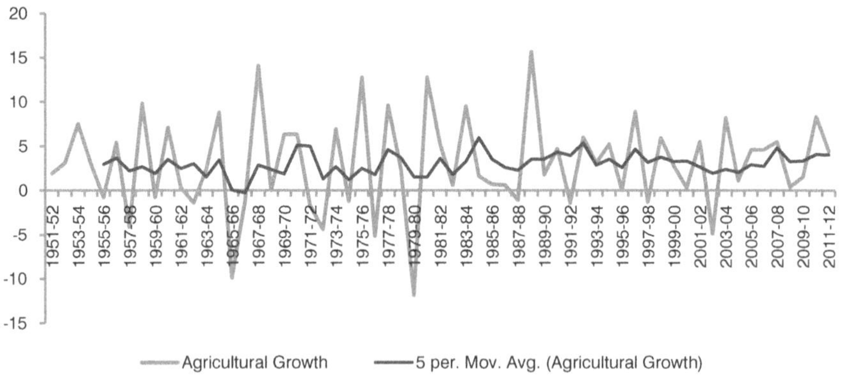

Figure 3.4 Agricultural growth

countries (Ghosh 2016). Fourth, just when all these developments made farmers more financially vulnerable, concessional flows of credit to farmers were reduced.

Indian agriculture, therefore, has come to suffer from shrinking growth, rising landlessness, under- and unemployment despite considerable inter-rural migration from areas of low rural employment to those with some employment opportunities, and, alarmingly, declining food intake. Rising indebtedness has also led to a spate of farmers' suicides (Patnaik 2007).

The one major positive development – a laudable diversification of agricultural products, particularly towards rising fruit and vegetable production – is also not without its dark side. It is part of the general pattern of production being skewed towards the demand of the well-to-do and away from an increasingly impoverished rural population. A worrying reduction in food grain production and consumption (Patnaik 2007) was the result, a reality that was recognized by the passage of the National Food Security Act in 2013, though it remains substantially unimplemented.

Conclusion

The fruit of decades of increasingly liberal economic policies, it should now be clear, have been rather poor, and thus evidence against FMFT positions and in favor of developmentalist ones. Notwithstanding all the free market rhetoric, growth in India has remained reliant on state spending and investment and state-provided opportunities for the corporate sector. It has been really high only under the exceptional circumstances of the 2004–8 period. The expansion of manufacturing, though impressive in aggregate terms, remains unremarkable in comparison to that in other fast-growing economies and of questionable quality with poor competitiveness, value added and employment effects. Indian exports, though they have diversified, have not established a secure competitive lead in any single product line. The expansion of services is really a morbid symptom of this pattern of growth, an effect of high informalization of the economy, a sort of holding tank for the excess labor "released" from a prematurely differentiated and capital-intensive agriculture and not absorbed in industry. And the crisis in agriculture bespeaks an acute human crisis in the Indian countryside.

The recent slump in export markets may represent, moreover, an underlying structural change: a greater tendency for growth in the larger economies at least to be most robust when stimulated by domestic demand (Constantinescu *et al.* 2014). This is, in itself, a hopeful development for the majority of the people of all economies: everywhere decades of marketist policies has depressed wages, increased inequality and constrained home demand under "export oriented" forms of development where domestic demand does not matter. Expanding it as export markets shrink would entail raising wages and productivity and addressing inequality, all of which would benefit working people and create a more sustainable pattern of growth. This is precisely the set of policies against which India's corporate classes have set their face and, as long as the Modi government is in power, they can continue pretending that growth is just round the next neoliberal corner.

References

Ahluwalia, Montek. 2016. "The 1991 Reforms: How Home Grown Were they?" *Economic and Political Weekly* 16 July, LI, 29.

Amsden, Alice. 2001. *The Rise of "the Rest": Challenges to the West from Late-Industrializing Economies* (Oxford: Oxford University Press).

Amsden, Alice. 2007. *Escape from Empire: The Developing World's Journey Through Heaven and Hell* (Cambridge, MA: MIT Press).

Balagopal. K. 1987. "An Ideology for the Provincial Propertied Class", *Economic & Political Weekly*, 22, 36/37, pp 1544–46.

Banga, Rashmi. 2014. "Hollowing-out of Indian Manufacturing", *Economic and Political Weekly*, XLIX 40, 4 October, pp. 57–63.

Chandrashekhar, C. P. 2013. "The Forgotten Software Boom", *The Hindu*. 14 July.

Chandrashekhar, C. P. 2016. "The Myth of Growth", *Frontline* 20 July.

Chandrashekhar, C. P and Jayati Ghosh. 2002. *The Market that Failed*, 2nd rev. ed. (New Delhi: Leftword).

Chang, Ha-Joon. 2002. *Kicking Away the Ladder.* London: Anthem.

Constantinescu, Christina, Aditya Matto and Michelle Ruta. 2014. "Slow Trade", *Finance & Development*, 51, 4, pp. 39–41.

Crouch, Colin. 2011. *The Strange Non-Death of Neoliberalism* (Cambridge: Polity).

Das Krishna, Geetima. 2015. "Indian Exports", *Economic and Political Weekly* L, 34, 22 August.

Desai, Radhika. 2004a. *Slouching Towards Ayodhya: From Congress to Hindutva in Indian Politics*, 2nd rev. ed. (New Delhi: Three Essays).

Desai, Radhika. 2004b. "Forward March of Hindutva Halted?" *New Left Review* 30, second series, November–December 2004, pp. 49–67. Reprinted in Arvind Sivaramakrishnan, *Short on Democracy: Issues Facing Indian Political Parties*, New Delhi: Imprint One, 2007.

Desai, Radhika. 2006. "Neo-Liberalism and Cultural Nationalism: A Dance Macabre", in Dieter Plehwe, Bernhard Walpen and Gisela Nuenhoeffer (eds.), *Neo-Liberal Hegemony: A Global Critique* (New York: Routledge).

Desai, Radhika. 2008. "Die Gegenrevolution im Zeitlupentempo: Von Entwicklungsstaat bis Neoliberalen Staat in Indien", in Ingo Schmidt (ed.), *Die Heimatfronten der Globalisierung: Nationale Klassenkompromisse, Neuzusammensetzung des Proletariats und Transnationale Opposition*, (Berlin: VSA Verlag).

Desai, Radhika. 2010a. "Consumption Demand in Marx and in the Current Crisis", *Research in Political Economy*, 26, pp. 101–41.

Desai, Radhika. 2010b. "Hindutva's Ebbing Tide?", in Sanjay Ruparelia, Stuart Corbridge, John Harriss and Sanjaya Reddy (eds), *Great Transformations*, pp. 172–85 (New York: Routledge).

Desai, Radhika. 2011. "Gujarat's Hindutva of Capitalist Development", *South Asia: Journal of South Asian Studies*. 34:3, pp. 354–81.

Desai, Radhika. 2013. *Geopolitical Economy: After US Hegemony, Globalization and Empire*. (London: Pluto).

Desai, Radhika. 2014. "A Latter Day Fascism?" *Economic and Political Weekly*, XLIX: 35, 30 August, pp. 48–58.

Desai, Radhika. 2015a. "South South Cooperation", in Immanuel Ness (ed.), *Palgrave Encyclopedia of Imperialism and Anti-Imperialism*. (New York: Macmillan).

Desai, Radhika. 2015b. "Geopolitical Economy: The Discipline of Multipolarity", The Valdai Club, http://valdaiclub.com/publication/79640.html

Desai, Radhika. Forthcoming. "The Slow-Motion Counterrevolution: Developmental Contradictions and the Emergence of Neo-liberalism", in Kenneth Bo Nielsen and Alf Gunvald Nilsen (eds), *Social Movements and the State in India* (London: Palgrave Macmillan).

Economic and Political Weekly. 2014. "Anger, Aspiration, Apprehension", Editorial, 24 May, XLIX: 21, p 7.

Frankel, F. 1978. *India's Political Economy 1947–1977: The Gradual Revolution.* (Princeton, NJ: Princeton University Press).

Gerschenkron, Alexander. 1962. *Economic Backwardness in Historical Perspective: A Book of Essays* (Cambridge, MA: Harvard University Press).

Ghosh, J. 1998. 'Liberalization Debates'. Byres, T. J. (ed.). *The Indian Economy: Major Debates since Independence*, New Delhi: Oxford University Press.

Ghosh, Jayati. 2016. "25 Years of Economic Reforms: Agriculture", http://www.networkideas.org/blogs/2016/07/25-years-of-economic-reforms-agriculture/ Accessed on 16 August 2016.

Hensman, Rohini. 2014. "The Gujarat Model of Development", *Economic & Political Weekly*, 15 March, available online at: www.epw.in/node/129173/pdf

Keynes, John Maynard. 1936/1967. *General Theory of Employment, Interest and Money.* (London: Macmillan).

Kolli, Ramesh and Anindita Sinharay. 2011. "Share of Informal sector and Informal Employment in GDP and Employment", *The Journal of Income and Wealth*, 33, 2, July–December, pp. 61–78.

List, Fredrick. 1841/1856. *National System of Political Economy* (Philadelphia, PA: J.B. Lippincott and Co).

Mair, Peter. 2011. *Ruling the Void: The Hollowing Out of Western Democracies* (London: Verso).

Mallett, Victor. 2016. "India Stays at top of growth table with 7.3% GDP rise", *Financial Times.* 8 February.

Murphy, Craig. 1983. *The Emergence of the NIEO Ideology.* Boulder, CO: Westview.

Nagraj, N. 2013. "India's Dream Run: Understanding the Boom and its Aftermath", *Economic and Political Weekly,* LXVIII, 20, 18 May, pp. 39–51.

O'Neill, Jim. 2001. "Building Better Global Economic BRICs", Global Economics Paper No. 66.New York: Goldman Sachs.

Panagariya, Arvind. 2014. "The Promise of Modinomics", 10 June. http://www.foreignaffairs.com/articles/141556/arvind-panagariya/the-promise-of-modinomics, accessed on 28 June 2014.

Patel, Surendra. 1993. "India's Hanuman Leap Towards Globalization", IDS/IEC Reprint Series, No. 1, 1993.

Patnaik, Prabhat. 1985. "On the Political Economy of Economic Liberalization", *Social Scientist*, July–August. Vol 13, nos 146–7, pp. 3–17.

Patnaik, Prabhat. 1998. "Some Debates on Indian Planning". Byres, T. J. (ed) *The Indian Economy: Major Debates since Independence* (New Delhi: Oxford University Press).

Patnaik, Prabhat. 2009. "Neoliberalism and the Food Crisis". In Wendy Doniger and Martcha C. Nussbaum (weds), *Pluralism and Democracy in India: Debating the Hindu Right* (Oxford: Oxford University Press),

Patnaik, Prabhat, C.P Chandrashekhar and Abhiit Sen. 1996. "The Proliferation of the Bourgeoisie and Economic Policy", in T. V. Satyamurthy (ed.), *Class Formation and Political Transformation* (Delhi: Oxford University Press).

Patnaik, Utsa. 2007. *The Republic of Hunger and other Essays* (New Delhi and London: Three Essays Collective and Merlin Press).

Polanyi, Karl. 1944/1985. *The Great Transformation* (Boston, MA: Beacon Press).

Reinert, Erik and Arno Daastøl, 2004. "The Other Canon", in E. Reinert (ed.), *Globalization, Economic Development and Inequality* (Cheltenham: Edward Elgar).

Stern, Robert. 2003. *Changing India: Bourgeois Revolution on the Subcontinent* (Cambridge: Cambridge University Press).

Toye, John. 2014. "Assessing the G77: 50 years after unctad and 40 years after the nieo", *Third World Quarterly*, 35:10, 1759–1774.

Trotsky, Leon. 1934. *The History of the Russian Revolution* (London: Gollancz).

Van der Linden, Marcel. 2012. "Gerschenkron's Secret: A Research Note", *Critique: Journal of Socialist Theory*, 40:4, 553–562.

Wade, Robert and Frank Veneroso. 1998. "The Asian Crisis: The High Debt Model Versus the Wall Street-Treasury-IMF Complex", *New Left Review* 1/228: 2–23.

Wilson, Dominic and Roopa Purushothaman. 2003. "Dreaming With BRICs: The Path to 2050", Global Economics Paper No. 99, New York: Goldman Sachs.

4 Political economy of China

From socialism to capitalism, and to eco-Socialism?

Minqi Li

According to the current definition given by *Wikipedia*: "An emerging market is a country that has some characteristics of a developed market, but does not meet standards to be a developed market" (Wikipedia 2016). According to French economist Julien Vercueil, an "emerging economy" should be defined by the following characteristics: intermediate income (with per capita income measured by purchasing power parity ranging from 10 to 75 percent of the European union average); rapid economic growth that has allowed the country to narrow the income gap with the "advanced economies" over the last decade; and commitment to neoliberal economic restructuring (the country has undertaken "profound" institutional transformations which contributed to integrate it more deeply into the global capitalist economy) (Vercueil 2012, 232).

In 2010, the term "emerging economies" was applied to more than 50 countries, representing more than 60 percent of the world population and about 45 percent of the world economic output (Vercueil 2012, 10). China is the largest "emerging market" or "emerging economy" by population and economic size.

From the world system perspective, most "emerging economies" are best understood as "semi-peripheral" countries within the capitalist world system. The countries in the capitalist world system are divided into three structural positions: core, semi-periphery, and periphery. Historically, the wealth of the capitalist world system was concentrated in the core but the great majority of world population lived in the periphery. As China "emerges" or advances from the periphery into the semi-periphery, the distribution of world wealth and geopolitical power has been fundamentally transformed. The transformation has profound implications regarding not only the operations of the capitalist world system but also whether the system can survive the twenty-first century.

The capitalist world system

The modern capitalist world system emerged in the sixteenth century and became the first global system in human history by the late nineteenth century. The capitalist world system is an unique historical system based on the pursuit of "endless accumulation of capital," with a strong and constant tendency to use a significant portion of the society's surplus product (the part of a society's economic output that is over and above what is required to replace the society's production inputs and meet the population's basic consumption) for "expanded reproduction" or economic growth (Immanuel Wallerstein, for example, defined "the essential feature of a capitalist world-economy" as "production for sale in a market in which the object is to realize the maximum profit," in which "production is constantly expanded as long as further production is profitable"; see Wallerstein 1974a).

The accumulation of capital within the capitalist world system is motivated by high profit rate or monopolistic "large profits" that historically have required the concentration of wealth in the "core countries" of the capitalist world system. The large profits concentrated in the core have allowed the core capitalist classes to use some economic resources to co-opt the domestic working classes and middle classes, accommodating their economic and political demands without undermining the basic requirements of capital accumulation.

The concentration of wealth in the core has been achieved through the transfer of economic surplus ("surplus value" in the Marxist sense or the surplus "socially necessary labor time) from the periphery to the core. The transfer of economic surplus has been accomplished through either direct use of force or "unequal exchange" (a trade mechanism that allows the core countries to exchange their own goods embodying comparatively less labor for goods produced in the periphery embodying comparatively more labor).

Figure 4.1 shows the historical distribution of population between various structural positions of the capitalist world system as well as the external areas (the geographical areas that were outside the capitalist world system) from 1600 to 2013. China was one of the external areas from 1600 to 1820. Since 1870, China has been a part of the periphery of the capitalist world system. From 1870 to 2013,

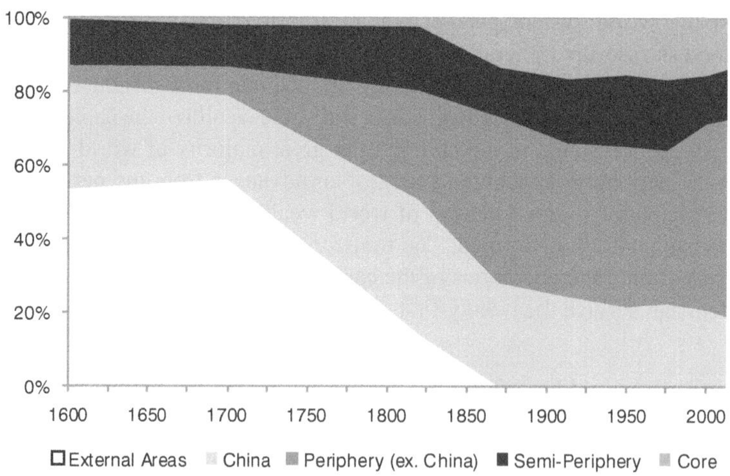

Figure 4.1 The capitalist world system, population, % of world total, 1600–2013

Sources: See Li (2015), Table 4.1 through Table 4.9

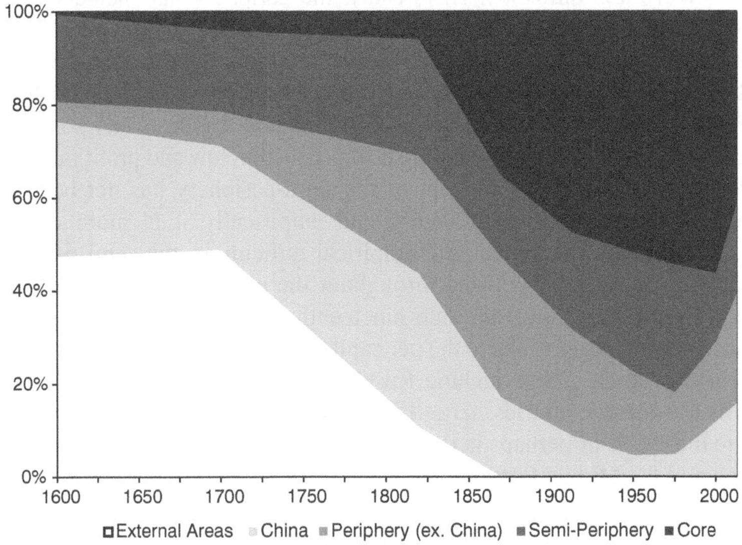

Figure 4.2 The capitalist world system, GDP, % of world total, 1600–2013

Sources: See Li (2015), Table 4.1 through Table 4.9.

the periphery had accounted for about two-thirds of the total population of the capitalist world system and the core population had varied between one-seventh and one-sixth of the total population.

Figure 4.2 shows the historical distribution of economic output between various structural positions of the capitalist world system as well as the external areas from 1600 to 2013. From the sixteenth century to the twentieth century, the western core capitalist countries had steadily widened their economic and geopolitical advantages relative to the rest of the world. By 1870, 35 percent of the world economic output was concentrated in the core. The core share of the world economic output increased to 52 percent in 1950 and peaked at 56 percent in 2000.

However, since 2000, the long-term historical trend towards the concentration of wealth in a few western core capitalist countries has been dramatically reversed, largely because of the rise of China as a new global economic power. By 2013, the core share of the world economic output was reduced to 41 percent. Does this reversal simply represent a redistribution of wealth and power within the capitalist world system? Or, does it signal a more fundamental turning point – that the basic laws of motion of the capitalist world system can no longer operate as it used to and, consequently, the system itself can no longer be sustained over the twenty-first century?

The semi-periphery

Within the capitalist world system, both the core and the periphery play clearly identified functions and their empirical definitions can be established with comparatively less difficultly. Historically, the periphery has included the great majority of the world population. This has been necessary as the periphery is the geographical zone that generates large economic surplus to be extracted by the core. In addition, the periphery has served as a strategic reserve within the capitalist world system. Its large reserves of cheap labor and natural resources can potentially be mobilized to keep the system-wide costs of production low and profit rates high.

On the other hand, the concept of the semi-periphery has not been clearly defined in the world system theory and empirically it is more difficult to grasp. Despite the theoretical and empirical difficulties, the semi-periphery as a structural position has existed throughout the history of the capitalist world system. Empirically, since the late nineteenth century, the semi-periphery has included several regions where the per capita GDP has (or had) fluctuated around the world average. These include Russia (or the former Soviet Union), large Eastern European countries, large Latin American countries, Southern Europe (before the 1970s or perhaps in the twenty-first century again), Japan (before the 1970s), and the Middle East oil exporters.

In the world system theory, the semi-periphery plays an indispensable stabilizing role for the capitalist world system. Politically, a layer of the semi-periphery (that is distinguished from the periphery) is necessary to prevent the combined rebellion of the great majority of the world population against the concentration of wealth in the core. To play this politically stabilizing function, the semi-periphery has an economically intermediate position, "exploiting" the periphery in international trade (that is, exchanging its own goods that embody comparatively less labor for goods produced by the periphery that embody comparatively more labor) but being "exploited" by the core.

For the capitalist world system, the semi-periphery also plays an economically indispensable role. From time to time, the core capitalist economies would suffer from decline of profit rates, leading to prolonged economic and political instabilities. The profit rate tends to fall because capitalist accumulation drives up costs of production and creates new competition that depresses the system-wide "effective demand". To overcome the accumulation crisis, the core capitalist countries need to search for new "leading industries" that can provide large monopolistic profits and relocate the old industries to places with lower costs of production. The semi-periphery was the place where the core countries traditionally chose to relocate their industrial capital during time of crisis (Wallerstein 1974b).

During 1914–1945, the capitalist world system suffered from a major crisis that included the Great Depression and two world wars. During and immediately after the crisis, several semi-peripheral regions (the Soviet Union and large Latin American countries in the 1930s; Southern Europe and Japan in the 1950s and 1960s) were the main beneficiaries of the system-wide capital relocation. In fact, these were the "emerging economies" in the mid-twentieth century.

By the 1960s, the semi-periphery as a whole had succeeded in rapidly narrowing the gap with the core. However, with a few exceptions (notably Japan succeeded in advancing into the core), the semi-peripheral "success" proved to be short-lived.

China and the capitalist world system

For about 2,000 years before modern times, China was one of the world's largest economies by population and total economic output. According to the historical data compiled by Angus Maddison, in 1500, China accounted for 25 percent of the world economic output. By 1820, China's share of world economic output increased to 33 percent (Maddison 2010).

During the second half of the eighteenth century, Britain conquered much of the Indian sub-continent. British rule in India played a pivotal role for the emerging British hegemonic power. Without the massive tributes collected from India, Britain would not have had the economic resources to defeat Napoleon and establish monopoly in the world's capital goods industries. Without India acting as an "English barrack in the Oriental Seas," Britain would not be able to fight numerous wars in Asia and Africa throughout the nineteenth century.

In the meantime, British imports of Chinese tea and silk had cost the East India Company a massive amount of silver. Britain was on the gold standard. Exchange of British gold for silver to pay for the Chinese goods involved large exchange losses. Eventually, the East India Company found opium as the commodity that could make a significant entry into the Chinese market. The opium trade in effect became the mechanism through which Indian tributes could be transferred to Britain without heavy exchange losses (Arrighi *et al.* 2003: 287–293).

Opium trade led to massive outflows of silver from China, disrupting the Chinese economy (in addition to the harmful effects on the Chinese population's health). In 1839, the Chinese emperor sent Lin Zexu to Canton to ban the opium trade. This was followed by the notorious "Opium War". China's defeat resulted in the unequal Nanjing Treaty. China was forced to cede Hong Kong, open several ports to foreign trade, and pay a large war indemnity.

The Opium War and the Nanjing Treaty marked the beginning of China's incorporation into the capitalist world system. By the early twentieth century, China was reduced to a "semi-colonial" peripheral member of the system that was unable to defend its own sovereignty and historical territories. China was confronted by an unprecedented national crisis. The nature of the national crisis had to do with whether China was able to respond to the challenge imposed by the forced incorporation into the capitalist world system by consolidating itself as an effective nation-state that was capable of mobilizing economic resources for rapid capital accumulation.

Various layers of the Chinese ruling elites attempted to respond to the crisis. From the 1860s to the 1890s, several provincial warlords led a limited program of military modernization known as the "Westernization Movement". The "Westernization Movement" failed miserably when China lost the 1894–1895 war to Japan, in which China's Beiyang naval fleet was completely annihilated.

The Nationalist Party led by Sun Zhongshan began as a political party that represented the interests and ambitions of China's indigenous capitalists (the "national bourgeoisie") and the overseas Chinese diaspora. By the 1930s, when the Nationalist Party ruled much of China under the dictator Jiang Jieshi, it had degenerated into a military-bureaucratic clique based on comprador capitalists in the big cities and the gentry-landlords in the rural areas.

According to Carl Riskin, the Chinese economy had a sizable actual and potential economic surplus which amounted to 27–37 percent of the national income in 1933. However, 94 percent of China's national income was absorbed by personal consumption expenditures and the remaining 6 percent was mostly divided between military expenditures, government consumption, and payments of foreign debt and war indemnities. Productive investment was no more than 2 percent of China's national expenditures in 1933 (Riskin 1975).

Without a fundamental transformation of China's class structure, it was not possible to establish a functioning modern state that could mobilize economic resources for modern economic growth. Such a fundamental transformation could not happen without a massive social revolution that could mobilize the entire lower layers of the Chinese society.

Chinese socialism

In Marx's original conception, "communism" would be a post-capitalist classless society that would be made possible by the development of "material productive forces" under capitalism and would resolve the economic and social contradictions of capitalism. Lenin first made the distinction between "socialism" and "communism" and defined "socialism" as the "first phase of communist society" which would be "stamped with the birthmarks of the old society". Significant economic inequalities (in the form of "bourgeois law") would continue to exist under socialism (Lenin 1973[1918]).

After the Russian Revolution, faced with the reality of failure of revolutions in Western Europe, the Bolsheviks were compelled to adopt the strategy of "socialism in one country". By the 1930s, Soviet socialism had evolved into a strategy of rapid industrialization through state ownership of basic means of production and centralized economic planning. In Asia, the communist movement had become a radical variant of the national liberation movement.

According to the official theory of the Chinese Communist Party, the Chinese Revolution was a "New Democratic Revolution" that was to complete a bourgeois democratic revolution under the "proletarian leadership". In reality, the Chinese Revolution had succeeded in creating a new state structure by completely destroying the old ruling elites (the "three big mountains" of "imperialism, feudalism, and bureaucratic capitalism"). This was made possible by the massive mobilization of the lower social classes (especially the peasants). The new People's Republic was able to mobilize economic surplus for rapid industrialization.

Given that the new state was the historical product of a massive popular revolution, it had to reflect some of the historical aspirations of ordinary peasants and workers. In effect, the socialist state entered into an implicit social contract with the urban working class and the rural peasants. The workers and peasants were expected to make material sacrifices and contribute to "socialist construction" at the national and the local levels. In return, the state and the rural collectives would meet the population's basic needs and provide basic social security (through the social safety net known as the "iron rice bowl"). Moreover, the Communist Party promised that the Party "cadres" (Communist Party officials) would share the material hardship with the "masses". In the long run, economic and social inequality would be gradually eliminated and the growth of "material productive forces" would bring about material prosperity which would lead to the transition to classless communism.

The socialist social contract was already undermined during the First Five Year Plan (1953–1957) when the material privileges of the Party officials and technocrats were consolidated. Social tensions and internal conflicts within the Communist Party leadership were greatly intensified by the failure of the Great Leap Forward and the following famine. By 1966, Mao Zedong attempted to revive the socialist revolution by directly appealing to workers and students. The "Great Proletarian Cultural Revolution" was met with fierce resistance from the Party and state bureaucracy, weakened by the numerous internal divisions among the student and worker "rebels," and finally brought to an end by the intervention of the army.

By the early 1970s, both the Chinese and the international revolution were in retreat. Mao Zedong and his comrades were confronted with a situation not dissimilar to what confronted the Bolsheviks in the 1920s. Mao decided that the best way forward was to pursue *rapprochement* with the western capitalist countries. As China re-accelerated industrialization using imported western technology, China began to be re-integrated into the capitalist international division of labor.

Global capitalist restructuring and the rise of China

From 1914 to 1945, the capitalist world system suffered from a major system-wide crisis. The system barely survived two world wars and the Great Depression. Figure 4.3 compares the economy-wide profit rate (calculated as the ratio of total capitalist property income divided by the business sector capital stock) of the United Kingdom, the United States, and China from 1855 to 2014. The United Kingdom and the United States were the hegemonic powers in the nineteenth and the twentieth centuries respectively. China has been the leading engine of global capitalist accumulation since about 2000.

As the United States emerged from the Second World War as the undisputed hegemonic power, it led the post-1945 global capitalist restructuring. Big government institutions and Keynesian macroeconomic policies were established to stabilize the capitalist economy. The demands of the western working classes were accommodated through welfare state institutions and "capital-labor accords" that promised the western workers steadily rising living standards in exchange for their cooperation in productivity growth. The United States pressured Britain and France to abandon their colonial empires. The newly independent Asian and African countries were promised economic assistance and the future of modernization. Through the Yalta Agreement, the Soviet Union was provided

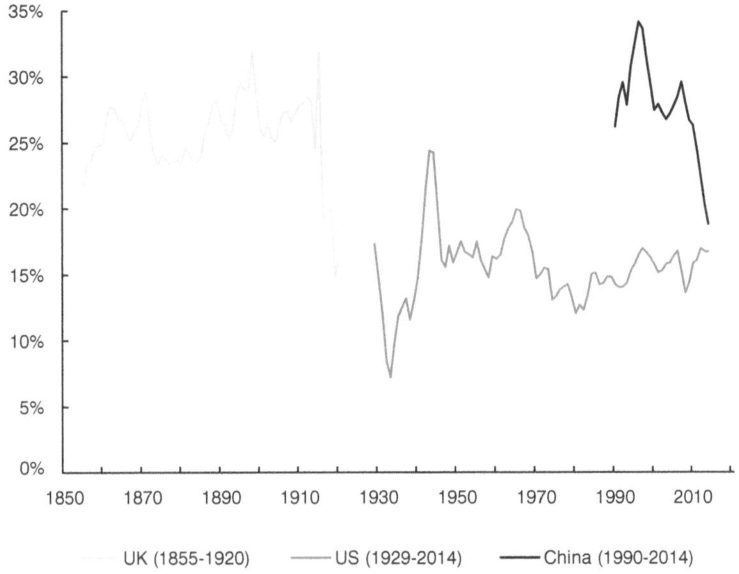

Figure 4.3 Profit rate, leading capitalist economies, 1855–2014

Sources: See Li (2015: 193–196; 202–203). The US and the Chinese profit rates are updated to 2014 using data from the US Bureau of Economic Analysis and China's National Bureau of Statistics.

with a sphere of influence and effectively given a stake in the system. During the "Cold War," the Soviet Union and the United States respected each other's spheres of influence and focused on competition in economic growth. For about a quarter of a century after the Second World War, global capitalism enjoyed unprecedented boom.

However, the long economic boom depleted the remaining rural surplus labor force in the core and the semi-periphery. Proletarianized working classes and urban middle classes demanded not only higher wages but also a wide range of economic and social rights. Their bargaining power was further increased by the welfare state institutions (or the "socialist social contract" in the socialist states). By the 1960s, working-class militancy grew throughout the core and the semi-periphery, leading to large and sustained declines of the profit rate and a global accumulation crisis.

Global capitalist classes responded with the neoliberal counter-offensive. In the core capitalist countries, monetarist policy was used to create high unemployment and a favorable environment for corporate attack on labor unions. In the semi-periphery, "structural adjustments" or "shock therapies" were imposed on highly-indebted Latin American and Eastern European countries, leading to de-industrialization and massive declines of living standards.

As a strategy to revive global capital accumulation, neoliberalism involved economic costs and political risks. It depressed global effective demand and threatened the global capitalist economy with frequent and destructive financial crises. Politically, it led to dramatic increase in global and national inequalities and seriously undermined the system's political legitimacy.

To turn the global balance of power decisively to the favor of the global capitalist classes without incurring unacceptable economic and political costs, it was necessary for global capitalism to relocate some of the old industries to a large geographical area with low costs of production (especially cheap labor). The industries could no longer be relocated to the historical semi-peripheral countries, which were suffering from accumulation crises themselves. The worker in the semi-peripheral countries demanded wages and other economic and social rights that had become too "expensive" for them to be profitably exploited given these economies' existing "comparative (dis)advantages" in the capitalist world system. The historical semi-peripheral countries were squeezed between their inability to compete with the core countries on the technology frontier and the political failures to meet the rising demands from the urban working and middle classes.

In this context, China's capitalist transition, by providing the capitalist world system with a large cheap labor force that was equipped with a relatively well developed industrial infrastructure built during the socialist era, had played a pivotal role in the global capital relocation in the late twentieth century.

After Mao's death in 1976, the "capitalist roaders" within the Party leadership took over the power. By the 1980s, it became apparent that it was not possible for the state owned industries to be competitive in the international markets while honoring the socialist social contract. To support China's growing demands for imported western technology and consumer goods, China needed to re-orient its domestic industries towards manufacturing exports based on exploitation of cheap labor.

During the 1990s, most state owned enterprises were privatized. More than 100 million migrant workers provided the capitalist sweatshops with a massive cheap labor force. China was admitted into World Trade Organization in 2001. Since then, China has become the "workshop of the world" or the leading platform of manufacturing exports in the global capitalist economy.

China and unequal exchange

In the previous global capitalist restructurings, semi-peripheral countries were the main beneficiaries of capital relocation. By contrast, in the late twentieth century, a large peripheral country (China) had to be mobilized to complete the global capitalist restructuring. However, as China advances towards the semi-peripheral status, the remaining strategic reserves (in terms of cheap labor force and ecological space available for effective exploitation) of the capitalist world system are being rapidly depleted, seriously undermining the system's capacity to restructure when it enters into the next major crisis.

China's economic rise contributed to the revival of global capital accumulation by providing the capitalist world system with a large cheap labor force. The exploitation of the Chinese cheap labor force has generated a large economic surplus, which is in turn transferred to the system's core.

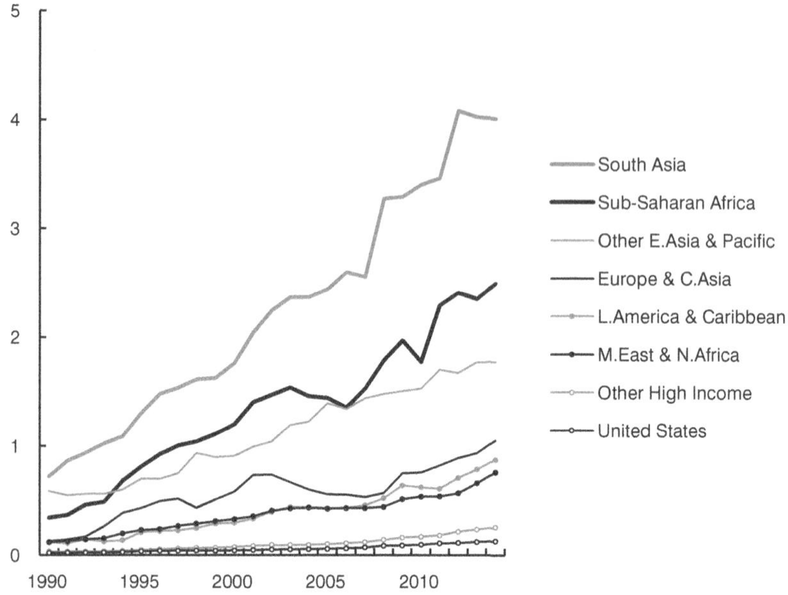

Figure 4.4 China's labor terms of trade, by geographical region, 1990–2014

Source: Calculated by the author using data from World Bank (2016). See the section on "China and unequal exchange" for details.

In the capitalist world system, economic surplus is transferred from the periphery to the core through unequal exchange. Figure 4.4 shows China's labor terms of trade against different regions in the global capitalist economy from 1990 to 2014. See the appendix to this chapter for the estimation of a country's labor term of trade.

In the early 1990s, China was unquestionably a peripheral country in the capitalist world system. China suffered from unequal exchange against every other region in the world. In 1990, one unit of Chinese labor traded for 0.02 of a unit of US labor, 0.03 of unit of other high income labor, 0.1 of unit of Latin American labor, 0.3 of unit of Sub-Saharan African labor, 0.6 of a unit of other East Asian labor, and 0.7 of a unit of South Asian labor. In 1990, on average, it took commodities embodying 16 Chinese worker-years to exchange for commodities embodying just one foreign worker-year.

By 2014, China had become an "exploiter" or beneficiary of unequal exchange in trade relations against several peripheral regions in the world. In 2014, one unit of Chinese labor traded for 4 units of South Asian labor, 2.5 units of Sub-Saharan African labor, and 1.8 units of other East Asian labor. China traded more or less on equal terms against Latin America, Eastern Europe and Central Asia, and Middle Eastern "developing countries". Although it still took about 8 units of Chinese labor to trade for one unit of US labor and 4 units of Chinese labor to trade for one unit of other high income labor ("high income countries" defined by the World

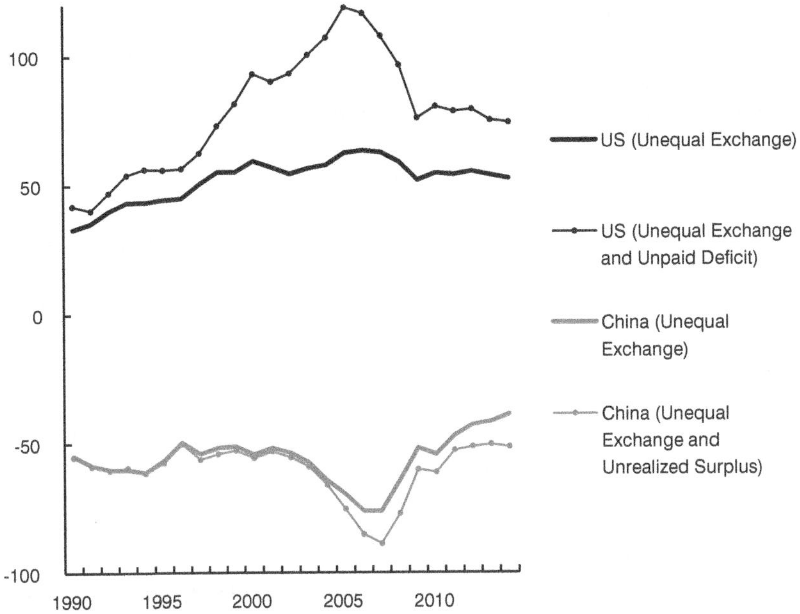

Figure 4.5 Net gain or loss from unequal exchange, million worker-years, 1990–2014

Source: Calculated by the author using data from World Bank (2016). See Appendix for details.

Bank include not only core countries but also some semi-peripheral countries, such as the high income oil exporters). In average, in 2014, one unit of Chinese labor traded for 0.6 of unit of international labor.

Figure 4.5 compares the total labor time that was transferred (that is, the Marxian "surplus value" that was transferred) into the United States from the rest of the world through unequal exchange with the total labor time that was transferred from China to the rest of the world through unequal exchange.

A country's net gain or loss through unequal exchange is defined as follows:

> net gain (loss) from unequal exchange = a country's domestic component of merchandise exports (The Country's Labor Term of Trade – 1)

The above formula tells what a country's gains or losses are as a result of transfer of labor through unequal exchange if the country were to have balanced trade given the country's labor term of trade.

By this measure, the US gained 33 million worker-years through unequal exchange in 1990, 44 million worker-years in 1995, 59 million worker-years in 2000, and 63 million worker-years in 2006. Since then, the US gain from unequal exchange has declined. Nevertheless, in 2014, the US gain from unequal exchange stood at 53 million worker-years or the equivalent of 35 percent of the US total employment.

The practical implications are that if there had been no unequal exchange, for the US to maintain its existing material consumption levels, about 50 million US workers would have to be transferred from the non-essential services back to the goods production sectors (assuming that the American workers will have the same labor productivity to produce the currently imported goods as the foreign workers). Statistically, this would lead to a reduction of the US economic output by about one-third.

In fact, the US trade with the rest of the world has not been balanced. Since the 1990s, the United States has been running chronic trade deficits. The trade deficits have been covered by net foreign capital inflows, mostly in the form of accumulation of foreign exchange reserves by the rest of the world. This has led to the perverse situation where instead of the rich countries lending to the poor countries to invest in raising living standards, relatively poor countries (such as China) have been lending to the wealthiest country in the world to consume. To the extent that China and other peripheral or semi-peripheral countries have been compelled to accumulate foreign exchange reserves to insure against the threat of capital flight and financial crises, their investment in the US treasuries may be interpreted as an implicit "tribute" to American imperialism.

If one also counts the foreign labor embodied in the US trade deficits that has not been repaid by real commodities, then the US total gain from both the "pure" unequal exchange and the unpaid trade deficit surged to 93 million worker-years in 2000 and 119 million worker-years in 2005. However, by 2014, the total gain fell to 74 million worker-years.

China's net loss from unequal exchange was 55 million worker-years in 1990, 57 million worker-years in 1995, and 54 million worker-years in 2000. It surged to 70 million worker-years in 2005 and peaked at 76 million worker-years in 2007. Since then, China's net loss from "pure" unequal exchange has declined sharply, falling to 38 million worker-years in 2014.

Since 1994, China has consistently run trade surpluses. The Chinese labor embodied in the trade surpluses that have not been repaid by real foreign commodities may be seen as another form of transfer of labor from China to the rest of the world. China's total loss from both the "pure" unequal exchange and the unrealized trade surplus surged to 89 million worker-years in 2007 and stood at 51 million worker-years in 2014.

In the early 1990s, China's net losses from unequal exchange were larger than the US net gains from unequal exchange, allowing China to generate economic surplus not only to be transferred to the United States but also to other core countries and some semi-peripheral countries. From 1995 to 2010, China's net losses were roughly comparable to the US net gains. Since about 2010, China's net losses have become smaller than the US net gains, requiring the United States extract economic surplus from other peripheral economies.

In the coming years, as China consolidates its position as a semi-peripheral country and China's labor term of trade improves further, China's net loss from unequal exchange will continue to shrink. It took just nine years (from 2005 to 2014) for China's labor term of trade to improve from one unit of domestic labor for 0.32 unit of foreign labor to one unit of domestic labor for 0.63 unit of foreign labor. At this rate, within a decade, about 40–50 million worker-years of "surplus value" would be withdrawn from the global unequal exchange and would no longer be available for the transfer to the core. China itself may begin to compete with the core countries for the extraction of surplus value from the periphery.

But can the smaller periphery (after China has been subtracted from the periphery) make up the 40–50 million worker-years of "surplus value" that has been lost because of the "rise of China" and on top of that, generate additional economic surplus to support China's bid for a position in the core of the capitalist world system? Or, perhaps, the basic laws of motion of the capitalist world system can no longer be sustained and the humanity has arrived at a historical turning point.

Profit squeeze

Historically, the semi-periphery has played an indispensable stabilizing role for the capitalist world system by acting as the political "middle layer" and providing a geographical space of relatively low costs of production that is ready for capital relocation from the core.

For the semi-periphery to play the economic and political stabilizing roles, the semi-periphery needs to be of a significant size. In the twentieth century, the semi-periphery generally accounted for between one-sixth and one-fifth of the world population and a similar share of the world economic output.

However, the semi-periphery cannot be too large relative to either the periphery or the core. If the semi-periphery is too large, it would reduce the world surplus value available for the core, making it impossible for the core to have monopolistic large profits or to have the necessary economic resources required to maintain internal social peace. It will also impose potentially unbearable burden on the smaller periphery by extracting excessively large amounts of natural resources and economic surplus.

As China advances into the semi-periphery, the world semi-periphery is expanding from the traditional size of between one-sixth and one-fifth of the world economy to a much larger size of between one-third and two-fifths of the world economy. In the long run, this is likely to result in substantially higher labor and resources costs for the capitalist world system.

Figure 4.3 shows that in the 1990s and the early 2000s, China's average profit rates were at levels about twice high as the US profit rate. China's very high profit rates were made possible by the intense exploitation of a large cheap labor force, massive resources consumption, and rapid growth of exports that allowed China to claim an increasingly large share of the core capitalist markets. All these conditions have been undermined. Since the Great Recession of 2008–2009, China's exports growth has slowed down sharply. As China's various ecological systems approach collapse and mass protests against environmental damages grow, the Chinese capitalism now has to begin to pay for the rapidly escalating ecological costs.

Historical experience of other semi-peripheral countries has shown that at a certain stage of capitalist (or "socialist") development, as a country's social structure was transformed through industrialization and urbanization and the proletarianized working class began to account for the majority of the total labor force, the working class and the urban middle class (the social class of highly-skilled professional workers or the "petty bourgeoisie") would demand a widening range of economic, social, and political rights. The rising working-class and middle-class militancy often led to both an accumulation crisis and a political crisis. This was what happened in the Soviet Union, Eastern Europe, Latin America, South Korea, and Taiwan in the 1980s and 1990s.

After several decades of capitalist industrialization, China's social structure has been fundamentally transformed. China's non-agricultural employment was 40 percent of the total employment in 1990, 48 percent in 1995, 50 percent in 2000, 55 percent in 2005, 63 percent in 2010, and 70 percent in 2014. Historical experience from countries such as Poland, South Korea, and Brazil indicates that when a semi-peripheral country's non-agricultural employment exceeded 70 percent of the total employment, the country often experienced a surge of working-class struggles and major political instabilities.

As China's rural surplus labor force begins to be depleted, Chinese working-class struggles have visibly increased. The Chinese workers' growing bargaining power has been reflected by the reversal of falling wage share in China's national income. By this author's estimate, China's total labor income (including the urban formal-sector workers' wages, urban private-sector workers' wages, the estimated informal-sector workers' wages, the agricultural laborers' incomes, and the employers' social insurance contributions) as a share of China's GDP declined sharply from 46 percent in 1990 to 37 percent in 1995 and to 34 percent in 2000. From 2000 to 2010, it stabilized around 34 percent. However, by 2014, China's labor income as a share of GDP recovered to 40 percent. On the other hand, China's capitalist income as a share of GDP rose from 31 percent in 1990 to 43 percent in 1995. It fell to 39 percent in 2000 and stabilized at the high level of around 40 percent between 2000 and 2010. But by 2014, the capitalist income share fell back to 33 percent.

The growing strength of the Chinese working class is also reflected by the relative positions of the Chinese wages in the capitalist world system. The Chinese manufacture sector workers' average wage (calculated as the weighted average of the formal-sector workers' wage and informal-sector migrant workers' wage) was 1.8 percent of the US manufacturing sector average wage in 1990, 2.1 percent in 1995, 2.6 percent in 2000, 4.1 percent in 2005, 8.8 percent in 2010, and 16.6 percent in 2014.

Figure 4.6 compares the manufacturing sector's wage cost per dollar of value added in China and the United States from 1990 to 2014.

In the early 1990s, the Chinese industries were still dominated by state owned enterprises. China's wage cost was around 25 cents per dollar of value added, about three-quarters of the US wage cost per dollar (about 33 cents). For China's state industrial sector, the wage cost per dollar was between 31 and 35 cents.

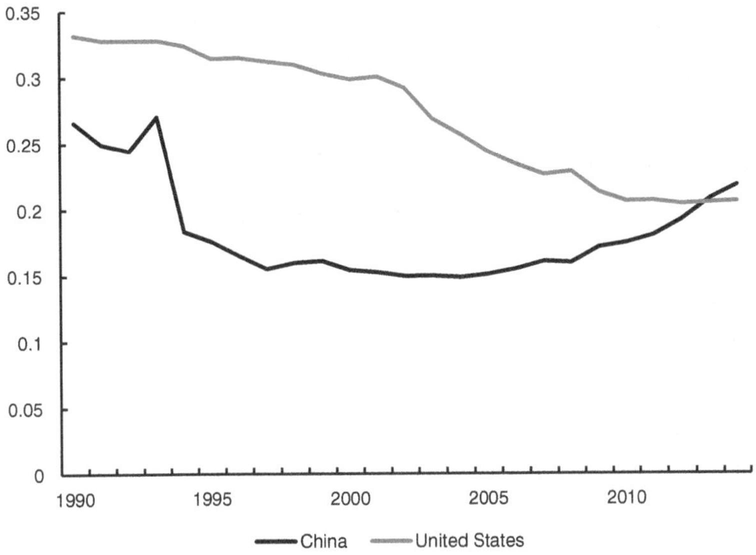

Figure 4.6 Wage cost per dollar of value added, China and the US manufacturing, 1990–2014

Sources: The Chinese manufacturing workers' wages are from China's National Bureau of Statistics (National Bureau of Statistics 2016). The Chinese manufacture sector's average wage is calculated as the average of the formal sector (the "urban units") workers' wage and the migrant workers' wage weighted by their employment in the manufacturing sector. The US manufacturing workers' wages are from ERP (2015), Table B-15, "Hours and Earnings in Private Non-Agricultural Industries, 1970–2014". The US workers are assumed to work 45 weeks a year. China's manufacturing employment is estimated using data from National Bureau of Statistics (2016). The US manufacturing employment is from BEA (2016), Table 6.5. China's and the US manufacturing value added are from World Bank (2016).

From the capitalist point of view, the Chinese state owned industries were not competitive enough in the global market.

In 1994, a large depreciation of the Chinese Yuan (*renminbi*) from 5.8 Yuan per dollar to 8.6 Yuan per dollar helped to open up a large gap between the Chinese wage cost and the US wage cost. By the late 1990s, China's wage cost per dollar was reduced to about one-half of the US level, turning China into a major source of global surplus value.

From 2000 to about 2010, the gap between the Chinese wage cost and the US wage cost narrowed as the US manufacturing workers' wages stagnated despite rising productivity. In effect, the low Chinese wages helped to pull down the manufacturing workers' wages in the US and other core capitalist countries as the neoliberal "race to bottom" operated on a global scale.

However, the Chinese wage cost per dollar began to rise after 2005 and the rise accelerated after 2010. By 2014, the Chinese wage cost per dollar exceeded the US level. As the Chinese workers claim a bigger share of the value of output, the Chinese capitalist industries are losing "competitiveness" in the global capitalist market.

Indeed, China's economy-wide profit rate has fallen sharply since 2007 (see Figure 4.3). From 2007 to 2014, China's profit rate fell from about 30 percent to about 19 percent. At this rate, in just a few years, China's profit rate could fall into levels that were historically associated with major crises of American capitalism (between 10 and 15 percent).

China and the global climate catastrophes

One of the most important world-historical consequences of the "rise of China" as a major semi-peripheral economic power has to do with the dramatic acceleration of global ecological crisis, especially the rapid rise of global carbon dioxide emissions. From 2000 to 2014, world carbon dioxide emissions from fossil fuels burning rose from 25.5 billion tons to 35.5 billion tons. China's emissions grew from 3.5 billion tons to 9.8 billion tons, accounting for 62 percent of the world emissions growth during the 14 years (BP 2015).

The year 2015 proved to be the hottest year since the modern records of global surface temperature began. The global average surface temperature is now about one degree Celsius higher than the pre-industrial era. According to James Hansen, one of the world's leading climate scientists, if global warming exceeds two degrees Celsius, sea level will rise by 5–9 meters in the next 50–200 years (largely because of the collapse of the West Antarctica ice sheets). "It is unlikely that coastal cities or low-lying areas such as Bangladesh, European lowlands, and large portions of the United States eastern coast and northeast China plains could be protected against such large sea level rise" (Hansen *et al.* 2015). Many of the world's major cities, such as Tokyo, Shanghai, Hong Kong, Mumbai, Kolkata, Karachi, Buenos Aires, St. Petersburg, New York, Miami, and London, will be at risk of flooding (Spratt and Sutton 2008).

If global warming rises above 3 degrees Celsius, sea level is likely to rise by 25 meters. The Amazon rainforest may collapse and water flows into Asia's great rivers (the Indus, Ganges, Brahmaputra, Mekong, Yangzi, and Yellow rivers) will fall by up to 90 percent. Drought and famine may turn large terrestrial areas uninhabitable and billions of environmental refugees may be forced to move from the sub-tropics to mid-latitudes (Spratt and Sutton 2008).

It is obvious that to preserve civilization as we know it, humanity should strive to limit global warming to no more than 2 degrees and should prevent global warming of more than 3 degrees at all cost.

According to the Fifth Assessment Report of the United Nations Intergovernmental Panel on Climate Change, to prevent the atmospheric concentration of carbon dioxide equivalent from rising above 450 parts per million by the end of the twenty-first century (a level of greenhouse gases that roughly corresponds to long-term global warming of 2 degrees), the cumulative world carbon dioxide emissions from 2011 to 2100 need to be no more than about 1 trillion tons (IPCC 2014). From 2011 to 2015, the world had already emitted about 175 billion tons of carbon dioxide from fossil fuels burning. The remaining 825 billion tons of "emissions budget," to be used up over the last 85 years of the century, implies average annual emissions of 9.7 billion tons. This is about the same as China's annual emissions today. As the world population is projected to rise to about 9 billion by the mid-twenty-first century, world average per capita carbon dioxide emissions need to fall from the current level of about 4.9 tons to about 1.1 tons (an emissions level that is lower than today's per capita emissions in Georgia, Namibia, Vietnam, and India). For all practical purposes, it is no longer possible for the world to limit the long-term global warming to no more than 2 degrees Celsius.

According to IPCC's Fifth Assessment Report, to prevent the atmospheric concentration of carbon dioxide equivalent from rising above 550 parts per million by the end of the twenty-first century (a level of greenhouse gases that roughly corresponds to long-term global warming of three degrees), the cumulative world carbon dioxide emissions from 2011 to 2100 need to be no more than about 2 trillion tons (IPCC 2014). Subtracting the 175 billion tons that had been emitted between 2011 and 2015, the remaining "emissions budget" is 1.83 trillion tons. Averaged over 85 years, the implied average annual emissions are calculated to be about 21 billion tons or approximately 2.4 tons per person for a future world with a population of 9 billion.

In 2014, China's per capita energy consumption reached 2.2 tons of oil equivalent and per capita carbon dioxide emissions reached 7.2 tons (BP 2015). To bring China's carbon dioxide emissions down to a level that is consistent with the per capita emissions required for limiting global warming to no more than 3 degrees, China's per capita emissions will have to fall by about 67 percent.

Using China's energy balance tables, it can be calculated that in 2012, 43 percent of China's carbon dioxide emissions were produced in various industrial production processes; 41 percent were produced in electric power generation, 7 percent in the transportation sector, and 9 percent in the rest of the economy (including agriculture, construction, services, and the residential sector) (National Bureau of Statistics 2016).

Although the renewable energies have made rapid advances, both the renewable energies (such as hydro, wind, and solar) and the nuclear energy are currently best used for electricity generation. Renewable and nuclear energies cannot substitute for fossil fuels in various high-temperature industrial processes, cement production, and primary steel production. They cannot be chemical raw materials or replace oil as liquid fuels in the transportation sector (Heinberg 2015). Assuming that in the future, 100 percent of electricity generation can be de-carbonized (a very optimistic assumption as wind and solar electricity is intermittent and currently needs coal-fired or gas-fired electricity to provide back-up) and 50 percent of the transportation sector can be electrified (essentially assuming that all road passenger transportation can be electrified), this would only reduce China's emission intensity of energy consumption by about 45 percent.

In 2014, China's emission intensity of energy consumption was about 3.3 tons per ton of oil equivalent. A 65 percent reduction of China's emission intensity of energy consumption (much more ambitious than the 45 percent reduction that seems to represent the maximum extent of possible technological progress in the short- and the medium-term) would bring China's emission intensity down to about 1.2 tons per ton of oil equivalent. Assuming that this can be accomplished, China's per capita energy consumption still needs to be reduced to and then stabilized at about 2 tons of oil equivalent in order to keep the per capita carbon dioxide emissions at no more than 2.4 tons.

Towards eco-socialist dictatorship?

The capitalist world system is based on the highly unequal distribution of wealth across the three structural positions of core, semi-periphery, and periphery and the pursuit of endless accumulation of capital. Historically, the operations of the system have been made possible by the concentration of wealth in the core that has allowed the core to function as the center of the system-wide capital accumulation.

When rising costs of production and growing competition reduced the profit rates in the core capitalist countries, the semi-periphery was traditionally the geographic zone where industrial capital from the core could be relocated. Global capital relocation helped to restore the profit rates in the core and re-create favorable conditions of capital accumulation.

By the late twentieth century, the historical semi-periphery had become too "expensive" for capital relocation and a large peripheral country, China, was mobilized to actively participate in global capital accumulation. However, as the Chinese working class and urban middle class begin to demand a growing range of economic, social, and political rights, the Chinese capitalist profit rate has fallen sharply. Potentially, the Chinese working class may push up not only China's but also the global labor cost, undermining the global capital accumulation.

As China advances into the semi-periphery, the size of the periphery is substantially reduced in terms of both population and economic output. This may seriously reduce the economic surplus that can be generated by the periphery to be transferred to the core. If the massive amount of surplus value that is currently generated by China and transferred to the core is completely withdrawn from the global unequal exchange without compensation, the foundation upon which the capitalist world system has been built so far may begin to fall apart.

After centuries of relentless capital accumulation, the continuing existence of the capitalist world system is no longer compatible with the basic requirements of global ecological sustainability. The previous section makes it clear that to prevent global warming from rising above 3 degrees Celsius, it is necessary to limit per capita carbon dioxide emissions to no more than 2.4 tons and per capita energy consumption to no more than 2 tons of oil equivalent. Two tons of oil equivalent, roughly corresponds to the energy content of 600 gallons of gasoline, or the annual fuel consumption of a regular passenger car in the United States. Clearly, without highly egalitarian distribution of energy and other material resources, it will be impossible to meet the population's basic needs that are consistent with a decent life and simultaneously meet the requirements of climate stabilization.

Figure 4.7 compares per capita carbon dioxide emissions and human development indices for 135 countries in the world. Currently, only Cuba, a country that has maintained some essential socialist characteristics, has succeeded in achieving "very high human development" (based on the United Nations

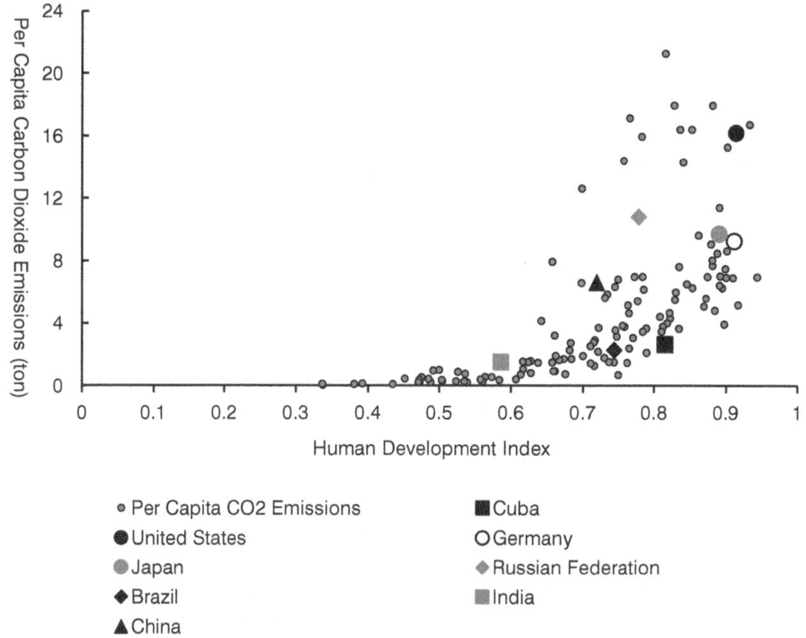

Figure 4.7 Carbon dioxide emissions and human development, 2013

Sources: Per capita carbon dioxide emissions for 2013 are from IEA (2015). Human Development Indexes for 2013 are from the United Nations' Human Development Report (UNDP 2014).

definition of having a human development index greater than 0.8) while keeping per capita carbon dioxide emissions very close to 2.4 tons (Cuba's per capita emissions in 2013 was 2.6 tons).

To keep per capita energy consumption at no more than 2 tons of oil equivalent while providing every citizen with a decent living, it is necessary for society as a whole to exercise democratic control over all the energy resources, democratically decide the social priorities of energy uses (food production, basic residential heating and lightening, essential public transportation, health care, education, and certain basic industries), minimize and possibly eliminate various luxury and unessential consumption (such as the fuel consumption of private passenger cars and personal air travel).

To the extent that ecological sustainability requires egalitarian distribution of material resources and social control over the basic means of production, it can only be achieved through some form of "socialism". Moreover, in the sense that the future socialism will have to "dictate" the population's material consumption levels in accordance with social equity and ecological sustainability, decide the social priority of various consumption purposes, and greatly reduce the material privileges of the wealthier sections of the population, it may be said to be based on "eco-socialist dictatorship".

In the coming decades, we will find out whether China can play a leading role in the global transition towards eco-socialist dictatorship.

Appendix: estimating labor terms of trade

A country's labor term of trade is defined as the ratio of the labor embodied per million-dollar of *the domestic component of* merchandise exports over the labor embodied per million-dollar of *domestically used* merchandise imports. The domestic component of merchandise exports is the merchandise exports less the estimated imported component of exports. The domestically used merchandise imports are the merchandise imports less the estimated imported component of exports.

The imported component of exports is estimated by assuming that the imported component as a share of the exports is the same as the imported component of domestic expenditures as a share of domestic expenditures:

> Imported component of exports / exports = imports / (GDP + imports) = imports / (household consumption + government consumption + gross capital formation + exports)

Total labor embodied in the domestic content of merchandise exports is the sum of the labor embodied in agricultural raw material exports and the labor embodied in the domestic content of industrial exports. Labor embodied in agricultural raw material exports is estimated as the dollar value of agricultural raw material exports divided by the agricultural value added per worker. Labor embodied in the domestic content of the industrial exports is estimated as the dollar value of the domestic content of industrial exports divided by the industrial value added per worker. Labor embodied per million-dollar of the domestic content of merchandise exports is then calculated using the total labor embodied in the domestic content of merchandise exports divided by the dollar value of the domestic content of merchandise exports.

Total labor embodied in domestically used merchandise imports is the sum of the labor embodied in the domestically used merchandise imports from each of the following regions: East Asia and Pacific (developing countries), Europe and Central Asia (developing countries), Latin America and Caribbean (developing countries), Middle East and North Africa (developing countries), South Asia, Sub-Saharan Africa (developing countries), the United States, and other high income countries. For each region, labor embodied per million-dollar of its domestic content of merchandise exports is calculated, which is then multiplied by the dollar value of a country's domestically used merchandise imports from that region to derive the labor embodied in the domestically used merchandise imports from that region.

The dollar value of a country's domestically used merchandise imports from a region is estimated by using the region's share in the country's total merchandise imports multiplied by the country's total domestically used merchandise imports.

A country's labor embodied per million-dollar of domestically used merchandise imports is then calculated using the total labor embodied in domestically used merchandise imports divided by the dollar value of the domestically used merchandise imports.

References

Arrighi, Giovanni, Po-keung Hui, Ho-fung Hung, and Mark Selden. 2003. "Historical Capitalism, East and West," in Giovanni Arrighi, Takeshi Hamashita, and Mark Selden (eds.), *The Resurgence of East Asia: 500, 150 and 50 Year Perspective*, pp.259–333. London and New York: Routledge.

BEA (Bureau of Economic Analysis, the United States) 2016. "Income and Employment by Industry." http://www.bea.gov/iTable/iTable.cfm?ReqID=9&step=1#reqid=9&step=1&isuri=1.

BP (British Petroleum) 2015. *Statistical Review of World Energy*. http://www.bp.com/en/global/corporate/energy-economics/statistical-review-of-world-energy.html.

ERP (Economic Report of the President, United States) 2015. *Economic Report of the President*, Statistical Appendixes. https://www.gpo.gov/fdsys/browse/collection.action;jsessionid=24W0VqSLb7p1z2hqqZhjgW58mvhMVQwNT2VTnsGbvpvrnnQnmhjz!1896643129!-731145847?collectionCode=ERP&browsePath=2015&isCollapsed=false&leafLevelBrowse=false&isDocumentResults=true&ycord=0.

Hansen, James, Makiko Sato, Paul Hearty, Reto Ruedy, Maxwell Kelley, Valerie Masson-Delmotte, Garry Russell, George Tselioudis, Junji Gao, Eric Rignot, Isabella Velicogna, Evgeniya Kandiano, Karina von Schuckmann, Pushker Karecha, Allegra N. Legrande, Michael Bauer, and Kwak-Wai Lo. 2015. "Ice Melt, Sea Level Rise and Superstorms: Evidence from Paleoclimate Data, Climate Modeling, and Modern Observations That 2°C Global Warming Is Highly Dangerous." *Atmospheric Chemistry and Physics Discussion* 15: 20059-20179. http://www.atmos-chem-phys-discuss.net/15/20059/2015/acpd-15-20059-2015.pdf.

Heinberg, Richard. 2015. "Renewable Energy After COP21: Nine Issues for Climate Thinkers to Think about on the Journey Home." December 14, 2015, Published by Post Carbon Institute. http://www.postcarbon.org/renewable-energy-after-cop21/.

IEA (International Energy Agency) 2015. *Key World Energy Statistics*, October 2015. https://www.iea.org/publications/freepublications/publication/key-world-energy-statistics-2015.html.

IPCC (Intergovernmental Panel on Climate Change) 2014. *Climate Change 2014: Mitigation of Climate Change. Contribution of Working Group III to the Fifth Assessment Report of the Intergovernmental Panel on Climate Change*, Summary for Policy Makers. http://mitigation2014.org/report/summary-for-policy-makers.

Lenin, Vladimir I. 1973[1918]. "State and Revolution," in *Collected Works of Vladimir Lenin*, Volume 25, pp. 381–492. Moscow: Progressive Publishers.

Li, Minqi. 2015. *China and the Twenty-First Century Crisis*. London: Pluto Press.

Maddison, Angus. 2010. "Statistics on World Population, GDP, and Per Capita GDP, 1-2008 AD." http://www.ggdc.net/MADDISON/oriindex.htm.

National Bureau of Statistics, People's Republic of China. 2016. *Statistical Yearbook of China*, various issues. http://www.stats.gov.cn/tjsj/ndsj/.

Riskin, Carl. 1975. "Surplus and Stagnation in Modern China," in Dweight H. Perkins (ed.), *China's Modern Economy in Historical Perspective*, pp.49–84, Stanford, CA: Stanford University Press.

Spratt, David and Philip Sutton. 2008. *Climate Code Red: The Case for a Sustainability Emergency*. http://www.climatecodered.net.

UNDP (United Nations Development Programme) 2014. *Human Development Report 2014: Sustaining Human Progress: Reducing Vulnerabilities and Building Resilience*. http://hdr.undp.org/sites/default/files/hdr14-report-en-1.pdf.

Vercueil, Julien. 2012. *Les pays émergents. Brésil-Russie-Inde-Chine: Mutations* Économiques *et Nouveaux* Défis (Emerging Countries. Brazil-Russia-India-China: Economic Change and New Challenges), 3rd ed. Paris: Bréal (English summary cited from Wikipedia on "Emerging Markets").

Wallerstein, Immanuel. 1974a. "The Rise of Future Demise of the Capitalist World System: Concepts for Comparative Analysis." *Comparative Studies in Society and History* 16(4): 387–415.

Wallerstein, Immanuel. 1974b. "Dependence in An Interdependent World: The Limited Possibilities of Transformation within the Capitalist World-Economy." *African Studies Review* 17: 1–26.

Wikipedia. 2016. "Emerging Markets." https://en.wikipedia.org/wiki/Emerging_markets (accessed on January 16, 2016).

World Bank. 2016. *World Development Indicators*. http://databank.worldbank.org/data/reports.aspx?source=world-development-indicators.

5 The BRICS re-scramble Africa

Patrick Bond

Introduction

Systems of capital accumulation left Africa "scrambled" long before the infamous 1884–1885 border carve-up was completed in Berlin. There, negotiators from the colonial powers Britain, France, Portugal, Germany and Belgium created scores of dysfunctional national units without reference to prior indigenous social organization. Setting the stage for colonial domination, the transatlantic enslavement of approximately 12 million Africans from the fifteenth to nineteenth centuries was followed by the first systematic Western extraction projects: Kimberley diamonds (1867), Johannesburg gold (1884) and the myriad other mineral and petroleum outflows that followed. Then, over the next century, came repeated disasters for Africa: the colonial project's catastrophic distortions; the "false decolonization" and neo-colonial power relationships after 1950s–1970s independence struggles were won; the durability of settler-colonialism especially in Southern Africa through the late twentieth century; the Cold War machinations until 1990; the foreign debt enslavement and structural adjustment policies of the neoliberal era, especially the lost decades of the 1980s–1990s; calamities associated with ongoing wars and terrorism; scores of African dictatorships supported by Washington, London and Paris; the looming destruction posed by climate change; and the resource cursing alongside "Africa Rising" myth-making of recent years. All these largely resulted from capital accumulation processes that favored Western corporations and their African comprador partners. The geopolitical arrangements and multilateral economic management strategies associated with this historic trajectory have – since even before Rosa Luxemburg wrote the seminal text in 1913 – earned the tag "imperialism," because it is (as she showed using Africa as her main research base) in the combination of periodic global capitalist crises, the expansion of corporations' geographic reach, the growing ambitions of financiers, and the fusion of capitalist/non-capitalist exploitative prowess that Western-dominated accumulation continues to underdevelop Africa.

Would the advent of the Brazil-Russia-India-China-South Africa (BRICS) "bloc" (or network) herald a dramatic change in these arrangements? After all, since 1990 when the Cold War ended, formidable changes have beset African political economy. With the USSR becoming (an initially impoverished) Russia during the 1990s, the dramatic decline of Western overseas development aid to Africa reflected new power balances and geopolitical calculations. The liberation of South Africa from apartheid in 1994 portended a more aggressive economic role – which has ebbed and flowed, with Johannesburg firms still the largest source of FDI in Africa – as well as Pretoria's PanAfrican political leadership, in the 2001 New Partnership for Africa's Development (Nepad), the 2003 African Peer Review Mechanism (APRM), in the controversial election to the African Union's chair of President Jacob Zuma's ex-wife Nkosozana Dlamini-Zuma from 2012–2016 and in Zuma's 2015 push for a military-oriented "African Capacity for Immediate Response to Crises". South Africa intervened to "keep peace" in nearly a dozen African sites (but with mixed results and occasional disasters).

Simultaneously, other BRICS increased their footprint in Africa. The 1990s–2000s rise of Chinese trade and parastatal investment (albeit with uneven flows) raised the continent's level of GDP – apparently justifying $200 billion in new Sub-Saharan African foreign indebtedness from 2006–2016 (a 50 percent increase, mostly to China) – at the same time the continent's overall wealth shrunk dramatically due to (net negative) natural capital depletion in nine out of ten countries (World Bank 2014). The Forum on China-Africa Cooperation met every three years from 2000–2015, and at the last summit in Johannesburg announced notional Chinese commitments of $60 billion, along with a "reindustrialization" strategy for light manufacturing enterprises with Ethiopia in the vanguard. From 2003–2016, Brazil's Workers Party leaders made encouraging sounds about a benign approach by its corporations and development aid mechanisms in Lusophone Africa (Angola, Mozambique and Cape Verde). In New Delhi, an India-Africa Forum Summit to promote interstate and business relations was held in 2008, and again in Addis Ababa in 2011 and New Delhi in 2015, with the latter meeting generating a $10 billion Indian commitment before 41 heads of state in attendance (up from 10–15 in the prior two). Even the least active of the BRICS, Russia, was meanwhile promoting nuclear energy, arms, transport, mining and petroleum deals in more than a dozen African countries. (In competition, Barack Obama's 2014 meeting with most African leaders in Washington had a $37 billion deal-making headline.)

In short, prospects for an ever-greater BRICS role in Africa were the source of enormous optimism. But reality has begun to set in. From 2011, the crash in commodity prices signified the exhaustion of Chinese Keynesian infrastructure expansion and left African materials exporters with enormous excess capacity and debt (mostly to China). The BRICS countries' role in world trade amplified economic and political contradictions associated with generalized world capitalist overproduction and global governance failure; this was evident at the World Trade Organization's (WTO's) revitalization in December 2015, as the Nairobi summit had devastating implications for food sovereignty in Africa as well as in the BRICS themselves. The same month in Washington, International Monetary Fund (IMF) vote restructuring featured four BRICS countries' increases (led by China with 35 percent) but also dramatic setbacks for Nigeria (–41 percent) and South

Africa (−21 percent) as well as smaller economies which were not as capable in supporting the institution's recapitalization. Finally, the December 2015 Paris Agreement confirmed Africa's victimization by climate change, mainly because the BRICS allied with historic greenhouse gas emitters, especially the United States and European Union, in a deal celebrated by polluters because not only are (weak) emissions cut commitments non-binding (with no legal accountability for violations), there is no longer a prospect of legal liabilities (the "climate debt") against the wealthy countries for their role in what are likely to be 200 million additional African deaths this century due to extreme weather, droughts and increased temperatures.

In this context of worsening political-economic and political-ecological devastation traceable to both the BRICS and Western powers, there are also worrying socio-cultural backlashes against BRICS firms and citizens operating in Africa (and likewise within BRICS against Africans – especially African immigrants to South Africa). The one example of constructive intra-BRICS solidarity, which has saved millions of lives of HIV+ Africans already, is the Indian and Brazilian violation of Intellectual Property on AntiRetroViral (ARV) medicines that South African activists and allies forced to become available as generic supplies through protest against Big Pharma, the WTO's Trade Related Intellectual Property System and the South African and US governments. That model of "brics from below", which will be required to link hinterland-African anti-extraction and debt activists to South African and other BRICS counterparts, is probably the only positive feature of the transition of the "emerging powers" into what now appear to be, at least in the cases of Brazil, Russia, China and South Africa, *submerging*, albeit still explicitly *sub-imperial* powers (Bond and Garcia 2015).

In nearly all African countries, infrastructural and productive investments are desperately needed, along with life-saving medicines and access to new technologies. Development aid, trade, loans and Foreign Direct Investment (FDI) are considered vital for these purposes, yet indisputably, the world's main political-economic and political-ecological processes have been hostile to the continent since slavery, unequal trade, colonialism, durable settler-colonialism and neo-colonial modes of extraction began in the fifteenth century. Nearly without respite, Africa has witnessed external actors whose imperial, colonial and now multilateral institutional power bases have largely drawn surpluses from the continent without reinvestment (aside from the twentieth century's settler colonial societies – South Africa, Rhodesia, Mozambique and Angola – which prospered from the 1930s–1960s). There have been exceptions to the despair, including two high-growth high-investment countries (Botswana and Mauritius). And there have been inspiring, victorious resistance struggles in many African countries and international solidarity campaigns against slavery, colonialism, apartheid and illegitimate debt.

But writing in mid-2016, the main forces drawing Africans into the world economy appear uniformly destructive. The 2002–2011 commodity super-cycle peaked just at the point that Africa Rising rhetoric was ramped up, apparently so as to encourage the continent's elites to continue trade and investment liberalization aimed at more intense extractivism, even when this was obviously not in their economies' interests. In part because the value of minerals and petroleum exports shrunk, the continent's foreign debt doubled to more than $400 billion after the West's (partial) debt relief in 2006. FDI flowed into Africa more rapidly until a 2015 reversal, but was mostly directed at the extraction of primary commodities in a process that (unlike Australia, Canada and Norway with similar commodity export orientations) left African countries "resource cursed", losing far more in depleted minerals and petroleum than regained via the capital account (World Bank 2014). The West's foreign aid to Africa shrunk dramatically after the Cold War ended in 1990, and subsequent increases after 2000 translated only into marginal gains (e.g. in education and health). However, the Forum for China-Africa Cooperation has recently heralded a dramatic increase in aid and credit availability, though not without complications discussed below.

In this context of apparent shifts in world power, in March 2013 Durban hosted the heads of state summit of the BRICS: Brazil, Russia, India, China and South Africa. The BRICS have been heralded not only as major "emerging markets" in terms of their GDP growth – although, at least from 2014–2016, three were economically *sub*merging (Brazil, Russia and South Africa) – but as the main forces reshaping multilateral institution governance. To illustrate, just before the G20 meeting in China in mid-2016, an experienced journalist for a major Johannesburg Sunday newspaper, Godfrey Mutizwa (2016), applauded the BRICS:

> From a desire in 2009 to advance the reform of the Bretton Woods institutions – the International Monetary Fund and the World Bank – the group has moved from cooperation to a commitment in 2015 to act jointly on key international issues ranging from UN Security Council reform to global conflict and climate change.

To be sure, this is conventional wisdom in mainstream South Africa, especially in the wake of the Durban summit. Yet in reality, such "joint action" (albeit rarely with all five BRICS aligned) has *amplified* not ameliorated the underdevelopment of Africa, *where it has been effective,* e.g. in the December 2015 decisions taken in Paris, Nairobi and Washington.[1] To make this case, the structure of the argument that follows is that the BRICS have risen up to a point in the global division of labor, then suffered intense fall-out from the broader crisis of capital accumulation (reflected in Africa most spectacularly in the end of the commodity super-cycle), and have as a result intensified the metabolism of exploitation. This exploitative role in Africa is worsening in part through the BRICS' current strategy of assimilating into (not offering genuine alternatives to) the multilateral finance, trade and climate systems, all of which have devastating implications for this continent.

In part this strategy of weakening many African countries is entirely coherent, as seen through the predatory actions of BRICS' corporations. This is especially obvious in the extractive sectors where to a large extent the BRICS' corporate reaction to falling commodity prices is increased volumes of output in search of a stable supply of profits. Space constraints do not permit a cataloguing of these experiences (see, e.g. Burgis 2015, Carmody 2013). But revealing cases of BRICS-based looting have emerged, such as:

- Chinese entrepreneur Sam Pa's Queensway Group in Marange, Zimbabwe where in 2016 Robert Mugabe alleged $13 billion in diamonds extracted over the prior decade are unaccounted for (only $2 billion of revenues were officially recorded);
- Vedanta's purchase of Africa's largest copper mine (Zambia's Konkola) for $25 million followed by at least $500 million in externalized profits *annually*;
- AngloGold Ashanti's collaboration with Democratic Republic of the Congo (DRC) warlords during a period in which 5 million civilians were killed;
- displacement by Brazil's Vale mining house of thousands Mozambican villagers during its search for coal;
- sales pitches for Russian Rosatom nuclear power plants to corruption-prone governments in South Africa, Zambia, Uganda, Egypt and Nigeria;
- tax-dodging in various African countries (using Mauritius as a hot money center) by South Africa's cellphone giant MTN (when chaired by subsequent deputy president Cyril Ramaphosa), as well as MTN's failure to cut off Boko Haram's Nigerian cellphone accounts in 2015 which led to a $1.9 billion fine;
- the dubious roles of South African politicians Tokyo Sexwale and Khulubuse Zuma – both in league with Israeli mining tycoon Dan Gertler – in central African deals; and
- the 2013 South African National Defense Force armed intervention to support the authoritarian regime of François Bozize in Bangui, Central Africa (leaving more than a dozen fatalities but also more than 800 rebel deaths) on behalf of Johannesburg businesses.

But these are some of the more extreme cases of corporate-driven underdevelopment, and what this chapter dwells on instead is the broader context in which the BRICS are re-scrambling Africa.

Stressed BRICS on uneven global economic and geopolitical terrain

Together as a bloc, the five BRICS control 26 percent of the earth's land mass but 42 percent of its population. Although hosting 46 percent of the global workforce, the BRICS are responsible for just 14 percent of world trade and 19 percent of world Gross Domestic Product, which rises to 27 percent if measured in purchasing power parity (PPP). In per capita GDP (also in PPP terms), only Russia has a higher figure than the world average ($11,800). The bloc was, however, initially named and celebrated – as BRIC, without South Africa until Beijing invited Pretoria to join in 2010 – by Goldman Sachs Assets Management chair Jim O'Neill in 2001. The first formal BRIC event was in 2006 when foreign ministers met at the United Nations, followed by heads-of-state summits in Yekaterinburg in 2009, Brasilia in

2010, Sanya in 2011, New Delhi in 2012, Durban in 2013, Fortaleza in 2014, Ufa in 2015 and Goa in 2016. There is usually a degree of pageantry and back-slapping associated with these events though they last just two days, typically. And there are parallel, often overlapping conferences of business leaders which have access to the state officials, as well as meetings of labor (since Durban in 2013) and "civil BRICS" (innocuous civil society groups, starting in Russia in 2015). Dozens of other BRICS-related events occur in between on different schedules, including meetings of ministers responsible for economies, security, agriculture, health and municipal government, as well as the alliance of think-tanks and interested academics. There have been three counter-summits (and protest marches) dedicated to expanding the terrain of critical analysis, in Durban, Fortaleza and Goa.

In Durban, "gateway to Africa" rhetoric was justified by the dedication of a half-day discussion between BRICS and more than a dozen heads of state from the continent. (This strategy of drawing in the host's friendly neighbors was repeated in Brasilia in 2014 and Ufa in 2015.) Then deputy foreign minister Marius Fransman (2013) expressed conventional wisdom just before the 2013 summit: "South Africa presents a gateway for investment on the continent, and over the next 10 years the African continent will need $480 billion for infrastructure development". The Durban event's focus on Africa undergirded the renewed local emphasis on mega-project economic development strategies focusing on an "aerotropolis", the Dube Trade Port, harbor widening and deepening in what is already Africa's largest container port, and a new "Dig Out Port", anticipated to cost hundreds of billions of rands. In the latter cases, however, Durban's leaders believe their main competition is from African ports, e.g. Maputo in Mozambique which is more favorably suited to eventually supplying the huge Johannesburg market and northerly transport routes.

As a bloc, BRICS issues periodic communiqués and occasionally acts in concert, for example successfully lobbying against the proposed expulsion of Russia from the G20 Brisbane summit following sanctions imposed on Moscow by the West after the March 2014 transfer of power over Crimea. But BRICS will ultimately be known not for its generally anti-Western rhetoric, but for what it does, concretely, to change the world. The most important institutional innovations – discussed below – are the BRICS New Development Bank (NDB) for project loans, and the Contingent Reserve Arrangement (CRA) which stands ready to augment the IMF in the event bail-out credits are required by BRICS members. There was also talk of an internet cable rerouting to avoid United States interference and a credit rating agency alternative to Moody's, Fitch and Standard & Poors, but these have not come to fruition.

Starting in mid-2013, the "tapering" of US Federal Reserve "Quantitative Easing" (i.e. slightly tighter monetary policy) lowered the value of four BRICS currencies (all aside from the yuan). Full-fledged economic depression has characterized Brazil and Russia since 2014, partly because commodity prices plummeted, and South Africa was pushed to the brink of recession in 2016. India's extreme uneven and combined development threatens to leave the vast majority of citizens behind, notwithstanding the world's fastest growth rates in what will soon be the world's most populous country. China's lower growth rates, much-reduced commodity imports and stagnation of major new investment (as a result of massive overcapacity) became the world's main economic threat by 2014. The Beijing-Shanghai-Shenzhen capitalist and state elites themselves stand vulnerable, having suffered:

- stock market crashes of over 7 percent that caused "circuit-breaker" panics on two days in the first trading week of 2016, with panicky trading forcibly halted within a half hour on the second occasion, after mid-2015 market crashes costing an estimated $3.5 trillion over the course of a fortnight;
- capital flight that reduced China's peak $4 trillion in foreign reserves in 2013 to $3.3 trillion by 2016, at a pace rising to a record $120 billion/month outflow by the end of 2015 (in contrast, the average annual "illicit financial flows" from China were $140 billion from 2003–2014, according to a study by the NGO Global Financial Integrity);
- massive industrial and commodity overcapacity especially in coal, steel and cement, requiring a new round of subsidies to avoid massive local bankruptcies;
- an inability by many Chinese borrowers to repay the fast-rising $27 trillion domestic debt, given the profusion of zombie companies and individuals who over-borrowed;
- such an over-saturation of commodities that the dependency generated elsewhere during China's import splurge is now the cause of many exporters' collapse;
- real estate overbuilding in an even more maniacal fashion, resulting in a 20 percent crash in 2014–2015, a problem far worse in the provincial cities (the ratio of real estate to GDP – 23 percent – in China had reached a level three times higher in 2016 than the US at its most property-bubbly in 2007);
- several attempts at devaluing the yuan – in late 2015 named an IMF "reserve" currency – that could start a currency war;
- bouts of regulatory incompetence and other corporate-captive maladies that include extreme urban pollution;
- the rejection of worker rights including occupational health and safety, the banning of non-sweetheart trade unions, an apartheid-style rural-urban migrant labor system, and marketing prowess (pioneered in the US) to foist consumption of especially shabby products, whose planned obsolescence is even more rapid than US corporations' slovenly standards; and
- a willingness to continue putting down citizen and worker uprisings with police violence and arrests of a couple of dozen key labor leaders here, a few hundred human rights lawyers there, thousands of environmentalists here, 15,000 internet activists there, and more hundreds of thousands of ethnic minorities.

These are some of the main socio-economic and environmental contradictions in just one BRICS country. Another debilitating financial meltdown is likely to arrive while the BRICS are suffering severe economic stresses. At the global scale, capital had, by 2016, become dangerously "overaccumulated" due to overcapacity in production, especially the basic materials Africa exports such as petroleum, iron ore (and steel and aluminium in South Africa's case), coal, platinum and nickel, all of whose prices had fallen drastically from 2011–2015 peaks to trough, as well as in labor-intensive manufacturing. The backlash in the world market was reflected in the one-third drop in the value of world trade from early 2014 to late 2015. The peak in trade was in 2008, when the Baltic Dry Index – the main measure of world shipping prices – exceeded 12,000; it subsequently fell to less than 300 by early 2016.

Profit rates are another symptom of the overaccumulation crisis, and at the global scale they fell steadily from mid-twentieth-century levels of around 30 percent to 20 percent since the neoliberal age began in the 1980s. During the years 2006–2008 and 2010–2015, year-on-year profit rates fell precipitously. Once a substantial problem of overaccumulation arises in production (from the mid-1970s), it inexorably moves to finance. The system reacts to overcapacity pressures by attempting to displace them through credit creation. After the 2008–2009 meltdown destroyed vast financial assets, the world's debt markets rose again thanks to loose monetary policy and bail-out loans, adding $15 trillion to the 2008 total debt stock of $165 trillion, but on the basis of only $8 trillion in new GDP (from $62 trillion in 2008). World stock markets continued bubbling at unprecedented levels, far out of any relation to real underlying asset values.

By July 2016, the G20 (2016) trade ministers diagnosed the overaccumulation crisis at their Shanghai meeting: "We recognize that the structural problems, including excess capacity in some industries, exacerbated by a weak global economic recovery and depressed market demand, have caused a negative impact on trade and workers. We recognize that excess capacity in steel and other industries is a global issue which requires collective responses". With such excess capacity at the global scale, ameliorative moves to cut Chinese output in steel and coal were marginal. Even former US Treasury Secretary Larry Summers (2016) declared that the world suffered "secular stagnation … an increasing propensity to save and a decreasing propensity to invest" notwithstanding inordinately low interest rates. But the best way to way to understand this "propensity to save" was because of capitalist crisis tendencies. As explained by Richard Westra (2016), "With the disarticulating of production through globalization, there existed no possibility for bloating funds to ever be converted into real capital with determinate, socially redeeming use. Instead, systemic rule changes empowered big banks, big investment firms and finance wings of giant corporations to unleash vast oceans of funds in a global orgy of money games".

Loose monetary policy had encouraged the reflation of financial bubbles and by 2013, the president of the US Federal Reserve System's Dallas bank branch, Richard Fisher, identified this contradiction in his Fed colleagues' third Quantitative Easing (QE). Central banks in the US, EU, UK and Japan can print money to bail out fragile financiers no matter how foolish the cause and corrupt the recipient bankers, or run a Negative Interest Rate Policy and devalue currencies to spur investment or compete with other economies. Though he described QE3 as "monetary Ritalin" on that occasion (losing the Fed vote by 1 to 11), Fisher had supported QE the first two times, in 2008 and 2012 due to the extreme dangers of financial meltdown. As he conceded to a stunned CNBC (2016) reporter, "What the Fed did, and I was part of it, was front-load an enormous market rally in order to create a wealth effect". The $15 trillion in QE paper wealth loaded into the world's largest banks trickled upwards to the top 0.1 percent of the richest societies, i.e. to enterprises where speculation has replaced production. Thanks to the hollowed-out Western economy that resulted from the repeated QE fix, financial crisis is again brewing. "An uncomfortable digestive period is likely now" because "The Fed is a giant weapon that has no ammunition left," Fisher remarked.

The resulting indigestion – what David Harvey (1982) termed the "devalorization of overaccumulated capital" – ebbs and flows in what appear as unpredictable surges of capital to and fro. Rising inequality plays a major role in assuring that devalorization is resisted by the wealthier markets and costs imposed on the poorer regions. BRICS are particularly susceptible to having large shares of their paper wealth devalued, especially in currency runs. There are defense mechanisms, to be sure, and the two most forward-thinking BRICS economic management teams – in China and Russia – began preparing for a coming collapse in several ways: tighter financial regulation (China ordering major international commercial banks to cease dealing in early 2016, for example); de-dollarization (e.g. in their bilateral energy relations, although Chinese T-Bill holdings still exceeded $1 trillion); purchasing gold (the world contains 35 000 tons of gold, of which China and Russia have together bought 5,000 in recent years); and shifting towards IMF Special Drawing Rights (especially China), which may become the global economic managers' next edition of the QE strategy (similar to April 2009 when $750 billion were issued to spur global demand).

Until recently, China has been immensely functional to Western capitalism, what with its banning of trade unions from Western corporate factories, its rural-urban migration controls that cheapen labor supplies, and its local ecological despoliation. Together these shifted substantial costs of production to workers, to women left in the countryside, and to nature. Yet as Johns Hopkins University sociologist Ho-fung Hung (2015) argued, "Capital accumulation in China follows the same logic and suffers from the same contradictions of capitalist development in other parts of the world. To understand the recent booms and busts of Chinese capitalism, we first have to understand capital's international trends and cycles". In a 2015 London School of Economics lecture (2015), Harvey remarked on how China served the world economy during the last decade: "There is a tale to be told here about the overaccumulation of capital … and surplus capital and labor which had to be absorbed in order to keep stability within the global system of capital accumulation". Hung (2015) agreed that this is "a typical overaccumulation crisis, epitomized by the ghost towns and shuttered factories across the country".

Not only has the unevenness of capital accumulation never been more obvious, so has extreme ecological damage risen, e.g. in Chinese and Indian cities to the extent that pollution-related health warnings are now commonplace. With China and India also representing the main threat to the world's planet due to growing greenhouse gas emissions – albeit at per capita rates far lower than the industrial countries – it has never been more important to reconcile capitalism and catastrophic climate change (and if that is impossible, then to reach beyond the former to prevent the latter). African countries (aside from South Africa) have done the least to create greenhouse gases yet are anticipated to be the ones that will suffer most from extreme weather, enduring droughts, flooding, sea-level rise and acidification, and coming carbon taxes that will lower exports. The inadequacy of the BRICS countries' inadequate Intended National Determined Contributions (INDCs) correlates to their role in global climate policy, which as codified in Paris cannot address the likelihood of catastrophic damage, with Africa the most adversely affected continent.

Political dynamics in the BRICS are diverse at the time of writing, with one head of state – Dilma Rousseff – suspended in an impeachment vote in May 2016 (generally seen as unfair given the circumstances, with impeachment and an appeal likely to follow in late 2016), while three others have strong mandates from democratic elections – Narendra Modi, Vladimir Putin and Jacob Zuma (albeit the latter suffered a frightening 8 percent decline in his party's electoral support between 2014 and 2016) – and one is a Communist Party dictatorship, led by Xi Jinping. The potential for solidarity between Brazil's Workers Party and other BRICS was dashed when the Indian foreign ministry immediately signaled that the "coup" president, Michel Temer, would be perfectly welcome at the October 2016 Goa summit.

Africa also suffers extreme political turmoil and occasionally this is reflected in tense BRICS relations. South Africa has the most active set of African interventions underway, as discussed below, but China's placement of troops in South Sudan is also a harbinger of the overlap between commercial and military interests. China's recent roles in the South African foreign affairs and finance ministries also undermine Beijing's advertised neutrality and non-interference, for Chinese officials regularly bragged about forcing the South African foreign minister to deny an entrance visa to the Dalai Lama (Bond 2013). And the Chinese were allegedly instrumental in reversing the appointment in December 2015 of finance minister Desmond van Rooyen (widely seen as a dangerously ill-equipped crony of Zuma), according to *Business Day* publisher Peter Bruce (2016): "I have reliably learnt that the Chinese were quick to make their displeasure known to Zuma. For one, their investment in Standard Bank took a big hit. Second, they've invested way too much political effort in SA to have an amateur mess it up. Their intervention was critical". The overarching political importance of the BRICS to Africa is propping up undemocratic regimes, just as political leaders from the US, Britain and France do (Bond 2013).

But it is the economic logic that is most worthy of examination in the sections below regarding BRICS' assimilation into world capitalism, and the adverse implications for the African continent. Leonce Ndikumana (2015) argues that because of the adverse power relations, Africa is both "more integrated but more marginalized". The marginalization associated with IFFs is well established, and this occurs particularly when Western and BRICS corporations externalize profits from mining. The United Nations Economic Commission on Africa (2013) showed how $319 billion was transferred illicitly from Africa during the commodity super-cycle (from 2001–2010), with the most theft in metals, $84 billion; oil, $79 billion; natural gas, $34 billion; minerals, $33 billion; petroleum and coal products, $20 billion; crops, $17 billion; food products, $17 billion; machinery, $17 billion; clothing, $14 billion; and iron and steel, $13 billion. During this period, African FDI fell from its $66 billion peak annual inflow in 2008 to a level of $50 billion by 2015, but each year, in addition to *illicit* financial outflows, there were licit flows in the form of dividend expatriation that created extreme balance of payments deficits in many countries.

Some of the deficits follow from debt repayment on mega-projects that failed to realize the returns that were promised. Chinese projects in particular have been criticized, e.g. Botswana's coal-fired power-plant failed, and Zambia's disastrous hydro-electricity expansion suffered allegations of sub-standard Chinese equipment that excessively reduced the Kariba Dam's water level. Other notorious mega-project failures, according to the *Wall Street Journal* (2014), include China Railways in Nigeria ($7.5 billion) and Libya ($4.2 billion), Chinese petroleum in Angola ($3.4 billion) and Nigeria ($1.4 billion), and Chinese metal investors in the DRC and Ghana ($3 billion each). The renewal of the Forum on China-Africa Cooperation in December 2015 did nothing to assuage critics of the type of Chinese investment and credits, and their appropriateness in a post-commodity super-cycle environment.

Even though the soured deals should offer a warning, and though commodity prices began falling in 2011, Africa has recently witnessed a dramatic increase in infrastructural project investment – real and planned – to support extraction. It was logical for BRICS leaders to identify port, bridge, road, rail, hydropower, thermal coal, nuclear energy and other infrastructure projects for subsidized investment, given that their countries' corporations would benefit from the associated extraction of minerals, petroleum and crops. The Programme for Infrastructure Development in Africa (PIDA) was the coordinating system. In 2016, the most ambitious of the PIDA projects included the Inga Hydropower Project in the DRC, which at $100 billion will be the most expensive development project in history if taken to fruition with 43,200 megaWatts of electricity (compared to the second largest, China's Three Gorges Dam at less than half that). But with commodity prices crashing, even China attempted in mid-2014 – on the eve of Obama's summit with African leaders in Washington – to get Washington's support. Two years later, the World Bank withdrew its financing, on grounds of the DRC's (and other Inga project participants') failure to comply with socio-economic and environmental agreements. Another controversial form of BRICS investment in Africa was in land, a process that has often been caricatured as "land grabbing". Thomas Ferrando (2013) developed a database to track this, discovering extensive holdings especially by Indian and Chinese firms.

These top-down processes are not uncontested. Seen from below, resistance initiatives by many African grassroots communities and shop-floors – most spectacularly in the three largest economies (Nigeria in 2012, Egypt in 2011 and South Africa throughout) – have intensified in recent years. These protests are regularly repulsed by states hostile to democracy, mostly with Western backing (although successes in Tunisia in 2011 and Burkina Faso in 2014–2015 put dictatorships onto the retreat). But Western hypocrisy is not the only factor. In many cases when African tyrants face popular critique, notably Zimbabwe, social unrest also threatens the stability of investments made by BRICS countries and corporate interests; indeed in several important African sites of struggle, the primary battle was between BRICS mining interests and affected communities and workforces. Other modes of resistance to either political tyranny or economic misery include refugee status or migrancy; in the case of South Africa, either path has been enormously difficult for Africans, as a result of malgovernance at the Department of Home Affairs and SA Police Services, as well as in working-class communities which have hosted immigrants but with periodic sites of xenophobic upsurges (2008, 2010 and 2015).

Only in the sole case of access to anti-retroviral (ARV) medicines did concerted international support dramatically improve African life expectancies, as expensive branded medicines were replaced by generics in the early 2000s. Two of the BRICS were exceptionally important allies of Africa's HIV+ community and health officials: Brazil and India had provided innovative pharmaceutical development of generic ARVs, and were unintimidated by Western corporations whose patents they abused. However, this may be seen in retrospect as an exception that proves the rule, for in 2016 right-wing governments in both countries heralded a new era of respect for intellectual property rights at the expense of their sick citizenries, with Modi pressured by Obama to retract Indian opposition to a new round of intellectual property protections that aid Big Pharma at a time when many treatable diseases continue to ravage Africa. It is in this sense that the sub-imperial role of BRICS, assimilating into international capitalism, is obvious, given the alternative that the ARV case presented. This sort of power reversal – from one genuinely anti-imperial instance to a pattern of sub-imperialism – is explained with theoretical inputs that draw especially upon Brazilian intellectuals.

Sub-imperial and anti-imperial stances

Given the intense contestation underway across these issue areas, this uneven record of Africa-BRICS relations deserves a theoretical explanation as well as strategic insights for the sake of social, economic and environmental justice. These are values regularly expressed by BRICS' own lead officials in their communiqués, sometimes in opposition to critical analysts (including this author) as well as analysts and journalists from competing Western powers. In Durban, for example, *Business Day* newspaper ran a non-stop barrage of hostile commentaries about BRICS in March 2013. One reaction was a talk given to the Academic Forum that month, by South Africa's Minister of International Relations and Cooperation Maite Nkoana-Mashabane (2013):

> The emergence of BRICS has not been well received by all of us. There are those who do not have a positive appreciation of BRICS because they believe that its continued existence will threaten the status quo and tamper with the current international balance of forces. At the other end, we find critics of

> BRICS who see it as a body of what they call "sub-imperialist" countries that are joining the club of traditional powers. These critics talk of what they call a "new scramble" for Africa, comparing the growing interest on our continent by BRICS countries to the late nineteenth century when European colonial powers partitioned Africa among themselves.

What these two groups of critics have in common is their lack of appreciation of multi-polarity for the geopolitical health of our international system. The first groups views multi-polarity in a negative sense, as a threat; while the second group would rather remain in the old system than to see it being shaken by emerging players from the South.

To see BRICS countries as "sub-imperialists" is the result of a dogmatic application of classical notions of imperialism and Immanuel Wallerstein's center-periphery model to a situation that is fundamentally different from what these theories were trying to comprehend and explain. Our scholars have to be innovative and courageous enough to develop new tools of analysis and theoretical models when history challenges us to do so. I am reminded, here, of a warning Franz Fanon made in his *The Wretched of the Earth* that, and I quote: "It so happens that the unpreparedness of the educated classes, the lack of practical links between them and the mass of the people, their laziness, and, let it be said, their cowardice at the decisive moment of the struggle will give rise to tragic mishaps". The tragic mishap in this case is that such intellectuals will be left behind and rendered irrelevant by history.

These reflections by Nkoana-Mashabane (and her then-speechwriter Eddie Maloka, subsequently head of the Africa Peer Review Mechanism) reflect a classic problem in analyzing South African public policy: "talk left, walk right" (Bond 2006). What, then, are the theoretical framings associated with sub-imperialism that upset her so much? The term originates in Brazil with the *dependencia* argument that after 1964, when a US-supported dictatorship was installed, Brasilia served as a strong US ally. According to Ruy Mauro Marini (1965: 22), "It is not a question of passively accepting North American power (although the actual correlation of forces often leads to that result), but rather of collaborating actively with imperialist expansion, assuming in this expansion *the position of a key nation*". Mathias Luce (2015) is one of the contemporary followers of Marini:

> Sub-imperialism is considered the result of the laws of dependent capitalism in combination with the world economic system configured by post-World War II capital movements. The arrival of a few socio-economic formations at the highest stage of dependent capitalism along with the rise of intermediate links in the imperialist chain made room for a new hierarchical level in the global order. In this way these formations turn into countries that do not just transfer surplus value to imperialist centers but also succeed in appropriating weaker countries' surplus value by displacing some of the contradictions specific to dependent capitalism. And they develop a policy of antagonistic cooperation with the dominant imperialism ... Every sub-imperialist country

> is part of what used to be called the semi-periphery but not every semi-peripheral country is a sub-imperialist socio-economic formation.

For Marini (1974), three key features of a sub-imperial society were regional economic extraction, the export of capital typically associated with imperialist politics, and internal corporate monopolization. Having read Rosa Luxemburg's 1913 *Accumulation of Capital* analysis of Africa's underdevelopment (using case studies from South Africa, Namibia and the DRC), Harvey (2003: 185–186) added another feature to what he termed the *New Imperialism*:

> The opening up of global markets in both commodities and capital created openings for other states to insert themselves into the global economy, first as absorbers but then as producers of surplus capitals. They then became competitors on the world stage. What might be called 'sub-imperialisms' arose … Each developing center of capital accumulation sought out systematic spatio-temporal fixes for its own surplus capital by defining territorial spheres of influence.

Updated, consider these four features:

- *the systemic processes of imperialism,* within which sub-imperialism facilitates accumulation, rely upon extra-economic coercion found in relations between capitalist and non-capitalist spheres, i.e. what Harvey (2003) calls "accumulation by dispossession", under conditions of capitalist crisis;
- those *capitalist crisis conditions* become evident within the sub-imperial economies in the form of overaccumulated capital, specifically overproduction and resulting excess capacity given that demand cannot match supply, intensified uneven geographical development (in Harvey's terminology, the "spatial fix" because it displaces the crisis across space) and financialization (the "temporal fix" insofar as the day of reckoning is postponed through the credit mechanism which displaces the crisis over time);
- as crisis conditions mature and cannot be resolved internally, the sub-imperial powers turn increasingly to their *regional spheres of influence*, and their treasuries, central banks and allied state and capitalist institutions facilitate and legitimate multilateral trade, investment and financing relationships which both serve to strengthen the *regional platform for accumulation* (even as sub-imperialist manufacturing exports destroy hinterland productive capacity and economic sovereignty) and require *a regional gendarme role* to enforce business contracts and to extract needed raw materials (and sometimes workers who lower the cost of labor); and
- the *super-exploitation* of the internal labor market intensifies which, given the limits of consumption that result, in turn "would require external markets for the resolution of its profit realization crisis," as Sam Moyo and Paris Yeros (2011) remark. Likewise, sectoral biases exist within BRICS economies, Steffen Böhm, Maria Ceci Misoczky and Sandra Moog (2012: 1629) observe:

> the sub-imperialist drive has remained the same: while domestic capital continues to invest heavily in extractive and monocultural industries at home, it is increasingly searching for investment opportunities in other peripheral markets as well, precipitating processes of accumulation by dispossession within their broader spheres of influence.

There are, in the process, occasional territorial disputes, and it is always tempting for Western powers to provoke incursions in the BRICS' regional sites of accumulation and geopolitical influence (of which the North Atlantic Treaty Organization's conflicts with Russia in Georgia, the Ukraine, Syria and Turkey, and the US with China in the South China Sea, have been most important in recent years). Although the US dominates military spending, with $610 billion in direct outlays in 2014 (and myriad other related expenses maintaining imperial order), four of the five BRICS also spent vast amounts on arms: $385 billion in 2015 (of which 55 percent was China). There are various other sites of contestation, e.g. over Washington's (and its "five eyes' allies") capacity to tap communications and computers through the internet. After revealing the US National Security Agency's (NSA) snooping capacity in 2013, whistle-blower Edward Snowden has an apparently safe Moscow exile, after fears of extradition to the US or worse (on 15 August 2016, Snowden tweeted, "Reports of my death are greatly exaggerated"). A few months later, Rousseff canceled the first visit by a Brazilian head of state to Washington in 40 years, as a way to protest Snowden's revelation that the NSA was tapping her phone.

But seen in these macro geopolitical terms, the Zuma government's initial endorsement of the NATO bombing of Libya in 2011 was the most egregious case of sub-imperial reach into Africa, against the African Union's wishes (and to be fair, Pretoria did reverse course and opposed further intervention). But behind the scenes, US journalist Nick Turse identified the Pentagon's "war fighting combatant command" in dozens of African states. It soon transpired that there was a blunt division of labor at work between Washington and its deputy sheriff in Pretoria, as a strategist from the Africa Command explained why they are training so many African militaries, including SA National Defense Force soldiers: "We don't want to see our guys going in and getting whacked" (Cochran 2010). At the conclusion of his 2014 meeting with Obama as part of a US-Africa heads-of-state summit, Zuma (2014) offered a veritable sub-imperialist manifesto:

> There had been a good relationship already between Africa and the US but this summit has reshaped it and has taken it to another level … We secured a buy-in from the US for Africa's peace and security initiatives … As President Obama said, the boots must be African.

Still, to those who believe BRICS are anti-imperialist, Rousseff's impeachment in May 2016 confirmed a sustained attack on the bloc by Washington. According to *Counterpunch* commentator Eric Draitser (2016), "what's unfolding in Brazil is a multi-pronged effort to destabilize the country via a variety of political and economic means, with the ultimate goal of bringing to heel a key member of

BRICS". The former Assistant Treasury Secretary in the Reagan Administration, Paul Craig Roberts (2016), wrote even more explicitly, "This is Washington's move against the BRICS. Washington is moving to put into political power a right-wing party that Washington controls in order to terminate Brazil's growing relationships with China and Russia". Venezuelan Vice-President Aristobulo Isturiz warned South African leaders during a May 2016 visit to Pretoria: "Obama is using his remaining time in office to destabilize all progressive countries and undermine their emancipation movements. It is [Washington's] intention to weaken the BRICS countries" (Ebrahim 2016).

This remark coincided with revelations that a Central Intelligence Agency operative bragged about assisting the apartheid state's 1962 arrest and 27-year imprisonment of Nelson Mandela. (The US State Department kept Mandela on its terrorist watch list until 2008, and there was close collaboration between Washington and Pretoria throughout the twentieth century.) African National Congress spokesperson Zizi Kodwa (VOA, 2016) claimed that the CIA "never stopped operating here. It is still happening now. The CIA is still collaborating with those who want regime change". Another version of the anti-imperialist framing was heard at the South African Black Consciousness movement's Black First Land First launch conference two days after Rousseff's impeachment: "Brazil and South Africa are seen by the Western imperialist forces as the weak link in the BRICS chain. The strategy of imperialism is to get rid of presidents who support the BRICS process".

Likewise, a founder of Brazil's Movement of Landless Workers (MST), João Pedro Stedile, was asked by *Il Manifesto* (2016) about why "a group of deputies from right-wing organizations went to Washington before the last elections". He replied, "Temer will arrange his government in order to allow the US to control our economy through their companies... Brazil is part of the BRICS, and another goal is that it can reject the South-South alliance". As WikiLeaks cables revealed, Temer was a mole for the US State Department a decade earlier, but merely playing what Washington considered to be an incompetent, ideology-free role as a political "opportunist".[2]

But as concrete evidence of a US-led coup in Brazil, this fact seems insufficient. Moreover, Rousseff herself denied the role of imperialism a week after the impeachment, during a *Russia Today* (2016) interview: "I don't believe external interference is a primary or a secondary reason for what's happening now in Brazil. It's not. The grave situation we see now has developed without any such interference". She repeated this when pressed by the interviewer, so it was crystal clear that she blamed the old oligarchs for her downfall. This point was reinforced by subsequent revelations about the coup plotters' local motivations: the key men involved were aiming simply to derail the "Car Wash" and other corruption investigations that threatened to sweep a large share of the Brazilian legislature into jail.

Nevertheless, insisted widely-read Brazilian geopolitical analyst Pepe Escobar (2016), "The most important angle as far as I'm concerned is the global angle. What will happen in that next BRICS meeting in four or five months, and what happens to the BRICS projects, including the development bank that features collaboration between Brazilian, Russian, and Chinese executives"? The answer came the day after the coup from Indian Ministry of External Affairs spokesperson Vikas Swarup, who said Temer was welcome and the summit would "take place as scheduled".

In spite of the evident contradictions, all these (and other) contingencies sometimes call forth the claim of "anti-imperialism" for BRICS and this is nowhere more apparent when it comes to multilateralism. Endorsements of the BRICS' international financial agenda by progressive analysts highlight the potential for the bloc's resistance to the long, destructive US-European hegemony at the Bretton Woods Institutions (for a critique of arguments by Walden Bello, Radhika Desai, Horace Campbell, Mark Weisbrot, Mike Whitney and others, see Bond 2016). For example, Sunanda Sen (2015) of the Levy Economics Institute supported the BRICS' "alternative sources of credit flows, aiming for financial stability, growth, and development. With their goals of avoiding IMF loan conditionality and the dominance of the US dollar in global finance, these new BRICS-led institutions represent a much-needed renovation of the global financial architecture". And according to *Review of International Political Economy* writers Cornel Ban and Mark Blyth (2013), the BRICS' "autonomy relative to the coercive apparatus of the International Financial Institutions has enabled more state-led development interventions than would have been the case otherwise... [with] ever-widening policy space created by the growing weight of the BRICs in the global economy". Just after the coup against Rousseff, South African Institute for Global Dialogue director Siphamandla Zondi (2016), wrote,

> The [BRICS] platform has become the most powerful platform for the pursuit of global reform ... Brazil has been a crucial voice in global debates about the reform of global governance, including the IMF and World Bank, and about fair and just outcomes for the developing world in world trade negotiations ... Brazil is an important part of the effort today to shift global power from the former colonial powers and their diaspora in North America to all regions of the world. It is a key partner in South-South co-operation.

BRICS assimilation into the IMF and World Bank

These claims about the BRICS' alternative agenda are ambitious but are not shared by either progressive critics (this author included) or the technocrats who designed the CRA and NDB, for the latter repeatedly assured the international financial community that assimilation and collaboration is the best approach, e.g. in the words of BRICS NDB Vice-President Leslie Maasdorp: "We will and should benefit from the long years and decades of experience of these [Bretton Woods] institutions" (Mnyandu 2015). Indeed, when it comes to global finance, instead of establishing an alternative reality (e.g. as anticipated by Hugo Chávez's Bank of the South, which Brazil sabotaged), the BRICS are financing the old one. Vast quantities of US Treasury Bills are held by BRICS countries (especially China) as their main foreign reserve holding. While the NDB may eventually move to financing projects in local currencies, the articles of agreement specify contributions in US dollars.

The CRA is anticipated to be a dollar lender, since repayment of most foreign debts the BRICS countries have incurred will be in dollars.

To illustrate, while the first NDB loans – in April 2016 – promoted "sustainable" energy, they were rife with contradictions insofar as the $250 million (in dollars not rands) to expand Eskom's grid so as to draw in more renewable energy, reflected the Independent Power Producers' privatization of electricity generation (long opposed by South African progressives who insist on state-supported renewables). Yet a month later, Eskom's chief executive Brian Molefe announced he would no longer buy renewable electricity, as for long-term baseload supply especially to serve mining houses and smelters, Eskom would focus instead on nuclear. In mid-2015, NDB director Tito Mboweni had told Bloomberg news that the proposed $100 billion South African nuclear deal, probably with Russia, "falls squarely within the mandate of the NDB", in spite of enormous local controversy surrounding Zuma's corruption-prone deal-making regarding not only Putin but the Gupta family, whose firm Oakbay would be the main uranium supplier.

Other items on Molefe's BRICS Business Council (2015) project wish-list included new coal-fired generators, off-shore oil drilling, and Durban's $25 billion port-petrochemical complex expansion. These infrastructure mega-projects are all rife with social, economic, governance and environmental dilemmas (Bond 2014), which South Africa does not have a strong history of resolving in the public's interest. In another mega-dam project, what may be the world's most infamous case of construction company bribery in World Bank lending history occurred in Lesotho, where more than $2 million flowed from a dozen multinational corporations to the Swiss accounts of the leading dam official, Masupha Sole, who served nine years in jail but was then, to everyone's astonishment, reinstated thanks to his political influence. Lesotho's dam water flows to South Africa, even in times (such as 2016) when the country faces ruinous drought. Although the World Bank debarred some of the most corrupt companies (in the process catalyzing the bankruptcy of Canada's once formidable civil engineering firm Acres International), nothing was done to punish the firms by Pretoria officials.

BRICS NDB Vice-President Maasdorp (Mnyandu, 2015) discussed his own role at the helm of the institution responsible: "I served for example as chairman of TransCaledon Tunnel Authority, which is a state-owned enterprise with a mandate to finance and implement bulk raw water infrastructure projects in South Africa, and played an oversight role from a governance perspective for seven years of large infrastructure projects". Several of the same construction firms that were implicated in Lesotho reappeared in notorious collusion cases involving white-elephant World Cup 2010 stadiums and other mega-projects in which billions of dollars were stolen from South African taxpayers. *South African firms are obviously not alone;* in 2014, the World Bank debarred the China Three Gorges Corporation's subsidiary building dams in Africa after extreme corruption was identified in another African project.[3]

In what is the most revealing case of BRICS assimilation into this system, in 2012 the IMF was recapitalized (through a credit mechanism) with $75 billion from the BRICS: China gave $43 billion; Brazil, Russia and India gave $10 billion each; and South Africa gave $2 billion. In return, in December 2015, four of the five received major increases in their voting power: China by 37 percent, Brazil 23 percent, India 11 percent and Russia up 8 percent. Yet the US will not yet give up veto power – it is the only country with more than 15 percent required – and the BRICS' total vote is now just 14.7 percent. Worse, the restructuring deal that made this rise possible was detrimental to seven African countries which lost more than a fifth of their IMF voting share: Nigeria lost 41 percent of its voting power, along with Libya (39 percent), Morocco (27 percent), Gabon (26 percent), Algeria (26 percent), Namibia (26 percent) and even South Africa (21 percent).

One facet of Africa's decline at the IMF is its inability to maintain currency strength in the face of the commodity crash. This was especially apparent in the period after mid-2011 when, for example, the South African rand peaked at R6.3/$. By January 2016, after a run apparently begun by Goldman Sachs, the rate was R17.9/$, although by mid-year it recovered to R13.4/$. Other African currencies collapsed during 2014–2015, with Zambia losing half the kwacha's worth, and the values of currencies from Angola, Namibia, Uganda and Tanzania down more than a fifth over the 12-month period.

But aside from the quantitative loss of power, the loss of African "voice" (as it is known) at the IMF is important given the critiques often expressed about the institution's dogmatic neoliberal ideology and its qualitative power over Africa, dating back to the 1980s. Even Jacob Zuma voiced these concerns in mid-2015 in a *RussiaToday* interview "they want to dictate what you should do. You can't utilize that kind of assistance the way you want. So, in a sense, it has conditions that will keep you dependent all the time. That's what we're trying to take ourselves out of". Perhaps unwittingly, Zuma was reiterating the criticism offered by his nemesis, former Minister of Intelligence Ronnie Kasrils, of the IMF's $850 million loan to South Africa six months before democracy dawned, in December 1993.

Kasrils had in 2013 described this deal as "the fatal turning point. I will call it our Faustian moment when we became entrapped – some today crying out that we 'sold our people down the river'". Mboweni had a central role in the IMF deal and subsequent neoliberal strategies such as record-high interest rates and exchange control liberalization. As Mboweni (2004) once explained, he knew that "the apartheid government was trying to lock us into an IMF structural adjustment program via the back door, thereby tying the hands of the future democratic government". But, he claims, "We did not sell out!" Sampie Terreblanche (2012, 64), a former economist who worked in the apartheid government's highest echelons, firmly disagrees, arguing that the deal "committed the Transitional Executive Council to the ideologies of neoliberalism and market fundamentalism".[4]

Also in mid-2015, just before the Ufa summit, hopes were raised in Greece that its prime minister Alex Tsipras could persuade BRICS to advance credit to the indebted country so as to avoid an IMF and EU austerity deal: budget cuts (especially on pensions), higher Value Added Tax on poor people's consumption, privatization, labor casualization and deregulation. Tragically, because of the vast Greek foreign debt, Tsipras had already agreed to privatize one of Greek's main ports to Chinese merchant capital (against the wishes of port workers), so there was hope for Beijing's support. And according to Greek Environment and Energy Minister Panagiotis Lafazanis (ANA-MPA, 2015), "During my (May 2015) meeting with Russian Deputy Finance Minister Sergey Storchak, we secured the decisive Russian support to Greece's request for participation in the BRICS NDB … right after operations begin, it will be able to accept financial support". However, at the crucial moment in July 2015, when BRICS credit would have been vital to Tsipras' potential survival outside the IMF and EU's power, the BRICS failed to provide an alternative credit line. As a result, Tsipras won a 61 percent "No" vote on the IMF/EU austerity plan, but without the alternative, the fear of the financiers' ability to immediately bankrupt Greece by freezing its commercial bank accounts with the rest of the world compelled an historic U-turn by Tsipras.

Instead of searching for an alternative to the IMF, the BRICS CRA actually empowers the IMF to impose conditionalities. According to the articles of agreement adopted in Fortaleza, if a CRA member is in need of more than 30 percent of its borrowing quota, it must first go to the IMF for a structural adjustment loan and conditionality before accessing more from the CRA. For South Africa, whose foreign debt rose from around $30 billion in 2003 to more than $140 billion a dozen years later – i.e. more than 40 percent of GDP, which puts it in the debt-crisis danger zone – this would mean that only $3 billion is available from the CRA before recourse to the IMF would be necessary.[5] Other BRICS have a strong repayment commitment, even the leader most feared as a world rogue. Tellingly, at a December 2015 press conference highlighting the role of international financial sanctions in Russia's economic depression, Putin (2015) announced proudly, "Despite all limitations, we complied with all our commitments to our partners, including international credit institutions. We pay everything due on time and in full".[6]

It was the fear of non-assimilation into the Bretton Woods Institutions that most animated Obama when discussing BRICS in Africa with *The Economist* (2014 emphasis added):

The Economist: One of the big factors in Africa and the economy's emergence has been Chinese investment. And they bring a different model. Is that something that you need to confront?

Mr Obama: My view is the more the merrier. When I was in Africa, the question of China often came up, and my attitude was every country that sees investment opportunities and is willing to partner with African countries should be welcomed. The caution is to make sure that African governments negotiate a good deal with whoever they're partnering with. And that is true whether it's the United States; that's true whether it's China. And I do think that China has certain capacity, for example, to build infrastructure in Africa that's critical. They've got a lot of capital and they may be less constrained than the United States is fiscally in helping roads get built and bridges and ports. On the other hand, China obviously has a need for natural resources that colors their investments in a way that's less true for the United States. And so my advice to African leaders is to make sure that if, in fact, China is putting in roads and bridges, number one, that they're hiring African workers; number two, that the roads don't just lead from the mine to the port to Shanghai, but that there's an ability for the African governments to shape how this infrastructure is going to benefit them in the long term.

The Economist: You see countries like China creating a BRICS bank, for instance – institutions that seem to be parallel with the system, rather – and potentially putting pressure on the system rather than adding to it and strengthening it. That is the key issue, whether China ends up inside that system or challenging it. That's the really big issue of our times, I think.

Mr Obama: It is. And I think it's important for the United States and Europe to continue to welcome China as a full partner in these international norms. It's important for us to recognize that there are going to be times where there are tensions and conflicts. But I think those are manageable.

BRICS assimilation into the WTO

The WTO was the second multilateral institution whose neoliberal power was amplified in December 2015 thanks largely to the BRICS, at a ministerial summit in Nairobi that achieved a breakthrough in negotiations to great relief for the world's elites. A vital feature was that three of the BRICS are in formal alliance with the EU and US as the "G5", the most important bloc, one generally opposed to what in 2003 formed as the trading-bloc G20, comprising the larger poor and middle-income countries which traditionally opposed the West's power. The BRICS' own divisions are legion, starting with Russia's role as a "developed" not developing economy (Skrzypczyńska 2015). For many years South Africa acted decisively in opposition to the interests of Africa, with Pretoria's trade minister Alec Erwin even nominated by *Foreign Policy* journal to become the WTO's leader after he performed to the North's satisfaction in various of the insider "Green Rooms" and as a "Friend of the Chair" (Bond 2006). In 2013, after fruitless efforts by Director General Pascal Lamy to restart the stalled 2001 Doha Agenda, the WTO was given a new leader: the Brazilian negotiator Roberto Azevêdo, who pro-trade bias was just as strong.

Moreover, according to the (ordinarily pro-BRICS) Malaysian NGO Third World Network (TWN) (2015), Brazil conspired with the United States and the European Union at the WTO to ensure "that India did not get the language it proposed" to maintain vital food subsidies, a defeat which in coming years will lead tens of millions of Indian peasants to suffer. As TWN's Chakravarthi Raghavan (2015) put it, "on the eve of Nairobi, Brazil unilaterally abandoned the G20 alliance to join the US and EU, in trying to act against China and India," not to mention against the world's poor. Azevêdo and Kenya's hosting chairperson agreed, according to Horace Campbell (2016), "to exclude 'African issues' from the agenda while simultaneously pushing through the Expansion of the Information Technology Agreement, which benefits US corporations". The WTO thus became far more hostile to African interests thanks in part to a few of the BRICS countries' interventions.

Is there scope for change? South Africa's main WTO negotiator, Faizal Ismail (2015), has described world trade "a deeply asymmetrical system in favor of its main architects, the US and the EU [that] requires fundamental reform." The WTO reform strategy favored by Ismail (and his then trade minister Erwin) was the Doha "Development" Agenda of 2001. But the Doha Agenda was soon a victim of the institution's overall paralysis. Indeed the "new trade narrative", according to Ismail, is: "Doha dead! Emerging markets should 'graduate'... The emergence of Global Value Chains as a new reality of international trade where goods are no more manufactured in one country but are made in the world and the large share of intermediate goods exports provide a compelling reason for countries to have more open trade policies". Ismail blames the strength of this narrative on US officials, especially Susan Schwab (2011), backed by business lobbies and Washington think-tanks. But he then blames a fellow BRICS ally: "The Russian G20 Presidency has been persuaded to continue with the theme of Global Value Chains and to discuss its policy implications for Trade Liberalization".

Nevertheless South Africa signed on to the Nairobi WTO deal, in yet another case of talk-left walk-right. Reflecting Pretoria's tendency towards assimilation not opposition, Azevêdo (2016) remarked in March 2017 at the University of Cape Town,

> South Africa remains a central player in the system today, as a leading voice in the African Group of WTO members, and in all aspects of our work. In fact, your current representative in Geneva, Ambassador Xavier Carim has recently been appointed as chair of the WTO's Dispute Settlement Body. This is one of the most prominent positions in the organization ... It stands testament to South Africa's leadership in the trade debate today.

African reactions to the WTO debacle were muted, but at least in the wake of the mid-2016 Brexit vote by United Kingdom, there appeared to be increasing resistance to European Union neoliberal penetration in the form of Tanzanian and Ugandan state retraction of commitments to join the European's Economic Partnership Agreements. The other 2016 incident that showed a rethink of Africa's persistent trade deficit with a more advanced industrial power, namely South Africa, was a ban imposed on many imports that typically moved across the Zimbabwe border. The policy kicked in as Zimbabwe ran short on US dollars, so was less a strategic than desperation strategy to preserve the country's currency and reduce the trade deficit. South Africa also came under pressure from both local steel companies and trade unionists to block steel imports from China (whose net exports soared from −35 million tons to 100 million from 2005–2015 as China raised its share of world production from 30 to 50 percent over that decade), and as a result, trade minister Rob Davies imposed a 10 percent special tariff in 2015.

These were small initiatives by countries with highly erratic leaders known more for zig-zagging in diverse ideological directions than any consistent policy stance. Still, in opposition to the persistent ideology of free trade, such desperation-protectionism might in future years be repeated and become the basis of an import-substitution industrialization strategy. But that in turn would require new governments opposed to neoliberalism, whereas the trends in the BRICS were basically in the other direction, especially in Brazil and India, with South Africa still obeying the dictates of the major credit ratings agencies more than its own people. The other important development in the wake of the post-Cancún WTO malaise was the rise of bilateral trade and investment treaties. Ana Garcia (2016) clarifies how damaging these have been to Africa, especially where BRICS countries have dominance.

BRICS assimilation into the UNFCCC

A third multilateral agreement in December 2015 was the Paris UNFCCC agreement. According to Oscar Reyes (2015), seven fatal flaws in the agreement stand out:

1 the targets are ambitious, but unlikely to be met (hence serving as a greenwash);
2 there are no legally-binding targets to cut emissions;
3 there was no new money promised to developing countries;
4 reparations are now legally off limits (no "climate debt" can be sued for by victims);
5 oil, gas and coal producers are not compelled to leave fossil fuels unexploited;
6 the deal opens the same carbon-trading loopholes that undermined prior climate deals;
7 sources of greenhouse gas emissions from international shipping and flights, and from military-related emissions, are not included.

Summing up Paris, the world movement of peasants and landless people Via Campesina (2015) was clearest: "There is nothing binding for states, national contributions lead us towards a global warming of over 3°C and multinationals are the main beneficiaries. It was essentially a media circus". The world's leading North-South CJ organization, Friends of the Earth International (2015) concluded: "The reviews [of whether INDCs are adhered to and then need strengthening] are too weak and too late. The political number mentioned for finance has no bearing on the scale of need. It's empty. The iceberg has struck, the ship is going down and the band is still playing to warm applause". Reyes (2015) singles out the role of Brazil in combining forces with the EU – against Bolivia – to "open the same carbon-trading loopholes that undermined the last global climate deal". Finally, not forgetting the voice of climate science, James Hansen (2015) bluntly described Paris, simply, as "bullshit".

Since 2009, the BRICS were vital participants in the degeneration of global climate policy, as four of their leaders ("BASIC") were the original co-signatories (along with Obama) of the Copenhagen Accord. Perhaps by mistake, John Kerry (later US Secretary of State) labelled Zuma, Lula da Silva of Brazil, Wen Jiabao of China and Manmohan Singh of India the "four horsemen"; the tag is accurate, in terms of climate damage to Africa caused by the 2009 deal and its successors. The Copenhagen Accord was mainly authored by the US State Department and then, as leaks by the US military-intelligence whistle-blower Chelsea Manning in early 2010 proved, was adopted by many poor and climate-vulnerable countries in Africa only thanks to bribery and bullying by the State Department's Todd Stern (Bond 2012). Only one of the BRICS has hosted a COP, Durban in 2011, and Washington immediately claimed victory. As documented by WikiLeaks (after liberating Hillary Clinton's private email server), Stern (2011) bragged to Clinton that in relation to the Green Climate Fund, "We left Durban with virtually everything we sought". His team had destroyed the "firewall" between rich and poor countries (the latter were not, in the 1997 Kyoto Protocol, required to make emissions cuts), so as he reported to Clinton in a memo worth quoting at length:

> The main action here was to beat back efforts to undermine the parallel structure of mitigation commitments for developed and developing countries that we negotiated in Copenhagen … The developing countries insisted on another Kyoto "commitment period," largely because Kyoto embodies the firewall. The EU was the only major player willing to consider that, but insisted that the quid pro quo had to be assurance from other major emitters that they would commit to negotiate a legal agreement to follow the second Kyoto period. For our part, we said that we could not do that unless China and other majors also agreed, but prior to Durban they had never indicated any willingness to do so. So there appeared to be a stalemate. The open questions for us going into Durban were (1) whether the EU would stick to its guns in demanding a future legal agreement in exchange for a second Kyoto period, and (2) what the 'BASIC' group of China, India, Brazil and South Africa would do if the EU did hold firm.

As it happened, the EU hung tough, while the BASICs, evidently influenced by the intense push for a legal agreement from the poorest and most vulnerable countries, especially the small island states, showed unexpected flexibility. Brazil led the way on this issue for the BASICs, and we engaged intensively with them. Two long trilateral meetings (EU-US-BASIC) were held in the middle of the second week, which pushed the ball forward. The final two-page agreement, dubbed the Durban Platform by the South Africans, was negotiated over many hours Friday and Saturday in a group of around 35 countries, with the EU and the island states pushing hardest for strong language and the earliest possible start. The new agreement is to be completed by the end of 2015 and start to be implemented from 2020 onward.

The key points for us, each of which we insisted upon, are:

- "Applicable to all Parties." This language is a singular breakthrough – the first time China and other emerging economies have agreed that they too would be bound by legal obligations.
- The Bali Roadmap. The agreement sunsets the 2007 Bali mandate at the end of next year's COP. This is important because Bali is consistently read as enshrining the firewall and we thus could not allow it to become the basis for negotiating the new legal instrument.
- "Common but differentiated responsibilities." This phrase is read (not by us, but by most developing countries) to denote the firewall, but the phrase is conspicuously absent from the Durban agreement.
- 2020 implementation date. The 2020 date is also important. The EU and its small island allies pushed very hard to have the agreement take effect as early

> as possible. But this didn't work for the BASICs, who are determined to keep their Kyoto protection all the way to 2020; and it couldn't work for us to start earlier than 2020 if the BASICs did not, since such asymmetry would be lethal to developing political support in the U.S.

Taking all these points together, I think Durban amounts to a significant achievement.

> For Africa, the implications of multilateral climate imperialism, amplified by BRICS/BASIC sub-imperialism, are catastrophic. According to UN Secretary General Kofi Annan's Global Humanitarian Forum (2009), already more than 300 000 current deaths per year are attributable to climate change, mostly in the Global South. With the present trajectory of warming anticipated to break 4 degrees above normal by 2100, with inland Africa heating up by 6 to 7 degrees, not only are humans threatened, but so too is nearly every living species – biodiversity itself – reliant upon water and a stable eco-system. African scientists anticipate worsening weather chaos, not to mention 182 million Africans dead this century, early and unnecessarily, due to climate related disease (Christian Aid 2006).

Some on the continent will profit from ongoing emissions, especially South African capital. Accommodatingly, the Department of Environmental Affairs has a minister, Edna Molewa, who did nothing to shift power relations in defense of the climate, in spite of a relatively high profile in international negotiations. She played a central role in Durban's COP17 (Bond 2011, 2012), and in 2012, she was visible at the Rio+20 UN Earth Summit. Yet when it counted, in regulating South African polluters, Molewa knew how to avoid conflict. She was silent about the vast bulk of national infrastructure spending on carbon-intensive activities: three major coal-fired power plants, expanded coal exports via a $25 billion rail budget in the first Presidential Infrastructure Coordinating Committee (PICC), and in the second PICC project, the $20 billion expansion of Durban's port and petrochemical complex, aiming to raise container throughput capacity by a factor of eight by 2040 (Bond 2014). Government also gave permission in 2013 for Shell Oil to begin the process of "fracking" the arid Karoo. This was followed in mid-2014 by President Jacob Zuma's Operation Phakisa ("speed up") ocean-economy strategy, including $5 billion worth of deep-sea oil and gas exploration, especially by ExxonMobil. Other carbon-intensive state policies include ever-worsening suburban sprawl in Gauteng province (and other metropolitan areas), facilitated by the doubling of the Durban-Johannesburg oil pipeline at nearly four times the initial budget of $500 million. Pretoria also granted approval for a new $6 billion state oil refinery, and has plans for more smelter-intensive minerals beneficiation including a new Chinese steel factory (in spite of steel imports from China decimating the two main existing producers in 2015). The South African office of Greenpeace (2015) was scathing about the INDCs Molewa offered in Paris:

> The 'Discussion Document: South Africa's INDC: 1 August 2015' avoids quantifying any contribution to mitigation and fails to meet the very basic generic requirements agreed for the mitigation component of the INDC. If not rectified, such blatant evasiveness will undermine South Africa's credibility and any claim to moral authority in leadership of developing country negotiators.

This lack of ambition is consistent with Pretoria's traditional post-apartheid approach. When seen from the perspective of civil society, government turns a blind eye to pollution violations especially from coal mining, electricity generation and oil refineries (all associated with climate change) (groundWork *et al.* 2014). Confirming an inappropriate degree of state modesty, Molewa (2014) once remarked in a rebuttal to this author, "We are constantly addressing issues to do with climate change – mostly behind the scenes". Also behind the scenes, South African Deputy President Cyril Ramaphosa's massive coal mines and similar dirty coal corporations were, according to insiders, long pampered by Molewa's water officials. At least 40 major new mines were proposed to provide coal to at least two new power plants, not to mention new export-oriented coal digs to supply China and India. Residents of the coal-producing province of Mpumalanga was by 2014, quite literally, wheezing (groundWork *et al,* 2014), as the National Development Plan called for 18 billion tonnes of coal to be dug and exported through the Richards Bay port in the country's largest infrastructure project. In addition, Eskom applied to Molewa for "rolling postponements" on pollution reductions required by law at 14 power plants there. Eskom's assumption was that its own crises – and regular load-shedding that struck fear into the society – would persuade Molewa of the need for forbearance. By February 2015, Molewa had agreed to a five year extension on air pollution regulatory forbearance for Eskom, Sasol and dozens of other firms whose emissions both harmed local workers and residents and contributed to climate change.

With the South African population recording 47 percent awareness that climate change is the world's greatest threat, according to the 2015 Pew Research Center survey (i.e., the greatest international problem of local concern, ahead of second place "international financial instability") (Carle 2015). Turning that awareness into activism remains the only hope, given that Pretoria's elites appear unwilling to change course (Bond 2012). The same is true for the other BRICS countries, whose companies are not only carbon-intensive when operating in Africa, but also structurally committed to the continent's resource exploitation.

Conclusion

The BRICS stand accused of underdeveloping Africa in several respects, a process amplified by roller-coaster commodity price changes during the period 2002–2016. The BRICS are, according to the information and analysis developed above, best understood as a new, more malevolent force within a general framework of neoliberal extractivism, amplifying the already extreme uneven and combined development so damaging to Africa. There are exceptions, of course, in which

African leaders have helped their countries raise productivity and convert their natural resource wealth into investment (the main one being Botswana although the citizenry have witnessed very little trickle-down). But as the World Bank (2014) notes, mostly the African continent is losing natural capital and in only a very few countries (12 percent) can a net benefit be calculated from extraction, even by the (pro-extractivist) Bank. The BRICS capacity to take advantage of Africa's weaknesses justifies the use of the term sub-imperialism. Whatever name one might use, South Africa's own National Planning Commission (2012) sheepishly conceded a "perception [*sic*] of the country as a regional bully", such that the "gateway to Africa" logic often comes up against the harsh reality of extraction and exploitation (especially in March 2013).

Still, the most important reasons for Africa's prone position in the world economy are not the fault of the BRICS – which simply amplify pre-existing problems instead of offering alternatives – but of the West. The latest manifestation of Western imperialism in Africa is indicative: when the World Economic Forum (WEF) came to Kigali in May 2016, the organization highlighted "Fourth Industrial Revolution cyber-physical systems" as central to Africa's future: the continent is "the world's fastest growing digital consumer market" (though fewer than four Africans in ten have electricity). For good measure, the WEF's main speaker (the as-yet-unindicted war criminal) Tony Blair, celebrated the dictatorship of his host Paul Kagame. At the same time, the IMF's (2016) *Regional Economic Outlook for Africa* suggested that "a substantial policy reset is critical in many cases... Because the reduction in revenue from the extractive sector is expected to persist, many affected countries also critically need to contain fiscal deficits and build a sustainable tax base from the rest of the economy". This is the Western solution: a policy reset that represents more of the same, a reboot of an infected computer suffering Western-installed malware, rehacked by the BRICS so as to empty Africa's bank accounts.

The danger is, Obama agreed with *The Economist* (2014), quite straightforward: whether the BRICS institutions are "potentially putting pressure on the system [of Western capitalism] rather than adding to it and strengthening it … [and] whether China ends up inside that system or challenging it. That's the really big issue of our times". There are always contingencies, as noted earlier, and the Chinese geopolitical and economic strategy is known to shift dramatically from generation to generation. Still, under Xi Jinping, the tendency of talking left while walking right will continue. The alternatives are obvious, but so far the main BRICS have only begun to exert defensive mechanisms – e.g. banning certain foreign exchange transactions (especially China in early 2016) and imposing desperately defensive tariffs – while the bigger-picture reforms attempted by others remain essentially unexplored:

- default on unpayable, unjustifiable debt – taken out by corrupt elites – as did Argentina and Ecuador in 2002 and 2009;
- evict World Bank personnel, as did Ecuador in 2007;
- impose exchange controls against elites, as did Malaysia (1998), Venezuela

(2003), Cyprus (2013), Greece (2015);
- establish new common currency in order to avoid US$ transactions;
- provide solidarity financing for governments resisting financial imperialism, as was offered (by Russia's deputy finance minister) to Greece but then never materialized;
- adopt socially- and ecologically-conscious financing strategies tied to compatible trade (like ALBA), such as were proposed and seed-funded by Venezuela in the still-born Bank of the South.

Instead, the BRICS have chosen the course of undergirding multilateral agencies (the Bretton Woods Institutions and UNFCCC) whose role is disastrous for Africa. What that means for BRICS in the years ahead, it is fair to predict, is more top-down scrambling within Africa, and more bottom-up resistance (Bond 2016). Where African governments emerge that have more patriotic instincts, there will be scope for campaigning on matters of economic justice: e.g. against mining and petroleum extraction, IFF (and *licit* financial flow) extraction, and illegitimate debt. With the profits of so many Western firms in Africa hitting new lows and their share value nearly wiped out (e.g. the 2011–2015 cases of Lonmin, Anglo and Glencore, which each lost more than 85 percent of value), there are imperialist precedents for what BRICS firms now may find logical: yet more extreme metabolisms of extraction and more desperation gambits to keep BRICS-friendly regimes in power, at the expense of the reproductive needs of society and nature. But resistance is already evident, as the Africa Uprising against "Africa Rising" proceeds.

Notes

1 Where joint action has *not* been effective or not been attempted – e.g. where Russia and China join the US, France and Britain to *deny* UN Security Council seats to the other three BRICS in spite of a decade-plus campaign to democratize that body (for fear of diluting their own power), or in the BRICS' failure to even propose a candidate from their ranks to replace two disgraced IMF Managing Directors (Dominique Strauss-Kahn in 2011 and Christine Lagarde in 2016) and poorly-performing World Bank presidents (Paul Wolfowitz in 2007, Robert Zoellick in 2012 and Jim Yong Kim in 2016) – this chapter does not have the scope to delve.

2 South Africans witnessed a similar problem when Chelsea Manning released US State Department cable transcripts in 2010 revealing that the country's then lead spy, Moe Shaik, regularly offered the same sort of tell-all function to US embassy officials. He later switched jobs to become a key liaison to the BRICS New Development Bank (Bond 2016).

3 The World Bank "Vice President – Integrity" [*sic*] responsible for the decision, Leonard McCarthy, was himself declared in 2015 by the finest South African newspaper editor, Ferial Haffajee (2015), to have "ruined our criminal justice system" because of his own political corruption when serving as lead prosecutor of Zuma.

4 Even personnel conditions were attached to the deal: Mboweni had to wait an extra five years to become central bank governor because IMF head Michel Camdessus insisted informally in a January 1994 meeting with Nelson Mandela that apartheid-era neoliberals Chris Stals at the Reserve Bank and finance minister Derek Keys be reappointed to their jobs (Bond 2014).

5 In 1985, the last time this debt ratio was hit, the then leader of apartheid South Africa, P.W. Botha, found it necessary to default on $13 billion in short-term debt payments coming due, to close the stock exchange and to impose exchange controls (Bond 2014).

6 The contrast with his predecessor Boris Yeltsin is obvious, for on the eve of his $40 billion default in 1998, Yeltsin's pro-Western government had borrowed $5 billion from the Bretton Woods Institutions, which disappeared without a trace. Nevertheless, the IMF quickly advanced a $20 billion bail-out loan, which if it occurred today would probably be vetoed by the US government's IMF representative (Bond 2003).

References

ANA-MPA, 2015. Energy Minister Lafazanis: Greece Will Probably Submit Request to Participate in BRICS bank. *ANA-MPA*, 29 May.

Azevêdo, R., 2016. *University of Cape Town Seminar – 'The Future of the WTO Doha Round of Trade Negotiations and the Implications for Africa's Regional Integration'.* [Online] Available at: https://www.wto.org/english/news_e/spra_e/spra114_e.htm

Ban, Cornel and Mark Blyth 2013. "The BRICs and the Washington Consensus: An Introduction." https://www.academia.edu/3640601/The_BRICs_and_the_Washington_Consensus_An_Introduction

Böhm, S., Misoczky, M. C. and Moog, S., 2012. Greening Capitalism? A Marxist Critique of Carbon Markets. *Organization Studies,* 33(11), pp. 1617–1638.

Bond, P., 2003. *Against Global Apartheid.* London: Zed Books.

Bond, Patrick 2006. *Talk Left, Walk Right.* Pietermaritzburg: University of KwaZulu-Natal Press.

Bond, P. (Ed) 2011. *Durban's Climate Gamble: Trading Carbon, Betting the Earth,* Pretoria, University of South Africa Press.

Bond, P., 2012. *Politics of Climate Justice.* Pietermaritzburg: University of Kwa-Zulu Natal Press.

Bond, Patrick 2013. "Subimperialism as Lubricant of Neoliberalism: South African 'deputy sheriff' duty within BRICS." *Third World Quarterly,* 34(2), pp. 251-270.

Bond, P., 2014. *Elite Transition.* London: Pluto Press.

Bond, P., 2016. BRICS Banking and the Debate over Sub-imperialism. *Third World Quarterly*, 37 (4), pp. 611–629.

Bond, P. and Garcia, A., 2015. *BRICS: An Anti-Capitalist Critique.* Johannesburg: Jacana Press.

BRICS Business Council, 2015. *Facing Challenges, Building Confidence: BRICS Business Council Second Annual Report 2014–201.,* Ufa: BRICS Business Council.

Bruce, P., 2016. Oops! Zuma, On Slope, Slips in Snow. *Business Day*, 22 January.

Burgis, T., 2015. *The Looting Machine.* London: William Collins.

Campbell, H. G., 2016. The Deathbed of the WTO. *CounterPunch*, 1 January.

Carle, J., 2015. *Climate Change Seen as Top Global Threat.* Washington, D.C.: Pew Research Centre.

Carmody, P., 2013. *The Rise of the BRICS in Africa.* London: Zed Books.

Christian Aid, 2006. *The Climate of Poverty: Facts, Fears and Hope.* London: Christian Aid.

CNBC, 2016. *Richard Fisher: Real Issue in China.* Washington D.C.: CNBC.

Cochran, S., 2010. Security Assistance, Surrogate Armies, and the Pursuit of US Interests in Sub-Saharan Africa. *Strategic Studies Quarterly,* pp. 111–152.

Draitser, E., 2016. BRICS Under Attack: The Empire Strikes Back In Brazil. *Global Research*, 22 March.

Ebrahim, Shannon 2016. "Obama sabotages left-wing states: ANC, BRICS targeted, warns Isturiz." *The Star*, 11 May.

Escobar, Pepe 2016. "Brazil's Dilma Faces Coup: 'Say Goodbye to BRICS, Say Hello to Washington'", *Sputnik News,* 12 May. http://sputniknews.com/news/20160511/1039466571/dilma-brics-impeachment-coup-cunha.html#ixzz496aiVoxS

Ferrando, T., 2013. *Thomas Ferrando (2013) Developed a Database to Track This, Discovering Extensive Holdings especially by Indian and Chinese firms.* Massachusetts: ZNet.
Fransman, M., 2013. *South Africa: A strong African Brick in BRICS.* Stellenbosch: Stellenbosch University.
Friends of the Earth International 2015. "Reaction to Paris Agreement." Paris, 12 December. http://oneworld.org/2015/12/12/too-weak-too-late-says-climate-justice-campaigners/
G20, 2016. *G20 Trade Ministers Meeting.* Shanghai: G20.
Garcia, A., 2016. *BRICS in Africa: More of the Same?* Rio de Janeiro: Oxfam Brasil and PACS, https://issuu.com/pacscomunicacao/docs/publicao_africa-brics-en
Greenpeace, 2015. *Greenpeace Africa Submission on the Draft South African INDC.* Johannesburg: Greenpeace Africa.
groundWork, 2014. *Slow Poison: Air Pollution, Public Health and Failing Governance.* Pietermaritzburg: groundWork.
Haffajee, F., 2014. He Ruined Justice. *City Press*, 5 October.
Hansen, J., 2015. *Isolation of 1600 Pennsylvania Avenue: Part I.* New York: Columbia University Press.
Harvey, D., 1982. *The Limits to Capital.* Chicago, IL: University of Chicago Press.
Harvey, D., 2003. *The New Imperialism.* Oxford: Oxford University Press.
Hung, H-f., 2015. China Fantasies: Illusions on both the Left and Right about China Miss How the Contradictions of Capitalism are Shaping that Country's Development. *Jacobin*, 19.
Ibrahim, S., 2016. Obama sabotages left-wing states. *The Star*, 11 May.
Il Manifesto, 2016. João Pedro Stedile: 'It's Time to Mobilize'. *Il Manifesto*, 13 May.
International Monetary Fund, 2016. *Regional Economic Outlook: Sub-Saharan Africa.* Washington, D.C.: International Monetary Fund.
Ishmail, F., 2015. *A BRICS Perspective for Reforming the World Trade Organization (WTO) – Reflections of a Negotiator.* Johannesburg: Human Sciences Research Council.
La Via Campesina, 2015. COP21: The Curtain Falls on a Masquerade. *Confédération Paysanne Press*, 13 December.
London School of Economics and Political Science, 2015. *The Power of Ideas: A Discussion with David Harvey.* London: London School of Economics and Political Science.
Luce, M., 2015. Sub-imperialism, the Highest Stage of Dependent Capitalism. In P. Bond and A. Garcia, eds. *BRICS An Anti-Capitalist Critique.* Johannesburg: Jacana Media, pp. 27–44.
Marini, Ruy Mauro. 1965. "Brazilian Interdependence and Imperialist Integration." *Monthly Review* 17(7), pp.10-29.
Marini, R. M. (1974) Subdesarrollo y Revolución, Mexico City, Siglo XXI Editores, translated at http://mrzine.monthlyreview.org/2010/bt280210p.html#_edn13
Mboweni, Tito, 2004. "BMF Corporate Update Gala Dinner," June 18, Black Management Forum Gala Dinner, http://www.polity.org.za/print-version/mboweni-bmf-corporate-update-gala-dinner-1862004-2004-06-18.
Mnyandu, E., 2015. BRICS Will 'Play a Profound Role' – Maasdorp. *Independent Online*, 6 July.
Molewa, E., 2014. SA in the Green When it Comes to Its Environmental Goals. *Mail & Guardian*, 12 September.
Moyo, S. and Yeros, P., 2011. *Rethinking the Theory of Primitive Accumulation.* Istanbul, 2nd IIPPE Conference.
Mutizwa, G., 2016. What BRICS Needs to Become a Global Force. *City Press*, 14 October.
National Planning Committee, 2012. *2030, Our Future – Make it Work: National Development Plan.* Pretoria: Minister in the Office of the President.
Ndikumana, L., 2015. *Integrated Yet Marginalized: Implications of Globalization for African Development.* Amherst, MA: Political Economy Research Institute.
Nkoana-Mashabane, M., 2013. *BRICS Academic Forum Welcome Dinner Speech,* Durban: Department of International Relations and Cooperation.

Putin, V., 2015. *Vladimir Putin's Annual News Conference.* Moscow: Presidency of Russia.
Raghavan, C., 2015. Doha SU diminished, not dead, and retrievable. *Third World News Network*, 23 December.
Reyes, O., 2015. Seven Wrinkles in the Paris Climate Deal. *Foreign Policy in Focus*, 14 December.
Roberts, P. C., 2016. Washington Launches Its Attack Against BRICS. The Destabilization of Brazil and Argentina. *Global Research*, 22 April.
Russia Today, 2015. South African President: BRICS Carries the Future for Our World. Interview, *Russia Today*, 6 July.
Russia Today, 2016. Dilma Rousseff: Old Brazilian oligarchy behind 'coup.' Interview, *Russia Today*, 19 May.
Schwab, S., 2011. After Doha. *Foreign Affairs*, May.
Sen, S., 2015. *The BRICS Initiatives in the Current Global Conjuncture*, New York: Levy Economic Institute.
Skrzypczyńska, J., 2015. BRICS stance in WTO. *Revolutions: Global Trends and Regional Issues*, 3(1), pp. 46–62.
Stern, T., 2011. Durban Wrap-Up. United States State Department Email to Hillary Rodham Clinton, Washington, DC, 13 December. https://wikileaks.org/clinton-emails/emailid/24887
Summers, L., 2016. The Age of Secular Stagnation. *Foreign Affairs*, 15 February.
Terreblanche, S., 2012. *Lost in Transformation: South Africa's Search for a New Future.* Johannesburg: KMM Review Publishing Company.
The Economist, 2014. The President on Africa. *The Economist*, 2 August.
TWN 2015. "Nairobi green signal for continued US trade-distorting agri-exports," *Third World Network Info Service on WTO and Trade Issues*, 23 December. http://www.twn.my/title2/wto.info/2015/ti151220.htm
VOA, 2016. South Africa's ANC Accuses US of Pushing 'Regime Change.' *Voice of America*, 18 May.
Wall Street Journal, 2014. Beijing Shows More Caution on Africa Deals. *Wall Street Journal*, 7 May.
Westra, R., 2016. *Unleashing Usury: How Finance Opened the Door for Capitalism then Swallowed it Whole*, Atlanta, GA: Clarity Press.
World Bank, 2014. *The Little Green Data Book*, Washington, DC: World Bank Group.
Zondi, S., 2016. Brazil's Neo-liberals' Threat to BRICS. *Independent Online*, 16 May.
Zuma, J., 2014. *President Zuma Welcomes US-Africa Leaders' Summit Outcomes.* Pretoria: Office of the Presidency.

Part III

Varieties of emerging markets in the global economy

6 Capitalism, contradiction and the onward march of variegated neoliberalism in Southeast Asia

Toby Carroll

This chapter addresses the grand historical processes and transformations that have increasingly led to the rise of variegated patterns of market governance in Southeast Asia and presents evidence of this trend. I argue that while postwar and post-independence contexts saw Southeast Asian states variously undertaking non-liberal and or heterodox development paths, the demise of the Cold War and the rise of what Harvey (2007, 75–6) has dubbed "flexible accumulation" has brought new challenges (and for some elites, significant opportunities) and narrowed the range of policy choices for these states considerably. This is reflected in the increased uptake of various broad-based neoliberal market-oriented policy sets evident within national development plans that look markedly different from their forebears and relatedly, new institutional reforms. Here, reinvigorated interest by Southeast Asian states in signing new trade and investment agreements and neoliberal efforts towards establish "enabling environments" for capital are paramount in institutional reform agendas to keep growth going, increase productivity and competitiveness, attract fresh sources of foreign direct investment (FDI) and escape "middle income traps". In detailing this trend, I specifically point to a combination of disciplinary world market pressures amplified and animated by various iterations of neoliberalism and the evolving alignments of elite interest in relation to world market challenges and opportunities. Taken together, these pressures and alignments of interest have played important roles in yielding "variegated market states" and "variegated capitalism", with the latter often generating particularly pernicious outcomes in Southeast Asia (Brenner *et al.* 2010; Carroll and Jarvis 2015; Jessop 2015). Here, elites have been able to asymmetrically profit and plunder from (and around) the neoliberal agenda with relative ease while transnational capital has been able to flexibly exploit new sources of cheap labor and new markets – realities accompanied by heightened inequality, colossal environmental degradation and stalling developmental possibilities.

I begin the chapter by outlining the grand historical processes and transformations that have led to the rise of the variegated market state and variegated capitalism, illustrating how the emergence of particular information and communication technologies and developments in logistics and production have dovetailed with neoliberalism – the broad and changing policy sets based upon the assumptions of liberal economics deployed over the last four decades to subject state and society to market and market-like discipline ("marketization") –

and financialization to render old state-oriented/directed development strategies increasingly unthinkable for mainstream policy elites. The second section of the chapter presents evidence from two vignettes – focused on Indonesia and Malaysia – of the variegated market state and variegated capitalism in Southeast Asia. These vignettes demonstrate the manner in which states and their attendant elite interests have been heavily incentivized, *without multilateral conditionality* from the likes of the World Bank and International Monetary Fund (IMF), to continue to make the right overtures to capital regarding risk and opportunity and further embrace liberal economic reform in order to keep accumulative opportunities and growth going. This said, there is nothing automatic or homogenous about these processes subject as they are to contradiction, political interest and contestation.

The shift from nationally-oriented development to the variegated market state and variegated (world market) capitalism

In this section I outline the grand political economy transformations and their ideological and policy accoutrements that have been instrumental in yielding variegated market states and variegated capitalism, with a particular focus on the evolving impact of these transformations on Southeast Asia. Here, I follow the footsteps of others (and my own earlier work) in describing a grand shift from Fordist/nationally-centered modes of accumulation constrained and characterized by sets of social relations and institutions to a new regime of flexible accumulation – a mode of accumulation that has seen important fractions of capital (both financial and production-oriented) increasingly freed from national constraints and which too has seen labor (and other sources of opposition) subjected to increasing vulnerability and precariousness (Bruff 2011; Carroll 2015; Harvey 2007: 75–76; Jessop 2015; McDonough 2015; Van Der Pijl 2015). The analysis here is set against the relatively recent trend to describe ostensibly nationally or regionally located "varieties of capitalism" characterized by their institutional architecture (see for example Hall and Soskice 2001). In contrast to such analyses I preference the overarching importance of capitalism – an increasingly globalized system characterized generally by private ownership of the means of production, profit-seeking behavior (by capitalists)[1] and exploitative and contradictory social relations – generally. This said, my argument eschews a totalizing analysis that elides the manner in which politics and context explain real-existing outcomes and contexts (in much the same way Bruff (2011) talks of the need to focus on varieties *in* capitalism and Jessop (2015) talks of "variegated capitalism"). In particular I emphasize the importance of globalized or "world market" capitalism (Cammack 2016)) specifically, and its particular characteristics (including amplified unevenness, hyper-competition and intensified contradictions) in relation to understanding the current drivers of state form, and the significance of social conflict in generating actual institutional (and other social) outcomes.[2]

To understand the various forces compelling and coercing countries towards the variegated market state and the broader production of variegated capitalism, it is vital to note multiple interrelated, often self-reinforcing trends that have proven catalytic and provided an important context for battles by social forces over the nature of political and economic systems. The first of these is the shift from nationally-oriented tendencies in economic organization (often around Fordist-Keynesian approaches or state-directed planning of one shade or another) to what David Harvey (2007) has called "flexible accumulation", with the latter referring to the combination of techno-logistical developments associated with production and the rise of neoliberal policy sets (especially in relation to trade and capital flows) that permitted – and indeed further demanded – capital to reorganize production and access new resources and markets.

In the postwar period, governments in the industrialized world, compelled by a combination of organized labor, the limits of nationally-bounded capital and the dual specters of communism and fascism, were variously ideologically inspired by Keynes' ideas about the ability for governments to assuage the excessive boom and bust nature of capitalism with particular policy levers while also often deploying more explicitly social democratic modes of redistribution, welfare and economic organization. Government spending and ownership of key industries and utilities were paired with progressive taxation and redistribution, a focus on full employment, and increased regulation and protection (in relation to wages, working conditions, banking, trade, capital flows and the environment for example) becoming standards (albeit unevenly) in developed world notions of *national development.* Capital, significantly constrained to national settings for advanced industrial production, was subjected to the relative leverage of organized labor, the latter enjoying significant political party representation often within consolidating two-party systems (one party representing labor and the other representing fractions of capital). Put succinctly, this was an era in which labor and other progressively-oriented interests, often through struggle, were able to realize and extend upon significant material and regulatory improvements during a period of rising productivity and growth (the so-called "golden age of capitalism"), imposing costs and restrictions on capital.

In Asia various forms of non-liberal and or highly selective policy approaches (including eliminating markets altogether to market controlling and government-guided industry cultivating measures) were famously deployed in a bid to achieve late development within the all-important context of the Cold War and the "golden age of capitalism". Moreover, forms of national planning (Chalmers Johnson divided these into "plan ideological" and "plan rational" (Johnson 1982: 18)) were variously deployed within post-revolutionary, post-colonial and postwar contexts – in a neo-mercantilist manner – to realize *national development* and *national advantage*. In the "plan rational" countries of Japan and, later, South Korea the state, through pilot agencies staffed with meritocratic bureaucrats (such as the Ministry of International Trade and Industry in Japan and the Economic Planning Board in Korea) was seen as playing a central role in fostering, first, import substitution industrialization (ISI) and, later, export oriented industrialization (EOI). *Developmental states* – echoing earlier ideas of List and Hamilton – engaged in "picking winners" for national productive advantage, directing credit strategically (often pooled from citizens through postal and other public banking systems) and protecting industries competing against importers (in the case of

South Korea, see for example Hart-Landsberg *et al.* 2007: 8; Pirie 2008: 4). All of this was associated with degrees of "bureaucratic insulation" (not to mention frequent labor repression), with the interests of nationally-constrained capital subordinated to greater national development goals (well-known scholars of the developmental state talked of "embedded autonomy", "governed interdependence" and "governing the market" (Evans 1995; Wade 1990; Weiss 1998)).

In capitalist Southeast Asia, the overt developmentalism was often less apparent than that in Japan and South Korea, although the use of dirigiste policies (including highly strategic trade and industry policy typically associated with ISI and EOI) by states that often retained strong control and influence over important sections of the economy and deployed lashings of labor and leftist repression (sometimes, as in the case of Indonesia, on a vast scale), could be seen in countries such as Indonesia, Thailand, Singapore and Malaysia, all of which enjoyed burgeoning reputations as fast growing "developing countries" up until the 1997–1998 crisis (see for example Hadiz 2013: 211). Efforts by governments towards cultivating particular areas of competitiveness in capitalist production (domestic automotive production and the information communication technology sectors, for example) were coupled with the strong influence of "government-linked companies" (GLCs) and state-owned enterprises (SOEs) (on the importance of GLCs in Singapore, often described erroneously as a free market economy, see Rodan 2016), which played important, though highly divergent, roles in utility provision, healthcare, banking, national education and public housing.[3]

In post-colonial Indonesia, first under Sukarno – who forged an alliance with the Indonesian Communist Party, combined nationalism and socialism in his ideology, and nationalized Dutch industry in the late 1950s during "Guided Democracy" period (Lane 2008: 29–30; Pluvier 1970: 13; Robison 1986: 213; Vickers 2005: 144) – and then throughout the "New Order" period of Suharto, the state was deeply engaged in non-liberal efforts in relation to the economy, despite the influence (which waxed and waned depending upon economic fortunes) of US trained classical economists that reversed some of the nationalization of Sukarno and pursued policies targeted to towards foreign exploitation of resources and manufacturing (Anderson 1998; Robison 1986: 110–111). Under Suharto, the precise pattern of nascent capitalist development that consolidated over time (a blend of nationalism, anti-communism, authoritarianism and neo-sultanistic oligarchic cronyism and kleptocracy), owed much to the influence of the state in economic affairs and the opportunities that this and the increasing importance of oil revenues afforded. Indeed, during the early New Order period the state-owned corporate sector constituted "the largest and most crucial element of domestic capital in Indonesia", a feature which variously kept the means of production out of the hands of international capital, played an important role in national industrialization strategies of the 1970s, served to support the emergence of private capital (via infrastructure and finance provision and the awarding of contracts), and provided important revenue streams for the military and elites (Robison 1986: 211–212). Writing of the country's post-colonial economy, Robison characterized it and the social forces (and their legitimating ideologies) that produced it thus:

> Liberalism was to be a slender reed in the early decades of Indonesia's postcolonial economic history. In the end, it was to be a complex amalgam of state-centred economic nationalism and predatory oligarchy revolving around the state and its corps of politico-bureaucrats that was to prevail.
>
> The path to 'free flight liberalism' was rejected in favor of the principle that the state has a legitimate economic role in ensuring the national interest and that market forces should be tempered by social objectives. But, although themes of populism and nationalism were to triumph, they did so under the umbrella of a highly-centralized state and its corps of officials in the guise of state capitalism and an authoritarian form of organic corporatism. It was the state in the three decades from 1960 to the mid 1980s that embarked on an ambitious program to construct an autonomous industrial base. Nationalism and populism were ideologies sustained by deep-rooted and concrete vested interests. They lay at the heart of the organic notions of power that legitimated de facto possession of the state by its officials and relieved them of problems of accountability and representation. At the same time, an extensive state sector and pervasive industry policy were the perfect mechanisms for entrenching the pervasive authority of the state and its officials in the economic sphere.
>
> (Robison 2001: 110)

In Malaysia, emerging out of the ashes of the colonial state's victory over "communists, left-wing nationalists, former wartime partisans, radical sections of the working class, and squatter farmers", a period of *laissez faire* capitalism owing much to the continuity of dominant colonial class interests gave way to greater degrees of state intervention in a bid to attend to increasing asymmetries ((Boo Teik 2001: 181–182). Given the inability of *laissez faire* to "resolve the problems of increasing unemployment, declining incomes, and widening inequalities", the state actively sought to "manage the class pressures and ethnic demands that an unregulated market had not satisfied" with state intervention and affirmative action policies (for the indigenous *bumiputera* population) under the "New Economic Policy" (NEP) and a series of economic plans (Boo Teik 2001: 183–184). State intervention initially supported industrializing activities centered largely upon foreign direct investment (FDI) into textiles and garment manufacturing and electronics in the 1970s. This was followed by another state-supported push in the 1980s into more substantive forms of industrialization in automotive production and construction and industrial input materials (such as cement and steel) (Boo Teik 2001: 178).

In Singapore, the People's Action Party (PAP) enjoyed relative political autonomy from both capital and labor, a reality that pre-dated the city-state separating from the Malaysian federation. The PAP, led by a cadre of "English-educated middle-class nationalists" whose interests were initially separated from a domestic bourgeoisie aligned with colonial capital, were able to formulate a manufacturing strategy autonomous of domestic bourgeois pressures and forge a central role for the state in relation to the country's economic development (Rodan 2001: 142–143). Although committed to private sector-led industrialization –

inspired by the experiences of Northeast Asian cases such as Taiwan and Hong Kong – the Singapore story would be one that would involve a massive role for the state that would make even institutionally-oriented neoliberals shudder – with the formation of a pilot agency (the Economic Development Board – EDB), the establishment of crucial industrial infrastructure, the creation of key government-linked corporations (GLCs) (including a development bank and postal office bank that made possible the harnessing of public savings for developmental purposes), forms of lending and investment that were not wholly market-based, and the systemic subordination of organized labor to the broader imperatives of capital and, relatedly, the nation (suppressing wages, working conditions, increasing working hours and limiting collective action) (Rodan 2001: 145).

While the strategies deployed by states in capitalist Southeast Asia differed in their precise composition, shaped as these were by historical specificity and the battles between constellations of social forces emerging out of colonialism and nascent independence, the general narrative was one that involved significant national developmental elements (and significant national development and nationalist rhetoric) undertaken by states and regimes. Put another way, the projects of "strong men" such as Lee Kuan Yew, Mahathir Mohamad, and Suharto were not *laissez faire* projects; nor were they passive efforts to simply provide capital with a hospitable set of territorially-blind institutions as per contemporary neoliberal designs for the state. These were national projects that were selectively (and often heavily, if somewhat surreptitiously) interventionist and developmentalist, with regime elites cognizant of the need to cultivate late development (and accumulative opportunities) using a combination of state control and retention of important sectors, actively attempting to build national industrial capacity using both non-market *and* pro-private sector (and pro-transnational capital) components (see for example Robison 1986: 107). Taken together this combination often gave rise to a new domestic capitalist super elite that were the beneficiaries of the awarding of contracts, licenses, concessions and other *state-ensured* privileges.

What tied various state strategies together – including those of socialist countries –throughout the postwar era prior to the rise of neoliberalism was a notion of countries constituting key "units of development" and that various non-market/market constraining strategies were required to realize improvements, the latter often seen in terms of notions of social justice, equitable improvements in material conditions and modernity more broadly, rather than – for example – simply economic growth. As Mark Berger put it:

> The new global order that emerged in the Cold War era was premised on the sovereign equality of all nation states, despite the substantial inequalities between and within them. Against this backdrop the nation-state was naturalized as the unit of (capitalist and socialist) development worldwide. The idea and practice of development was enshrined between the 1940s and 1970s as a national and state-guided process of modernization.
>
> (Berger 2004: 38)

This era of national development, of course, would not last very long – compromised as it was by capitalist contradiction (stagflation and declining profits for capital), the competitive challenges of globalizing production and value chains and, especially important for countries deploying neo-mercantilist policies in Asia, the demise of preferential treatment by the US of subordinate states during the Cold War. The great unwinding in industrialized countries began in the late 1960s and early 1970s with slowing growth and declining rates of accumulation and profit. In the US, the rather brief "golden age of capitalism" drew to a close with average rates in the five years up until 1973 close to half what they had been from 1960 to 1968. Japan's decline was particularly precipitous, with average annual growth between 1960 and 1968 of 10.4 percent falling to 3.6 percent for the five years up until 1973 (Harvey 1990: 40–43, 130). Around the same time, deepening patterns of emergent transnationalization would place increasing pressures on the broad variety of nationally-oriented policy agendas of the postwar period (Harvey 1990: 40–43, 130). Developments in information and communications technology (satellite and undersea telecommunications cabling), logistics (containerized shipping and, later, increased airfreight) and new innovations in production (just-in-time etc.) combined to make possible an ongoing reorganization of production that benefited large-scale capital (which could access cheaper wages and congenial regulatory regimes), resulting in powerful fractions of capital becoming increasingly *transnational* and realizing "spatio-temporal fixes" to crises of accumulation (Harvey 2014: 151; Prashad 2012: 5). The combination of these techno-logistical developments with the ascendancy of financialization[4] and the soft-infrastructure of neoliberalism – the latter rising to prominence with right-wing administrations in the United Kingdom (Thatcher) and the US (Reagan) amid the grand crisis of Keynesianism and the political imperatives of addressing the needs of capital – would be a formidable challenge to the national development strategies of states and the leverage of organized labor in the industrialized world, all but ending the "class compromises" between capital and labor that had been associated with what John Ruggie described in Polanyian terms as "embedded liberalism" (Ruggie 1982).

In much of capitalist Asia, the postwar period was one of relative expansion and growth – a tendency which extended into Southeast Asia well beyond the rise of the first phase of neoliberalism and its first development policy incarnation, the Washington consensus,[5] the latter heavily impacting sub-Saharan Africa and Latin America in the 1980s and 1990s. Here, Southeast Asia – with its relatively cheap labor and accommodating (for capital and western interests) regimes – continued to reap the benefits of the transnationalization of production while problems in the developed world (emergent deindustrialization) and other post-colonial settings (stalled development, high levels of indebtedness) became increasingly evident. Elites within the region presided over economies that were growing quickly (events like the appreciation of the yen after the 1985 Plaza Accord assisted matters, contributing to the rapid regionalization of Japanese production[6]), facilitating further patronage opportunities and making the maintenance of popular legitimacy – especially when combined with labor repression and anti-Communist rhetoric

– easier for those in power than might otherwise have been the case. Emergent capitalist classes were also able to make significant gains, often under the patronage of regimes with which they were deeply intertwined and in tandem with foreign capital within joint-ventures (see for example Hewison 2001). All of this meant that national development policies and policy-cherry picking were more possible than in countries where conditional lending from "lenders of last resort", such as the IMF and World Bank, constrained policy autonomy. Indeed, while the drying up of material and other support from western governments and multilateral institutions that had regularly been extended on a strategic basis during the Cold War compelled governments to pursue some financial and economic liberalization in order to access new sources of finance and market share (Rodan *et al.* 2001: 15–16), much of capitalist Southeast Asia (the Philippines aside) was able to stave off the forced structural adjustment reform of the Washington consensus up until the 1997–1998 crisis (Carroll forthcoming).

However, much like earlier crises opened up opportunities for capital and the politicians that represented it to pitch neoliberalism as a "there is no alternative" (TINA) solution, the 1997–1998 crisis proved to be a crucial juncture for Southeast Asia. The crisis – which Higgott dubbed the first crisis of globalization (Higgott 2000: 262) – signaled the all-but-final gasp of nationally-driven development strategies based upon selective combinations of dirigiste and market policies and the ushering in of *both* Washington consensus and post-Washington consensus "institution building" reforms (the latter marshaled to tackle "crony capitalism" and "governance issues") in a much greater way. While many countries in the region had previously been afforded some relative luxury to be more selective in their policy choices (a mix of market and non-market policies depending upon interests and national developmental agendas), the requirement of conditional lending from lenders of last resort would further drive interment into the world market and heighten exposure to market discipline, further diminishing the autonomy of states and other elite interests. Crucially, while many of the countries of both capitalist Northeast and Southeast Asia had been at the very center of debates between "statists" and neoliberals over the role of the state in development, the onset of the crisis would do considerable damage to positions that privileged an extensive role (well beyond that specified within what would become the post-Washington consensus – see below) for the state in the economy.

Starting in Thailand in mid-to-late 1997 and then unfolding in Indonesia and beyond, countries that had selectively opened their economies in a bid to continue and extend earlier patterns of growth suddenly found themselves at the sharp end of increasing global market connectivity and, more specifically, conditional lending from the IMF and the World Bank.[7] Countries experienced rapidly declining currencies and reversals of capital flows made possible by capital account liberalization that had in several cases – in tandem with financial market deregulation – led to real estate speculation and increased exposure to currency risk (Radelet and Sachs 1997: 47). As the crisis unfolded in Thailand, for example, the World Bank and IMF extended large bailout packages and loans that demanded Washington consensus-styled structural adjustment and large-scale restructuring (variously downsizing, opening, rationalizing and marketizing) of the public sector and the financial sector (see Hewison 2001: 92).

In Indonesia, the crisis hit at the very core of the family-oriented networks of power and patronage and the social fabric of the country more broadly. The plummeting rupiah, which continued to fall after its floatation, accompanied a triple crisis in the banking and corporate sectors and government finances, compelling the government to call in the IMF and causing considerable pain for the population when subsidies (including those for fuel and food) were cut. The IMF insisted on a host of reforms and austerity measures that specifically took aim at national developmental and state interventionist efforts, including national car and aircraft projects, state trade monopolies on important foodstuffs and the "liquidation of insolvent banks" (Robison 2001: 118). While elite resistance to reforms and adjustment was often palpable, if there was any doubt that leverage was shifting for formerly-fast growing countries in the region, the famous image of the then-IMF Managing Director Michel Camdessus standing behind the dictator Suharto with folded arms as the latter signed a letter of intent and the onset of riots and large demonstrations would put paid to this and be emblematic of the end of the New Order (Gill 1999; Lane 2008: 169–171). In Malaysia, which was less severely impacted by the crisis than Indonesia and Thailand, experimentation with austerity to address the onset of recession gave way to Mahathir's imposition of capital account controls and other government initiatives (lending targets and fiscal and monetary tools) to revive growth. However, in line with the increasing tendencies elsewhere, these efforts did not equate to a dramatic overarching push away from the reality of the global political economy, with the government exempting export manufactures from the currency restrictions and removing the equity restrictions on foreign ownership in manufacturing (Felker 2015: 138–139).

While the crisis was important in terms of the rapid shifts in leverage between multilateral institutions, such as the World Bank and the IMF, and previously-celebrated fast growing countries and impacting policy autonomy, it was far from the end of the story. Indeed if anything it emphasized shifting terrains of power in the global political economy and the importance of foreign capital – and in particular financial capital – under late capitalism, as the dangers of capital flight and unsettling capital markets became an increasingly dominant policy concern across the region. Importantly, it was now apparent that the interests and risk appetites of the "electronic herd" outside of national borders could no longer be easily ignored and or simply subordinated to domestic elite prerogatives and interests.

This recognition was crucial in shifting development policy towards a policy set – the key tenets of which would comprise the post-Washington consensus (PWC) (Carroll 2010; Stiglitz 2001) – that would largely relate to establishing *liberal market-friendly institutions,* to first and foremost, satiate the electronic herd and capital more broadly. Here, the dominant narrative evinced within *World Development Reports,* World Bank Country Partnership Strategies and the utterances of politicians and key government agencies would be one of fighting "crony capitalism" with "good governance", the latter neoliberal parlance for providing optimal institutional environments for idealized notions of capital accumulation (World Bank 1997; 2001; 2002). Discussions of industrial policy and any remaining legacy of dirigisme were to be further erased via neoliberal development policy's second significant phase: a grand attempt to re-craft the state's role in development through "institution building" efforts and agendas to establish "enabling environments" for capital (the latter essentially referring to the provision of market friendly institutions). Importantly, this institution building approach would also include limited social protection efforts and highly coordinated and constrained participatory processes to circumvent resistance to neoliberal reform agendas. In Indonesia, projects such as the World Bank's massive Kecamatan Development Program (KDP), which impacted every village in the country and later went on to be a key component within the Indonesian government's anti-poverty approach, and a similar program in the Philippines reflected this institution building push, combining constrained participatory processes (using trained facilitators) in an attempt build market-friendly institutions from the bottom-up (Carroll 2009; Carroll and Jarvis 2015; Li 2006).

Importantly, the PWC was far from a straightforward story of institutional transformation (indeed far from it – it was often highly resisted, contested and mediated by powerful domestic political interests), a fact particularly reflected in the rapid expansion of public-private partnerships (PPPs) – in contrast to state provision – of various forms to deliver utilities and services. In the Philippines, Indonesia and Malaysia, indicative of processes underway elsewhere, large-scale privatization efforts were undertaken in water services and power. And – much like had been the case with the transformations under shock therapy in the countries of the former Soviet Union – the outcomes of these privatizations often reflected the patrimonial social relations of their jurisdictions, with gains and opportunities disproportionately captured by local elites and local elites partnering with transnational capital (Carroll 2010: 115–132; Jarvis forthcoming; Schuyler House and Wu forthcoming) and questions over regulatory capacity and or autonomy. Nonetheless, that policy makers were increasingly pursuing such agendas captured both the new constraints and opportunities of a globalized political economy in which capital needed its risks assuaged and in which many governments had less room to move in terms of distributing resources and protecting vested interests to the exclusion of foreign capital.

While growth returned to Southeast Asia after the crisis (albeit with some serious downturns, such as that in the early 1990s which impacted the electronics manufacturing sector), things would be considerably different from here on in for states in the region. The increasing reconfiguration of global and regional production chains associated with the rise of China as "factory to the world" (the country joined the World Trade Organization in 2001), and the increased incorporation of other Southeast Asian countries – such as Vietnam and Cambodia – into the world market as low-labor cost manufacturing sites would place further pressure on countries such as Indonesia, Malaysia and the Philippines which, despite growth and state intervention, had largely failed to generate high value-added domestically-owned industry with accumulation and employment potential that could generate "golden age of capitalism" level gains for broad sections of their respective populations (see for example Anderson 1998; Felker 2003: 259–261). Increasingly too, FDI flows – which were now shared with China and other new Southeast Asian entrants to global production – were often once again commodity-oriented, with policy foci eschewing large-scale industry for the newly celebrated micro, small and medium enterprise (MSME) sector and services.

The variegated market state and variegated capitalism in Southeast Asia: two vignettes (Indonesia and Malaysia)

The last decade and a half has only seen Southeast Asian countries further subjected to world market dynamics and their attendant pressures. While concerns over China undermining the cheap labor comparative advantage of the region have been common, the increase in Chinese wages and the renewed importance of commodities have reignited pessimism among analysts and, importantly, refocused the attention of important multilateral actors and policymakers on *competitiveness* and *productivity* (neither of which are, as we will see, to be remedied with old state-guided industrialization efforts or the sort of industrial upgrading that came from important transfers of technology within the context of the Cold War). Much of the region benefited in simple economic terms from the broader emerging market boom fueled by post 2007–2008 crisis expansionary monetary policy in the developed world that diminished returns on safe assets such as US Treasury bonds. In this environment, developed world capital went in search – as it always does – of new sources of profit, new inputs, new markets and reduced production costs. Crucially, for many countries in Southeast Asia, this context saw increasing per capita incomes, reductions in absolute poverty and the expansion of consumption (along with the broader extension of access to finance) occurring alongside increasing inequality, further elite gain capture, massive damage to the environment and natural resources and rising governmental concerns over "middle income traps".

In this section I review some of the key indicators and patterns associated with regional growth and look at the policy sets and state institutions charged with taking the respective economies forward. I focus on Indonesia (the region's largest economy and the world's fourth most populous nation) and Malaysia (which in 2013 was Southeast Asia's second largest economy and which achieved impressive post-independence per capita developmental gains) to demonstrate the increasingly constrained operating conditions that countries in the region find themselves in. However, many of the same patterns and policies can be seen elsewhere (albeit unevenly) in the region, with processes of marketization and policy scrambles for FDI unfolding from Vietnam (since its *doi moi* reforms) to more recently-opened Myanmar (see for example Cammack 2012; Hatcher 2012; Jarvis 2012; London forthcoming; Wanner and Rosser 2012). What is particularly evident is an increasing tendency towards the pronouncements of neoliberal multilateral institutions aligning closely with the policy actions of governments, despite the declining leverage of multilateral organizations throughout the emerging and frontier market boom. Here, governments now regularly recite the multilateral mantra of improving competitiveness by attending to the business and investment climates (an extension of the PWC institution building project), fostering and supporting MSME sectors (over grand industrial policy, for example), improving access to finance and providing the private sector (as the 'main engine of growth') with its necessary inputs (such as education to address skills gaps and productivity challenges and infrastructure). Crucially, gone is any mention from elites and policy makers generally of developmentalist/state-oriented efforts that accompanied earlier state agendas.

Anybody that has made routine visits to Indonesia over the last 15 years or so would acknowledge obvious change in the country. The infamous *macets* (traffic jams comprised largely of new Japanese branded cars) that increasingly plague the country's cities and the seemingly endless sprouting of flashy malls full of global brands are perhaps some of the most obvious signs that would strike someone who has not visited for a while. Notably, despite the grave situation during the crisis, throughout the emerging market boom, Indonesia was regularly heralded as somewhat of a darling. While the tapering of commodities prices has recently curtailed some of this, the country (now the world's fifteenth largest economy and a member of the G20) is often seen as having made a relatively successful exit from authoritarianism to democracy and important gains in key economic indicators. With a per capita income of US$3,346.50 in 2015 (up from $1,263.50 a decade earlier),[8] the country saw declines in national poverty between 1999 and 2012 (cut in half from 24 to 12 percent), with post-1997 crisis growth returning on the back of emboldened patterns of consumption and private-sector investment (World Bank 2015b: 7). Between 2001 and 2012 the country's GDP nearly doubled (from US$580 billion to US1.1 trillion) and fiscal health has been relatively good (low fiscal deficits, much reduced debt-to-GDP ratios and, until recently, external surpluses (World Bank 2015b: 7). Importantly though, much of this positive-sounding aggregate story is attributed to gains from rising commodity prices between 2003 and 2011. Not surprisingly, the narrative also came with significant caveats with respect to manufacturing. As the World Bank's most recent "Systematic Country Diagnostic" notes:

> There is strong evidence that growth and poverty reduction were strongly influenced by global commodity markets in the first decade of the new millennium. Indeed, the significant rise in commodity prices in 2003–11 led to massive income and wealth effects in Indonesia. These fed into corporate revenues, household incomes and government revenues, leading to a significant jump in domestic demand for goods and services. On the supply side, the (largely non-tradeable) services sector rose considerably, contrasting with a quasi-stagnant manufacturing sector, which lost competitiveness due to a sharp appreciation of the real exchange rate and high logistics and trade costs.
>
> (World Bank 2015b: 7)

Added to lackluster manufacturing performance, the above has dovetailed with serious environmental consequences; for example, land clearing (often for palm oil plantations) creating havoc domestically and regionally in terms of air quality and greenhouse gas emissions (Indonesia is now one of the world's largest emitters), and serious issues of resource depletion. Moreover, this pattern of growth was accompanied by rapidly rising inequality (between 2003 and 2010 the consumption Gini coefficient rose from 30 to 42) and a massive portion of the population failing to experience the benefits of growth. Importantly, recent assessments note that poverty reduction has now stagnated and that the country is in danger of becoming stuck in the dreaded "middle income trap" (World Bank 2015a: 5).

Despite much being made of the frequently nationalistic rhetoric that accompanied the 2015 election campaigns (the infamous and intensely elite pedigreed ex-Suharto General Prabowo Subianto's campaign included nationalist and explicitly anti-neoliberal pronouncements) and selective nationalist efforts (many of which have since been reversed or softened), during the presidency of Joko Widodo the overarching push, if not the pace, has been one that the World Bank and the IMF would largely be happy with. The first major liberalizing policy switch made after Widodo's election was to increase fuel prices and then completely remove long-standing fuel subsidies (despite political sensitivities around this), pushing up the costs for vehicle users (including motorcycles) and increasing the cost of basic goods (including staples such as rice) and services (Lane 2015b: 2). The goal of this cut (one of several that drew disposable income from some of the countries' most vulnerable) was to address the shortage of funds for infrastructure that was now being targeted as the key bottleneck to be removed to improve competitiveness and foster growth. Notably, this focus on infrastructure as a key constraint, which was a central focus of the Masterplan for the Acceleration and Expansion of Indonesia's economic Development (MP3EI 2011–2025), was in line with World Bank and other recommendations (see below) emphasizing not only the importance of infrastructure but the need (echoing key tenets of the PWC) for infrastructure to be driven by *public-private partnerships* (PPP). Indeed, government expenditure under Widodo into state-owned enterprises was specifically undertaken in order to make them more attractive to PPP possibilities (Lane 2015b: 2).

By early 2016, with the country feeling the effects of a depreciating currency and declining commodity prices (the latter slowing to a six year low in 2015), both the *Financial Times* and the *Wall Street Journal* were celebrating the erosion of some of the more nationalist and conservative (often driven by Islamic groups) policy elements (such as requirements to exclusively use the rupiah, Bahasa language requirements for expatriates, an expansion of the Negative Investment List, and restrictions on the sale of alcohol) that had accompanied the early part of Widodo's presidency (Lane 2015a: 7–8). Widodo's talk of "big bang" liberalization – coming after the elevation of reform-oriented technocrats (Widodo appointed a former investment funds manager as Trade Minister) – related to a series of measures. These included the removal of 35 industries from the Negative Investment List (the film, pharmaceutical and restaurant sectors), with a further significant relaxation in 40 other industries (including telecommunications and warehousing) – an initiative explicitly undertaken to facilitate to the entry of foreign capital (Chilkoti 2016; *Wall Street Journal* 2016). Further recent liberalizing measures have included the establishing of a "one-stop shop" for business licenses – long an effort attracting positive feedback from neoliberal multilateral agencies and business environment ranking systems such as *Doing Business* – and efforts to start the revision of 80 business restricting regulations and a promise to cut the corporate tax rate from 25 percent to 18 percent and the greenlighting of prefinancing and prebidding for public works (*The Wall Street Journal* 2016). Crucially, on a trip by Widodo and his Trade Minister to the US Indonesia's intention to join the Trans-Pacific Partnership (TPP) was announced which, if it materialized, would (among other things) demand further liberalization measures and erase the preferential treatment between state-owned enterprises (SOEs) and non-SOEs regardless of domicile (Amindoni and Hermansyah 2016).

Suggesting increasing alignment between broader government policy trends and orthodox development policy, the World Bank's current Country Partnership Framework (CPF) is tellingly positive in terms of being able to support the Government of Indonesia's (GoI's) current (and expansive) mid-term Development Plan (RPJMN 2015–2019), which details the need to increase the productivity of the lower and middle strata without "reducing the flexibility of major actors" as agents of growth (World Bank 2015a: 17). The CPF notes three main factors as responsible for limiting growth and job creation in higher productivity sectors: large infrastructure gaps; skills gaps; and "a weak business and financing environment, with investment and trade regulations that are generally restrictive, often inconsistent, and uncertain (World Bank 2015a: 20)". Notably, the CPF's key section that outlines the bank's country strategy going forward begins with a very lengthy section on the bank's overarching emphasis on infrastructure support to address constraints on growth, competitiveness and job creation, service delivery, inclusivity and connectivity, repeatedly emphasizing the bank's intention to support further private-sector participation in infrastructure (using loans, equity and technical assistance), including within water and sanitation and energy sectors (World Bank 2015a: 21–27.). Likewise, a significant section entitled "leveraging the private-sector: investment, business climate and functioning of markets" highlights the importance of improving the conditions for the private sector to flourish, especially in relation supporting further PPPs and – a central focus of contemporary neoliberal development policy – in the MSME sector. In short, the current economic policy pushes of both the GoI and the World Bank cover much of the same ground, with considerable alignment (echoing the influence of the PWC, the latter also being discernible in emphases upon limited social safety nets and social inclusion). Notably, while the section on strategy implementation risks raises common concerns regarding "political economy and governance" challenges and both domestic and international economic environments, there are very few serious policy flags raised by the bank in the CPF regarding the GoI's current strategy which also endorses many of the activities undertaken under Widodo and notes the importance of continuing to "accelerate the country's structural transformation" (World Bank 2015a: 53).

In Malaysia, Southeast Asia's third wealthiest country by per capita income (US$11,307), the shift from old patterns of policy making that saw the state attempting to nurture particular sectors and catalyze high value-added domestic production has been particularly pronounced. Recent growth (projected at 4.4 percent for 2016) has been predominantly driven by consumption, with (as in the case on Indonesia) tough productivity challenges in the SME sector (SMEs in Malaysia account for 97.3 percent of firms and 35.9 percent of GDP in 2015 and are much less productive across all sub-sector areas) (World Bank 2016: 1–5). Moreover, the economy currently faces a nasty set of headwinds (several exogenously generated) that have increasingly fed into broader processes involving the state having to grapple with being stuck in a middle income trap (government reports directly use this term), with far fewer policy options than before. Declining FDI (with responsibility leveled at relatively high wages and skill constraints), a depreciating currency (underperforming at levels not seen since the 1997–1998 crisis), the abrupt slowing of Chinese growth (Malaysia is China's largest Southeast Asian trading partner) and declining oil receipts on the back of the dramatic drop in the price of oil (around a third of public revenues are attributable to oil-related taxation) have impacted the country and challenged the government's often stipulated goal of achieving high-income status by 2020 (World Bank 2015c).

Even prior to the slowing of Chinese growth and the drop in oil prices, the Malaysian government evinced recognition of the limitations inherent in previous state-led attempts at generating competitiveness and national advantage. Indeed, the demonstrated eagerness of the government to improve the country's *Doing Business* rankings (which essentially measure the ability of a government to provide a nurturing environment to capital) and its 2010 New Economic Model (NEM) (to be driven by an Economic Transformation Programme ETP – more below), are stark recognition of the realities of slowing productivity and hyper-competition under late capitalism and the need for new strategies to navigate these to avoid middle-income stasis and achieve key goals (such as high-income status) as part of an overarching agenda dubbed "Vision 2020".

> The old growth model provided three decades of outstanding performance, permitting Malaysia to provide health and education to its people, largely eradicate poverty, build world-class infrastructure and become a major exporter globally. …But the progress we have made over the past half-century has slowed and economic growth prospects have weakened considerably. We are caught in a middle income trap – we are not amongst the top performing global economies. Amid changes in the external environment, many of the policies and strategies we used to achieve the current state of development are now inadequate to take us to the next stage. The government must confront these realities and make tough decisions.
>
> We urgently need radical change in our approach to economic development which will be sustainable over the long-term, will reach everyone in the country and will enable Malaysia to reach high-income status. … The [National Economic Advisory Council] believes that by consistently implementing bold

> policies across eight [Strategic Reform Initiatives], the fundamentals of doing business in Malaysia will be changed from the old approach, enabling the private sector to step up and make a full contribution to growth.
>
> (NEAC 2010)

Importantly, the policy foci and even the language associated with these represent a dramatic shift from earlier periods; a point explicitly recognized in the NEM. Indeed, a table in the document explicitly sets the "Old Approach" (state-driven) against the "New Approach" (heavily private-sector led, with the state – in a very PWC manner – providing the necessary institutions for idealized patterns of accumulation). Under the old approach seven key foci are noted, many of which line up with old developmentalist and dirigiste strategies associated with the developmental state and some earlier patterns of industrialization in Europe. Here the emphases are on "growth primarily through capital accumulation", "dominant state participation in the economy", "centralized strategic planning", "balanced regional growth" (within the country), "favoring specific industries and firms", "export dependence on the G3 (US, Europe and Japan)" and restrictions on foreign workers. These foci are set starkly against those of the "New Approach", many of which could have been penned by policy wonks within the World Bank's private-sector arm, the International Finance Corporation (IFC), or OECD. Here emphases on "growth through productivity", "private sector-led growth", "localized autonomy in decision-making" and favoring technologically capable industries and firms via granting "incentives to support innovation and risk-taking to enable entrepreneurs to develop higher value added products and services" are clear signs of a recognition of the limitations of old approaches within a newly hyper-competitive era (National Economic Advisory Council 2010). Tellingly, the NEM explicitly extols the benefits to business of this new approach which, once again, could have come straight out of a *World Development Report* or *Doing Business* (see Table 6.1).

Rounding this picture out, the NEM proposes a table of policy measures that include the following cutting-edge neoliberal foci (for an analysis of cutting-edge neoliberal policy modalities see Carroll 2012; 2015): facilitating "FDI and DDI in emerging industries/sectors"; removing "distortions in regulation and licensing, including replacement of Approved Permit system with a negative list of imports"; introducing a "single-window" licensing process through e-Government portals to include local and state governments; reducing "direct participation in the economy"; divesting "[government-linked companies – GLCs] in industries where the private sector is operating effectively"; ensuring "GLCs operate on a strict commercial basis free of government interference"; leveling "the playing field for the private sector through transparent standard settings"; supporting "a stronger competitive environment with competition law"; providing "support for SMEs in innovative and technologically advanced areas"; facilitating "timely access to funding for business activities"; and encouraging "GLC partnerships with private-sector companies" (National Economic Advisory Council 2010: 19).

Moreover, the above has been coupled with the country embarking upon what has been described as a new generation of trade agreements (including signing

Table 6.1 Benefits to business from Malaysia's New Economic Model, 2010

An equitable environment in which investors will thrive includes:	*An effective ecosystem for business will include:*	*An efficient market will provide investment and growth opportunities through:*
• **Business Rights.** Due recognition of rights and responsibilities of business owners • **Rule of Law.** Ability to manage businesses with the assurance of a fair and credible legal system • **Ownership Freedom.** Freedom to fully own businesses and choose partners • **Intellectual Property.** Intellectual assets will be protected • **SME Recognition.** Regulations are appropriate and proportionate to small businesses • **Market Transparency.** Absence of rent-seeking and quotas, with support to businesses based on market principles	• **Public Services.** Faster approvals across the board • **Licensing Efficiency**. Elimination of unnecessary licensing and undue regulatory burden • **Dynamic Clusters.** Benefit derived from scale through industry clustering and networking • **Human Capital.** Improved access to the best talent based on ability to pay • **Funding.** Flexible and prompt access to SME funding under strong government rules • **Efficient Courts.** Swift resolutions of legal disputes • **Transformation Fund.** Fair access to special assistance during the economic transition period • **Regional Integration.** An integrated regional market and support to grow into regional champions	• **Transparency.** Confidence in the openness and fairness of government tenders • **Fair Market Pricing.** With minimal exceptions, subsidies and price controls will be eliminated • **Barrier Free.** Liberalisation of all sectors • **Fair competition.** Ability to operate on a level playing field created by enactment of a competition law • **Public-private Partnership**. More opportunities to collaborate with the public sector and GLCs (government-linked companies)

Source: (National Economic Advisory Council 2010: 13)

the Trans-Pacific Partnership) which are now seen as potentially assisting in leveraging the sort of change demarcated in the NEM. In a recent (June 2016) report the World Bank notes the openness of the country, the 14 free trade agreements signed by the country to date and the importance of trade and investment to the Malaysian economy (the report states that "about 40 percent of jobs in Malaysia are linked with export activities and total wages supported by exports have quadrupled from USD$13.2 billion in 1995 to USD54 billion in 2011" (World Bank 2016 2)). Referencing the government's stated aim of reaching high-income status, and dovetailing with many of the policy foci of the NEM, the report hones in on the importance of higher value-added services, improved investment policies to attract a new wave of FDI, creating a more competitive economy to innovate and raise productivity and the importance of SMEs (and enhancing their productivity). Importantly, trade liberalization has been increasingly paired with further investment liberalization. As the OECD notes, in 2009 (much like the recent efforts in Indonesia under Widodo) the Malaysian government started to remove foreign investment restrictions in service sub-sectors with, cognizant of the relationship between services and competitiveness, subsequent announcements to further liberalize investment in services for both domestic and foreign players. The substantive removal of the Guidelines of the Foreign Investment Committee, which previously covered all acquisitions by foreign parties but which now only cover particular investments in property, and efforts to countenance IP protection (through a national IP policy, IP courts and IP awareness programmes) all suggest concern towards creating the very pro-private sector "enabling environments" prized by multilateral actors such as the IFC and OECD (OECD 2013: 20).

Of course policy pronouncements are always refracted through extant power relations that in Malaysia center upon networks of political and economic interests associated with the United Malays National Organization – UMNO). These will no doubt play a role in how the sorts of policy sets are prioritized and how actual existing neoliberal reform unfolds: and the signs, despite overtures in the NEM regarding how this new model of economic policy will help the *rakyat* ("ordinary citizens"), are not encouraging. For example, Jarvis, notes the manner in which the vast patronage networks associated with UMNO and the unfurling of neoliberal modalities are combining to erode many of the developmentalist gains of before:

> [I]n the Malaysian context … marketisation, privatisation and broad based neoliberal policy prescriptions involving user-pay and full cost recover principles applied to an increasing range of government and government linked sectors (utilities and energy, construction, network infrastructure) represent not only an encroaching pattern of rent seeking capitalism by the political business state but more fundamentally the sublimation of race to class as a key factor aligning political interests. Marketisation and neoliberalism, in other words, are being used to deepen rents; a process that is stratifying Malay-class factionalism, adversely impacting wealth distribution and derailing the positive developmental outcomes historically associated with Malaysia's political business state.
>
> (Jarvis forthcoming)

Ongoing issues relating to corruption (the massive 1MDB scandal being currently prominent here), and the clamping down on dissent along with the unveiling of emboldened new security powers that can designate any area of concern for the government "a security area" (Reuters 2016; Sadiq 2016) bode poorly for the realization of some sort of PWC utopia comprised of idealized enabling environments nurturing highly productive private-sector activity that benefits a broad swath of the population. This said the very real structural constraints binding the Malaysian state and the need for elites to legitimize their rule (which for many Southeast Asian countries has involved authoritarian regimes presiding over impressive growth and combining it with subtle and not-so subtle forms of control and repression) has clearly played a role in compelling the government towards overhauling the guiding framework for the economy, with significant opportunities flowing to elites and fractions of domestic and foreign capital.

Conclusion

The foregoing chapter has outlined an emergent reality of constrained policy and institutional choice for countries in Southeast Asia and elsewhere under late capitalism. The demise of the Cold War and the ascendancy of neoliberalism and a competitive world market has compelled states towards making significant concessions that accommodate the interests of capital and, in particular transnational/financial capital. The reality of a world market and its disciplinary tendencies have not yielded uniform outcomes and nor should we expect them to given the manner in which capitalism has unfolded highly unevenly and given to the mediating influence of domestic politics. However, where before multilateral organizations such as the International Monetary Fund (IMF) and the World Bank previously relied upon "conditional lending" to extend reform – a reality that was paramount during the 1997–1998 crisis that constituted the real beginning of the end for non-neoliberal policies in both Northeast and Southeast Asia – this is no longer necessary, with policy and other elites beyond ministries of finance increasingly buying into a certain inevitability in having to prioritize new FDI pushes, private-sector-led infrastructure (through PPPs), cultivating MSMEs and MSME productivity, and providing "enabling environments" for business as the sole manner in which development can now be advanced.

The two vignettes above demonstrate the new policy tendencies (and their drivers) evident across much of the region. While there are always important caveats, such as those associated with Singapore, where the city-state's ruling party (with considerable resources at its disposal relative to the population) has embarked upon recent redistributive efforts to attend to the political realities of rising inequality (see Rodan 2016), the grand trend in the region is increasingly in step (albeit unevenly) with that of the international financial institutions. In an environment of declining commodity prices and where the high-value added means of production have largely been allocated (solidifying the dominance of northern-located capital), with the sorts of all-important catalyzing transfers of technology, capital and preferential market access under the Cold War a thing of the past, the opportunities for governments to pursue dirigiste policies with significant capacity for domestic accumulation have significantly diminished. Hence it is now common to hear talk of a "new normal" for Southeast Asia involving slowing growth, decreasing benefits from the so-called "demographic dividend", creative destruction pressures from robotization, automation and "reshoring", and fewer opportunities for industrial upgrading that could yield important domestic accumulation gains (especially given the size populations at hand). What we have instead is state-driven marketization mediated by elite-driven politics. Here, the various policy sets that are promoted by the variegated market state feed into patterns of variegated capitalism which appear far from edifying. These patterns are characterized by being "consumer-driven" in nature (despite countries still remaining in low and middle-income status and despite too often dramatically increasing inequality) and fueled by unprecedented flows of finance (debt), the latter often for the purchase of products in which significant value accrues to foreign capital and a narrow elite. Such growth trajectories also involve the production of lowly-differentiated goods based upon the relative cost of labor and in which the actual numbers of workers employed is low relative to populations. Importantly these trajectories also involve the (re)accelerated exploitation of natural resources (with little-to-no value added). Given the above, and given too, the weakened position of organized labor within the world market, the outlook for the variegated market state and variegated capitalism appears ominous in Southeast Asia, likely contributing to further contradictory forms of populism and nationalism (Prabowo and the recent election of Rodrigo Duterte in the Philippines are perhaps instructive here).

Notes

1 It should be noted here that states and state entities can be capitalist in nature too, such as when sovereign wealth funds make investments in companies and or investment vehicles that do the same, or when companies owned and controlled states operate according to capitalist interest.

2 I define the state as the socially produced and mediated sets of institutions (including policies, rules, laws and norms) related to governing a given territory and the dominant governing interests presiding over the selection and implementation of these institutional sets.

3 In the forward to his classic book, *Indonesia: The Rise of Capital*, Richard Robison captured well the role that the post-colonial Third World state often assumed in fostering a capitalist economy: "In the Third World the general pattern has been for the state to assume political leadership of the capitalist revolution given the relative weakness of the domestic capitalist class. The bourgeoisie has generally developed within the framework of state-led capitalism in which political ascendancy lies with the officials of the state itself. One of the more interesting questions relating to social and political change in the Third World is whether these state state-led capitalist societies constitute a new and enduring historical model or an interlude" (Robison 1986: viii).

4 By financialization I am referring to the "shift from productive to financial forms of capital accumulation" and the associated regulatory and political elements associated with this (Carroll and Jarvis 2014: 538; Duménil and Lévy 2011: 99–112; Foster and Magdoff 2009; Gunnoe and Gellert 2010: 266).

5 The term Washington consensus refers to the generally shared endorsement by the World Bank, the IMF and the US Treasury of fiscal discipline, privatization, secure property rights, redirecting public expenditure towards "pro-growth" areas and areas to improve income distribution, tax reform (and a preference for lower marginal rates and broader tax bases via value added and other similar taxes), liberalization of interest rates, trade and foreign direct investment and competitive exchange rates (Williamson 1990: 7).

6 UNCTAD's *World Investment Report* states that outward investments by Japanese firms increased by 62 percent annually from 1985 to 1989 (UNCTAD 1991: 4).

7 This was often complemented by the Asian Development Bank.
8 All per capita figures are in constant US dollars and are taken from the World Bank's World Development Indicators.

References

Amindoni, Ayomi and Anton Hermansyah (2016) "TPP Officially Signed, Indonesia to Amend 12 Laws". *The Jakarta Post*, Friday 5 February 2016, http://www.thejakartapost.com/news/2016/02/05/tpp-officially-signed-indonesia-amend-12-laws.html, downloaded on July 7 2016.

Anderson, Benedict (1998) "From Miracle to Crash" *London Review of Books,* 20 (8):n.p.

Berger, Mark T. (2004) "The Battle for Asia – From Decolonization to Globalization", in M. Selden (ed.), *Asia's Transformations*, London: Routledge.

Boo Teik, Khoo (2001) "The State and the Market in Malaysian Political Economy", in G. Rodan, K. Hewison and R. Robison (eds), *The Political Economy of South-east Asia*, South Melbourne: Oxford University Press, pp. 178–205.

Brenner, Neil, Jamie Peck and Nik Theodore (2010) "Variegated Neoliberalization: Geographies, Modalities, Pathways", *Global Networks,* 10 (2):182–222.

Bruff, Ian (2011) "What about the Elephant in the Room? Varieties of Capitalism, Varieties in Capitalism", *New Political Economy,* 16 (4):481–500. doi: 10.1080/13563467.2011.519022.

Bruff, Ian (2012) "Risk, Social Protection and the World Market", *Journal of Contemporary Asia,* 42 (3): 359–377.

Cammack, Paul (2016) "World Market Regionalism at the Asian Development Bank", *Journal of Contemporary Asia,* 46 (2):173–197. doi: 10.1080/00472336.2015.1086407.

Carroll, Toby (2009) "'Social Development' as Neoliberal Trojan Horse: The World Bank and the Kecamatan Development Program in Indonesia", *Development and Change,* 40 (3):447–466.

Carroll, Toby (2010) *Delusions of Development: the World Bank and the post-Washington Consensus in Southeast Asia*, London: Palgrave Macmillan.

Carroll, Toby (2012) "Working On, Through and Around the State: The Deep Marketisation of Development in the Asia-Pacific", *Journal of Contemporary Asia,* 42 (3):378–404. doi: 10.1080/00472336.2012.687628.

Carroll, Toby (2015) "'Access to Finance' and the Death of Development in the Asia-Pacific", *Journal of Contemporary Asia,* 45 (1):139–66. doi: 10.1080/00472336.2014.907927.

Carroll, Toby (forthcoming) "Multilateral Development Policy and Neoliberalism in Southeast Asia", in A. McGregor, L. Law and F. Miller (eds), *Routledge Handbook of Southeast Asian Development*, London Routledge.

Carroll, Toby and Darryl S.L. Jarvis (2014) "Financialisation and Development in Asia under Late Capitalism", *Asian Studies Review,* 38 (4):533–543.

Carroll, Toby and Darryl S. L. Jarvis (2015) "The New Politics of Development: Citizens, Civil Society, and the Evolution of Neoliberal Development Policy", *Globalizations,* 12 (3):281–304. doi: 10.1080/14747731.2015.1016301.

Chilkoti, Avantika (2016) "Indonesia Launches 'Big Bang' Liberalisation", *Financial Times*, February 11, 2016, http://www.ft.com/cms/s/0/52390634-d087-11e5-92a1-c5e23ef99c77.html, downloaded on July 6 2016.

Duménil, Gérard and Dominique Lévy (2011) *The Crisis of Neoliberalism*, Cambridge, MA: Harvard University Press.

Evans, Peter (1995) *Embedded Autonomy: States and Industrial Transformation*, Princeton, NJ: Princeton University Press.
Felker, Greg (2003) "Southeast Asian Industrialisation and the Changing Global Production System", *Third World Quarterly*, 24 (2):255–282. doi: 10.1080/0143659032000074583.
Felker, Greg (2015) "Malaysia's Development Strategies: Governing Distribution-through-growth", in M. Weiss (ed.), *Routledge Handbook of Contemporary Malaysia*, London: Routledge, pp. 133–147.
Foster, Bellamy, John and Fred Magdoff (2009) *The Great Financial Crisis: Causes and Consequences*, New York: Monthly Review Press.
Gill, Stephen (1999) "The Geolpolitics of the Asian crisis", *Monthly Review*, 50 (10).
Gunnoe, Andrew and Paul K. Gellert (2010) "Financialization, Shareholder Value, and the Transformation of Timberland Ownership in the USA", *Critical Sociology*, 32 (2):1–24.
Hadiz, Vedi R. (2013) "The Rise of Capital and the Necessity of Political Economy", *Journal of Contemporary Asia*, 43 (2):208–225. doi: 10.1080/00472336.2012.757433.
Hall, Peter A. and David Soskice (2001) "An Introduction to Varieties of Capitalism", in P. A. Hall and D. Soskice (eds), *Varieties of Capitalism: The Institutional Foundations of Comparative Advantage*, Oxford: Oxford University Press, pp. 1–68.
Hart-Landsberg, MartinSeongjin Jeong and Richard Westra (2007) "Introduction: Marxist Perspectives on South Korea in the Global Economy", in M. Hart-Landsberg, S. Jeong and R. Westra (eds), *Marxist Perspectives on South Korea in the Global Economy*, Aldershot: Ashgate, pp. 1–29.
Harvey, David (1990) *The Condition of Postmodernity*, Cambridge MA: Blackwell.
Harvey, David (2007) *A Brief History of Neoliberalism*, New York: Oxford University Press.
Harvey, David (2014) *Seventeen Contradictions and the End of Capitalism*, Oxford: Oxford.
Hatcher, Pascale (2012) "Taming the Risks in Asia: the World Bank Group and New Mining Regimes", *Journal of Contemporary Asia*, 42 (3):427–46.
Hewison, Kevin (2001) "Thailand's Capitalism: Development Through Boom and Bust", in G. Rodan, K. Hewison and R. Robison (eds), *The Political Economy of South-East Asia, Second Edition*, Melbourne: Oxford University Press, pp. 71–103.
Higgott, Richard (2000) "The International Relations of the Asian Crisis: A Study in the Politics of Resentment", in R. Robison, M. Beeson, K. Jayasuriya and H.-R. Kim (eds), *Politics and Markets in the Wake of the Asian Crisis*, London: Routledge, pp. 261–282.
Jarvis, Darryl (2012) "The Regulatory State in Developing Countries: Can it Exist and Do We Want It? The Case of the Indonesian Power Sector", *Journal of Contemporary Asia*, 42 (3):464–492.
Jarvis, Darryl (forthcoming) "The State and Development in Malaysia: Race, Class and Markets", in T. Carroll and D. Jarvis (eds), *Disembedding Autonomy: Asia after the Developmental State*, Cambridge: Cambridge University Press.
Jessop, Bob (2015) "Variegated Capitalism and the Political economy of Austerity", in R. Westra, D. Badeen and R. Albritton (eds), *The Future of Capitalism after the Financial Crisis: The Varieties of Capitalism Debate in the Age of Austerity*, Abingdon: Routledge, pp. 19–38.
Johnson, Chalmers (1982) *MITI and the Japanese Miracle – The Growth of Industrial Policy, 1925–1975*, Stanford, CA: Stanford University Press.
Lane, Max (2008) *Unfinsihed Nation*, London: Verso.
Lane, Max (2015a) "Amidst Indonesia's Nationalist Atmospherics: The Changing Politics of Jokowi's Economics", *Perspective*, 64:1–10.

Lane, Max (2015b) "The Politics of Widodo's Prioritisation of Accelerated Infrastructure Construction", *Perspective,* 43:1–9.

Li, Tania (2006) "Government Through Community: The Social Development Program of the World Bank in Indonesia", http://www.iilj.org/GAL_2006_3_Li.htm

London, Jonathan (forthcoming) "Varieties of States, Varieties of Political Economy: China, Vietnam, and the Making of Market-Leninism", in T. Carroll and D. S. L. Jarvia (eds), *Disembedding Autonomy: Asia after the Developmental State*, Cambridge: Cambridge University Press.

McDonough, Terrence (2015) "Comparative capitalisms and the theory of capitalist stages", in R. Westra, D. Badeen and R. Albritton (eds), *The Future of Capitalism after the Financial Crisis: The Varieties of Capitalism Debate in the Age of Austerity*, Abingdon: Routledge.

National Economic Advisory Council (NEAC) (2010) *New Economic Model for Malaysia*, Putrajaya National Economic Advisory Council.

Organisation for Co-operation and Development (OECD) (2013) *OECD Investment Policy Review: Malaysia 2013*, Paris: OECD.

Pirie, Iain (2008) *The Korean Developmental State*, London: Routledge.

Pluvier, Jan (1970) "Indonesia Before the Holocaust", *Journal of Contemporary Asia,* 1 (2):5–21. doi: 10.1080/00472337085390121.

Prashad, Vijay (2012) *The Poorer Nations: A Possible History of the Global South*, London: Verso.

Radelet, Steven and Jeffrey Sachs (1997) "Asia's Reemergence", *Foreign Affairs,* 76 (6):44–59.

Reuters (2016) "Malaysia PM Najib Razak Gets New Powers Amid protests Over 1MDB Fund Scandal", *Guardian*, 27 July, https://www.theguardian.com/world/2016/jul/27/malaysia-pm-najib-razak-gets-new-powers-amid-protests-over-1mdb-fund-scandal, downloaded on 4 August 2016.

Robison, Richard (1986) *Indonesia: The Rise of Capital*, Singapore: Equinox.

Robison, Richard (2001) "Indonesia: Crisis, Oligarchy and Reform", in G. Rodan, K. Hewison and R. Robison (eds), *The Political Economy of South-East Asia*, 2nd ed., Melbourne: Oxford University Press, pp. 104–137.

Rodan, Garry (2001) "Singapore: Globalisation and the Politics of Economic Restructuring", in G. Rodan, K. Hewison and R. Robison (eds), *The Political Economy of South-East Asia,* 2nd ed., Melbourne: Oxford University Press, pp. 138–177.

Rodan, Garry (2016) "Capitalism Inequality and Ideology in Singapore: New Challenges for the Ruling Party", *Asian Studies Review,* 40 (2):211–230.

Rodan, Garry, Kevin Hewison and Richard Robison (2001) *The Political Economy of South-East Asia,* Melbourne: Oxford University Press.

Ruggie, John (1982) "International Regimes, Transactions, and Change: Embedded Liberalism in the Postwar Economic Order", *International Organization,* 36 (2):379–415.

Sadiq, Jahabar (2016) "The Muzzling of the Malaysian Mind", *New York Times*, downloaded on. July 6 2016.

Schuyler House, Ruth and Xun Wu (forthcoming) "Public-Private Partnerships in the Water Sector in Southeast Asia: Trends, Issues, and Lessons", in T. Carroll and D. Jarvis (eds), *Disembedding Autonomy: Asia after the Developmental State*, Cambridge: Cambridge University Press.

Stiglitz, Joseph (2001) "More Instruments and Broader Goals: Moving Towards a Post-Washington Consensus", in H.-J. Chang (ed.), *Joseph Stiglitz and the World Bank, The Rebel Within*, London: Anthem Press, pp. 17–56.

United Nations Conference on Trade and Investment (UNCTAD) (1991) *World Investment Report 1991*, Geneva: UNCTAD.

Van Der Pijl, Kees (2015) "Varieties of Capitalism or Dominan Fractions? Two Forms of Money Capital in the Current Crisis", in R. Westra, D. Badeen and R. Albritton (eds), *The Future of Capitalism after the Financial Crisis: The Varieties of Capitalism Debate in the Age of Austerity*, Abingdon: Routledge, pp. 39–55.

Vickers, Adrian (2005) *A History of Modern Indonesia*, Cambridge: Cambridge University Press.

Wade, Robert (1990) *Governing the Market: Economic Theory and the Role of Government in East Asian Industrialization*, Princeton, NJ: Princeton University Press.

Wall Street Journal (2016) "Indonesia's Economic Opening", *Wall Street Journal*, 18 February 2016, http://www.wsj.com/articles/indonesias-economic-opening-1455841349, downloaded on July 6 2016.

Wanner, Thomas and Andrew Rosser (2012) "Building Neo-liberal Markets and Other Agendas: The Politics of Risk Management at AusAID", *Journal of Contemporary Asia*, 42 (3):447–463. doi: 10.1080/00472336.2012.687632.

Weiss, Linda (1998) *The Myth of the Powerless State*, London: Polity.

Williamson, John (1990) "What Washington Means by Policy Reform", in J. Williamson (eds), *Latin American Adjustment: How Much has Happened?*, Washington, DC: Institute for International Economics, pp. 5–20.

World Bank (1997) *World Development Report 1997: The State in a Changing World World Development Report*, New York: Oxford University Press.

World Bank (2001) *World Development Report 2000/2001: Attacking Poverty, World Development Report*, New York: Oxford University Press.

World Bank (2002) *World Development Report 2002: Building Institutions for Markets, World Development Report* Washington: Oxford University Press and the World Bank.

World Bank (2015a) *Country Partnership Framework for the Republic of Indonesia*, Jakarta: World Bank.

World Bank (2015b) *Indonesia: Systematic Country Diagnostic*, Jakarta: World Bank Group.

World Bank (2015c) "Malaysia: Overview", World Bank downloaded on 12 February 2016, available at: http://www.worldbank.org/en/country/malaysia/overview, updated October 2016.

World Bank (2016) *Malaysia Economic Moniotor June 2016: Leveraging Trade Agreements* Kuala Lumpur: World Bank.

7 Thailand

Sick man of Asia?

Sompong Sirisoponsilp and
Ake Tangsupvattana

Thailand is a patient with flu and arthritis – the flu being an export slowdown caught from the global economy and the arthritis being the country's own structural problems (Prasarn Trairatvorakul, ex-governor of the Central Bank of Thailand, cited in Suttinee Yuvejwattana 2015). In 2014, overseas export sales fell again for the second consecutive year. It was the first back-to-back decline in almost two decades, whereas Vietnam and the Philippines performed well. Thailand was also forecast to have the slowest economic growth in ASEAN apart from Singapore, which is the only nation in the region considered fully developed (Suttinee Yuvejwattana 2015). In this context, the chapter argues that if the Thai state cultivates no clear development strategy, Thailand will be ensnared in perpetuity in a middle-income trap and become a sick man of Asia. Indeed, the only clear economic strategy of Thai state today is export-oriented industrialization relying on labor-intensive industry. However, the global economic scenario has been subject to dramatic alteration over the past decade. Labor-intensive industry carries no innovation dynamic which is central to success in today's global economy. Furthermore, with labor shortage in the country from demographic change, Thailand's increasing labor costs are diminishing its competitiveness in relation to China, Vietnam and other ASEAN countries.

In the epoch of inequality and austerity in global political economy, it is crucial for each state to evolve its own development strategy. The collapse of communist regimes brought into being domination by neoliberal economic globalization driven by the Washington Consensus. Even China is no exception here. After double digit GDP growth for decades, in 2012, China's GDP dropped into single digits. In 2015 China's GDP was 6.9 percent, the weakest since 1990, and is estimated at 6.5 percent for 2016.

China is currently the second largest economy in the world, overtaking Japan. That has set up an economic rivalry between the US and China. In 2016, China assumed the presidency of the G-20. At the same time, China initiated new economic policies, such as the Asian Infrastructure Investment Bank (AIIB) and One Belt One Road (OBOR), which can be interpreted as opposing Western economic domination. This strengthens China's international profile and makes it a recognized power in competition with the US (Chandran 2016). As a regional economic power China will wield greater influence in Southeast Asia including over nearby countries such as Thailand.

Whether the Western camp led by the US in the mode of so-called stock market capitalism (Dore 2000) or Eastern camp led by China in the mode of so-called state capitalism will predominate in Asia is to be seen. China's economic prosperity or stagnation per se is not the main concern of this chapter. However, China's economic interest relating to the Thai economy in ways that may perpetuate inequality between the two in the context of the global political economy is essential to this chapter.

What we argue is not that China is becoming an economic predator in the Asian region but, under economic globalization by neoliberals (whether in the form of state capitalism or stock market capitalism), it is very crucial for Thailand to have a very comprehensive economic strategy. The case study here shows that the Thai state has no economic strategy or plan to deal with either the US or China. Therefore, Thailand can easily become a victim in the context of ramped up economic competition in the region under globalization.

To counteract this we propose a dual development strategy: at its upper boundary the emphasis is to be placed on innovation such as modernizing the inter-city railway system for domestic purposes. At the lower bound we stress sustainability in tourism development. If we compare the proposed dual development strategy with that of labor-intensive industry it is evident that our approach carries genuine benefit to Thailand rather than to multinational capital. Therefore, the evading of middle-income trap and sick man of Asia scenario is possible.

No one country can totally ignore forces euphemized as globalization. Each country, however, must carefully devise a correct set of strategies for internationalizing their economies in order to strategically exploit globalization for their own advantage. What virtues, if any, carried by globalization, however, remain highly controversial: globalization is not a win-win proposition. There are "winners" and "losers" and too often poor countries are the ones who lose. Even when poor countries are able to derive some economic gain from the globalization, those gains happen to be disproportionately small compared to those earned by their rich counterparts. Therefore, globalization has been particularly criticized for widening the inequality gap between rich and poor countries.

In addressing the issue of how to best engage the global economy, the so-called Global Value Chain (GVC) perspective offers an effective framework for better understanding the dynamics of modern international trade and for analyzing the complex interplays between individual economies and globalization forces. A GVC denotes a business model characterized by an international production and trade network of connected firms collectively engaging in the business of bringing a particular product from its conception to the end consumers. The entire business can be unbundled into numerous discrete value-added stages typically consisting of research and design, product development, branding, manufacturing, marketing and sales, logistics, and distribution.

The GVCs have traditionally been dominated by multinational corporations (MNCs) that act assertively in governing production and trade networks of the global economy. It is estimated that about 80 percent of global trade (in terms of gross exports) is carried on within international production networks of MNCs

(UNCTAD 2013, 135). It is pointed out that the proliferation of GVCs not only benefits large MNCs but also small and medium enterprises in developing countries which no longer need to develop everything on their own to get access to markets in the developed countries but can do so simply by joining the GVCs. Despite the expected economic gains, governments in developing countries still are required to exercise great care in motivating local firms to join the GVCs. As stated in an UNCTAD report: "Countries need to make a strategic choice to promote or not to promote participation in GVCs. However, the key question for most is how to incorporate GVCs in development strategy" (2013).

It is therefore expected that international agencies engaging in the promotion of globalization and large MNCs acting as lead firms in most GVCs will compel developing countries to speed up the implementation of trade facilitation measures and to invest more in the improvement of transportation networks for international connectivity under the premise that doing so will increase the prospects of the firms in the host countries extending GVCs. However the interests of MNCs do not necessarily synch with those of developing countries seeking sustainable economic growth. As stated above, the real challenge is not about whether firms and countries should take part in the GVCs but about the selection of the mode to insert themselves into the GVCs.

One of the ultimate truths about any GVC is that the benefits derived from the trade are not equally distributed among participants in the same chain. The relative benefit that a participant earns is closely correlated with its relative bargaining power which is determined largely by its inherent "niche" managerial and technological capability. MNCs and firms in developed countries join GVCs through their capability delivered by more skilled labor in product research and design, branding, logistics, and access to markets and customers. On the other hand, firms in poor countries usually serve in the GVCs in the capacity of the original equipment manufacturing (OEM) manufacturers given the abundance of low skilled labor. Firms from developing countries have less power in business bargaining and negotiation than their counterparts because their comparative advantage is highly substitutable. These firms are functioning at the bottom layer of the chain operation and are able to capture a small share of total value added within the GVC. The OECD-WTD database on Trade in Value Added (May 2013) reveals that 67 percent of value created in GVCs is attributed to OECD countries, 25 percent to Newly Industrial Countries (NICs) and BRICS, and the remaining 8 percent to all other developing countries and least-developed countries (UNIDO 2015, 23). More importantly, their participation in the chain is not sustainable because they can be replaced easily and at very low switching cost by other firms located in the countries offering lower wage. Trade liberalization and improved transportation connectivity in developing countries will likely yield much greater economic gains to the MNCs who are the leading actors of the GVCs than the firms in the host countries.

Firms and countries alike must always keep improving their value capture capability in order to thrive and endure competition under globalization. There exist four general modes for firms or countries wishing to upgrade their competitiveness in the GVCs:

- Process upgrading: upgrading is achieved through improving the efficiency of internal processes.
- Product upgrading: firms enhance the capability to produce new products that have better quality and price performance than the existing ones.
- Functional upgrading: firms improve managerial and technological skills to move up to a position which is less vulnerable and create more value.
- Inter-chain upgrading: firms utilize the inherent capability of a new chain which allows them to capture greater gain.

A study comparing the strategies adopted by China and Pakistan in inserting themselves in the GVCs of soccer ball production revealed how in embracing different strategies the outcome was divergent development results. Pakistan counted on the strategy of sustaining its low-cost advantage while China promoted technological upgrading, mechanization, and automation, all of which helps to enhance competitiveness. At the end, Pakistan lost its global market share of the soccer ball industry to China (Xue and Chan 2013). It is therefore no longer adequate for developing countries to be content only with the opportunities to participate in the GVCs. Governments should focus more on value capture capability, look beyond simple GVC participation and its immediate returns, and pay utmost attention to the fulfillment of advanced and long-term policy objectives such as the quality of jobs created, technology and knowledge transfer to bring about spill-over effects into other sectors, contribution to long-lasting economic diversification and sustainability, and environmental impacts (UNIDO 2015, 13).

Regarding Thailand, it has been a heavily export-dependent country, with exports of goods and services in 2014 accounting for about 69.3 percent of Gross Domestic Product (GDP).[1] The well-being of Thailand therefore depends essentially on how well the country is integrated into the global economy. Thailand has continuously made all possible attempts to attract GVC activities in order to enhance the prospects of Thai business to actively engage in global trade. Various policy instruments have been launched by Thai governments to expand the country's foot-print in the global production and trade processes. In the context of the service sector, tourism is of prime importance. In 2015 and 2014, travel and tourism total contribution of GDP were 20.8 and 18.1 percent whereas direct contribution to GDP were 9.29 and 8.02 respectively (World Travel and Tourism Council Data 2016). Since the 1980s when tourism superseded rice as the highest major export in Thailand, the Thai state has aggressively and heavily promoted and relied on international tourism. Especially in the time of economic stagnation or crisis, tourism is the key to economic growth in Thailand. This also shows that the economic interest overshadows environmental degradation and cultural image (Ake Tangsupvattana 1999).

An instrument that has been highly promoted lately to increase Thailand's involvement in the international and regional trade and service is the development of an extensive network of transportation infrastructure intended to strategically position Thailand as the logistics and tourism hub of the ASEAN region. It has been commonly envisioned that with excellent logistics connectivity made possible by first-tier infrastructure Thailand would be able to substantially boost its exporting capacity and transportation of passengers and goods, thereby strengthening the country's competitiveness in highly competitive international trade.

This chapter critically questions Thailand's deep obsession with developing mega-transportation infrastructures in the pursuit of becoming the logistics center of the region, as well as its promotion of tourism for economic gain, without careful consideration over balancing negative impacts. The former, the widely-publicized Sino-Thai high-speed rail project will be used as an illustrative example of mega-transportation projects being conceived and developed under such a policy framework. The tourism question is discussed at both the level of policy analysis and the gap between policy and implementation. The chapter basically provides a critical review of whether the process of development in both cases is well-rounded and whether the cases have the potential to uplift Thailand's long-term competitiveness and sustainability.

In next section, the case of Sino-Thai high-speed rail will be explored. Then the case of tourism development will follow. The last section will offer critique and propose alternative strategies for the two cases. Readers should be advised that, for the first case, because we have no direct access to the detailed factual information and dialog actually exchanged in the meetings between Thailand and China, all our discussions are based mostly on the project information as publicly appearing in the public media. Also, given the extensive details of the first case, we can provide only a brief summary here.

The case of Sino-Thai high-speed rail

The high-speed rail project developed under Sino-Thai cooperation has been one of the mega-transportation projects hotly addressed in the recent political discussion. The Sino-Thai high-speed railway saga actually took off in 2010 under the regime of the Democrat-party government led by Mr. Abhisit Vejjajiva. Late that year, the Thai parliament endorsed a framework for the negotiation between Thai and China governments on a high-speed train project which was originally planned to connect Bangkok and the city of Nong Khai in the northeast near the Thai-Laos border. The line could later link up with another high-speed rail line running through Laos to southern China, eventually creating the Thai-Laos-China transportation connectivity intended to promote the regional trade between China and ASEAN members. China also expected the project to showcase its technological capabilities in building high-speed railways. It was then agreed that China would take on most of the investment in the development of the railway infrastructure while Thailand provided the land rights necessary for the railway construction. However, the project came to a brief halt after the Democrat party lost the 2011 general election to the Pheu Thai Party and the leadership of the country was passed to Ms. Yingluck Shinawatra, the head of the Pheu Thai party.

Yingluck Shinawatra's government put forward a 2 trillion baht infrastructure development bill to secure the loans for the massive construction of transportation infrastructures including high-speed trains, mass transit lines in Bangkok, inter-city dual-track trains, sea ports, new highways, and cargo stations and custom houses by 2020. The crown jewel of this loan bill was an extensive network of high-speed rail lines connecting the capital Bangkok with four regions. Part of the planned network of high-speed railways consisted of two lines purposely linking Thailand with the southern China; one running to the city of Nong Khai in the northeastern region and the other one to the city of Chiangmai in the northern region. During the official visit of Premier Li Keqiang to Thailand in October 2013, Thailand and China signed the "Memorandum of Understanding between the Government of the Kingdom of Thailand and the Government of the People's Republic of China on Governmental Cooperation Project on the Railway Infrastructure Development in Thailand in Exchange for Agricultural Products from Thailand". The MoU stipulated the interest of the Chinese side to shoulder the construction of a high-speed rail system between NongKhai and Ban Pachi in exchange for payment in the form of agricultural products. However, the Sino-Thai high-speed rail projects were derailed again when the Constitutional Court ruled that the bill was unconstitutional in March 2014 about two months before the Yingluck government was toppled from the power by a military coup staged by General Prayuth Chan-ocha in May 2014.

Just two months after forcing the Yingluck government out, the ruling National Council for Peace and Order (NCPO) approved two ambitious high-speed train projects: the 737-km NongKhai-Map Ta Phut route and 655-km Chiang Khong-Ban Phachi route. The projects came with a total price tag of 741.4 billion baht and were scheduled to be built between 2015 and 2021. It was indeed ironic that the proposed projects were more-or-less the same two routes linking Thailand and southern China advanced by the previous government that was just overthrown by the military junta: and moreover, the initial funding plan had been rejected by the Constitutional Court as essentially illegal! Viewed by many as a tactic to avoid being accused of cloning the predecessor's initiative, the plan called for the operation of the trains at the "average speed" of 160–180 km per hour rather than in the "high-speed" range of more than 250 km per hour. The official overriding justification in hastily driving the project implementation was to promote ASEAN connectivity reinforcing Thailand's position as a regional hub and creating development opportunities.

Late November 2014, the military-installed government led by the Prime Minister General Prayuth endorsed a draft memorandum of understanding on railway development cooperation between Thailand and China. As postulated in the MoU, China would take a lead role in building a 737-km Nong Khai-Map Ta Phut route and a 133-km Kaeng Khoi-Bangkok route. The MoU was later approved by the military appointed National Legislative Assembly in December 2014. Immediately after that, Thailand and China signed the MoU under the Strategic Framework for Development of Thailand's Transportation Infrastructure 2015–2022 in December 2014. China would be responsible for system study and design, laying track, and construction of tunnels and bridges while Thailand would carry out the Environmental Impact Assessment (EIA) studies, land expropriation, general civil engineering and power supply, and the supply of construction materials. The operation of the rail system was split into three phases. China would operate and maintain the system for the first three years of operation. Between the fourth and the seventh years, both countries would share equal responsibility during which the

Thai side would have an opportunity to thoroughly learn about the operation and maintenance of the system before assuming the full responsibility of the operation with China serving as an adviser onward.

It was announced in January 2015 by the then Minister of Transportation Air Chief Marshall Prajin Juntong that according to the tentative roadmap and timeline for the development of the Sino-Thai rail projects (see Figure 7.1) the field survey of the construction site would commence in March 2015 and the investment budget would be finalized in August or September, allowing the construction of the Sino-Thai railway route to take off as early as September. Seven rounds of talks were planned to discuss and make all necessary arrangements prior to the construction.

However, after the seventh meeting, this roadmap failed. This was followed by three other meetings which ended in failure of agreement as well leaving the project implementation issue unsettled. A crucial setback to the project unpredictably emerged in February 2016 before the tenth round of meetings when the Thai Transport Minister upon returning from a meeting with Chinese officials in Beijing reported that in light of the notably higher cost of investment and lower traffic volume than expected Thailand was going to propose to scale down the project by replacing the planned dual track for the Nakhon Ratchasima-NongKhai section with a single track and to delay the construction of the Kaeng Khoi-Map ThaPhut section, leaving the construction of dual-track Bangkok-Nakhon Ratchasima and single-track Nakhon Ratchasima-NongKhai sections with a total cost of 340 billion baht in the first phase. In response to Thailand's call for China to share 60–70 percent of total investment, China retaliated with a request for the right of commercial land development at proposed rail stations and along the routes in exchange. This request was extremely contentious for the Thai public to the extent they were being availed of negotiations with China by the military government.

A really big surprise came in on March 23, 2016 when the Thai Prime Minister announced after a meeting with Premier Li during the first Lancang-Mekong Cooperation (LMC) Leaders' Meeting in Sanya, Hainan Island that the joint-venture model of the project was to be scrapped and Thailand would be the sole investor in the project which was extensively scaled down to include only the link between Bangkok and Nakhon Ratchasima with possible extension in the future. The maximum operating speed of those trains was raised to the high-speed range of 250 kph from the previously designated medium speed at 180 kph with the price tag of about 170–190 billion baht. There would be a delay of four to five months from May 2016 as scheduled earlier. The government clearly stated that Thailand would not call for an international bid but wholly acquire rail and construction technology, signaling systems, and equipment from China in order to honor the prior commitment. This shift of investment model gave China the best of both worlds, relief from all the financial risks associated with the project but at the same time guaranteeing a fat sale of its rail technology and equipment.

Yet, even now, the viability of the project is still questionable. The latest results of the project study indicated that the revised system would attract 23,000 passengers daily based on an entry fare of 80 baht and the distance-based one of

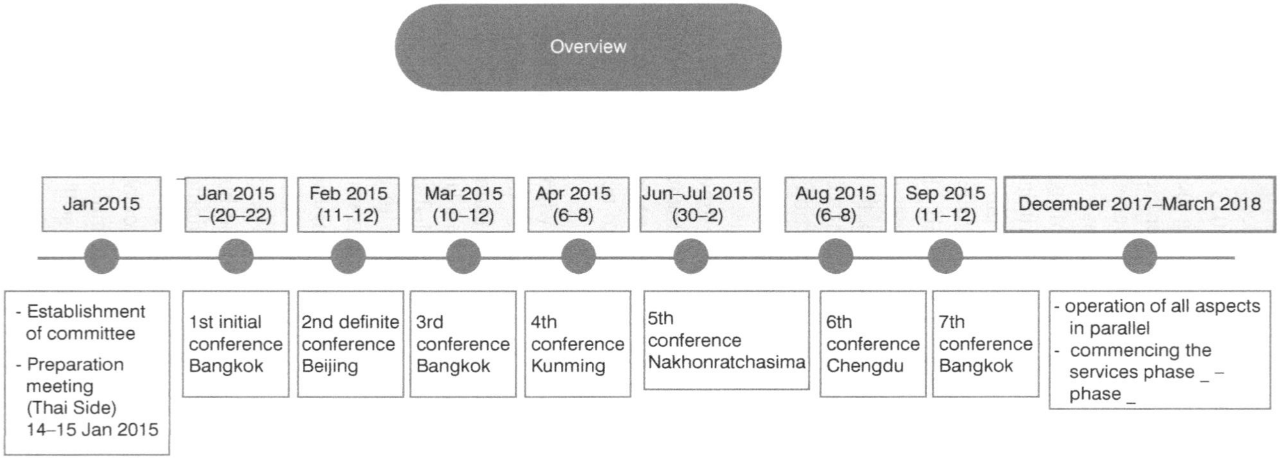

Figure 7.1 Timeline for the development of the Sino-Thai rail projects

Source: http://maps.mot.go.th/pao/products_EN.html, accessed June 5, 2016

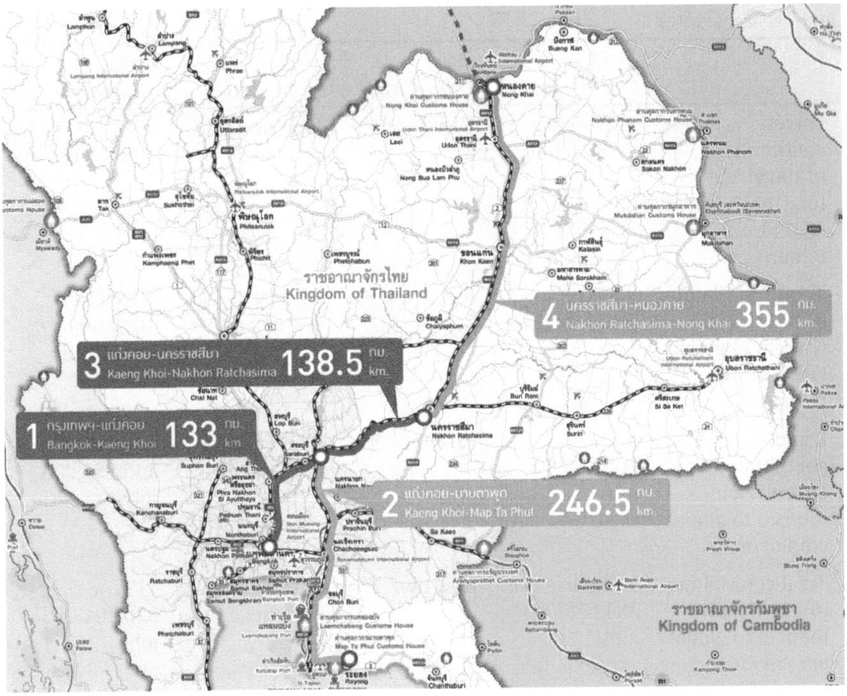

Figure 7.2 Rail project map

Source: http://maps.mot.go.th/pao/images/railway_banner.jpg, accessed June 5, 2016

1.8 baht per kilometer,[2] resulting in a 1 percent Financial Internal Rate of Return (FIRR) and a relatively low Economical Internal Rate of Return (EIRR) of 10 percent.

The case of tourism development

The Thai state's strategy for international tourism is driven predominantly by consideration of short-term economic gain at the expense of potential long-term environmental and cultural damages.

Indeed, the economic importance of global economy and tourism GVC is gigantic and evident as we can see in Table 7.1 below.

Economic contribution from tourism is really essential to Thai economy. Since the fourth National Economic and Social Development Plan 1977–1981, economic importance of tourism has been recognized and the data from Table 7.2 shows the recent economic impact of tourism for Thailand.

The data above shows why tourism is important to the economy and to the state at the expense of other potential investment areas. However, even on the issue of economic gain, the Thai state seems have lost its direction in the GVC

Table 7.1 Tourism contribution to global economy (all values are in constant 2015 prices and exchange rate)

	2015	*2016 (Forecast)*	*2016–2026 (Forecast)*	*2026 (Forecast)*
Direct contribution of travel and tourism to global GDP: USD billion	3.0% or 2,229.8 billion	Rise by 3.3%	Rise by 4.2% per annual	3.4 % or 3,469.1 billion
Total contribution of travel and tourism to global GDP: USD billion	9.8% or 7,170.3 billion	Rise by 3.5%	Rise by 4.0% per annual	10.8% or 10,986.5 billion
Direct contribution of travel and tourism to global employment	3.6% or 107,833,000 jobs	Rise by 1.9%	Rise by 2.1% per annual	4% or 135,884,000 jobs
Total contribution of travel and tourism to global employment	9.5% or 283,578,000 jobs	Rise by 2.2%	Rise by 2.5% per annual	11% or 370,204,000 jobs
Visitor exports: USD billion	6.1% of total export or 1,308.9 billion	Rise by 3.0%	Rise by 4.3% per annual	6.2% of total export or 2,056.0 billion
Travel and tourism investment: USD billion	4.3% of Total investment or 774.6 billion	Rise by 4.7%	Rise by 4.5% per annual	4.7% of total investment or 1,254.2 billion

Source: World Travel and Tourism Council (2016)

to the foreign tourism business-people. If this is the case, it also raises the further question of why the Thai state has to promote tourism business at the expense of negative impacts while economic benefits are sucked away.

The harmful impact of tourism on the natural environment can be divided into four areas: polluted tourist areas, land encroachment, the problem of construction itself, and inappropriate infrastructure and facilities which are incongruous with the natural geography and the balance of the eco-system. The first and second forms of degradation as a result of the tourist industry are the most serious cases, especially when they involve national parks. They are normally coincidental with each other. The utilization of national parks by the tourist trade usually causes a marked deterioration in their natural beauty and resources. The problems of garbage, sea-water pollution, dirty beaches, dumping untreated sewage into the sea, and damage to the sub-marine world, cause natural imbalances in both land and marine parks (Ake Tangsupvattana 1999, 271).

Table 7.2 Tourism contribution to Thai economy (all values are in constant 2014 prices and exchange rate)

	2014	*2015*	*2015 (Forecast)*	*2016–2025 (Forecast)*	*2025 (Forecast)*
Direct contribution of travel and tourism to Thailand's GDP: THB (Thai Baht) billion	8.02%	9.29%			
Total contribution of travel and tourism to Thailand's GDP: THB billion	18.1%	20.8%			
Direct contribution of travel and tourism to Thailand's employment	5.8% or 2,210,000 jobs	–	Rise by 0.2%	Rise by 4.6% per annum	8.6% or 3,476,000 jobs
Total contribution of travel and tourism to Thailand's employment	14.1% or 5,383,000 jobs	–	Rise by 1.0%	Rise by 4.1% per annum	20.2% or 8,140,000 jobs
Visitor exports: THB billion	14.4% of total export or 1,309.1 billion		Rise by 3.3%	Rise by 7.7% per annum	17.3% of total export or 2,828.6 billion
Travel and tourism investment: THB billion	7.4% of Total investment or 235.3bn billion		Rise by 5.4%	Rise by 6.0% per annum	9.6% of total investment or 444.2bn billion

Source: World Travel and Tourism Council Data (2016) and World Travel and Tourism Council (2015)

There have been many cases of tourist resorts encroaching public land or national parks. For instance, at Khao Yai National Park,Kirimaya Golf Resort and the spa in Nakhon Ratchasima's Pak Chong district, the resort's land ownership documents were allegedly issued for overlapping forest and public land (Bangkok Post 2015a). Bonanza Golf and Country Club was facing partial demolition and its owner criminal charges after it was discovered that part of its areas encroached on the Khao Yai National Park (Thai PBS 2015a). At seaside resorts, like Samui and Phuket, officials from the Royal Forest Department were conducting a survey to determine forest reserve areas on Samui Island after extensive illegal encroachment and over-exploitation of the environment by tourist developments in hilly areas (Nation 2012) and as part of the ongoing crackdown on public land encroachment, soldiers, sailors and police teamed up to search 80 locations in Phuket, including homes and resorts owned by local politicians (The Nation 2014). These are only some examples of the encroachment, which in the end, leads to environmental degradation from tourism development.

On cultural aspects of negative tourism impacts, sex tourism in Thailand is the cardinal example because this is what the country is most notorious for. Although the Thai state has neglected the relation of sex trade with tourism, sex tourism has been implicitly or explicitly permeated in tourism development in Thailand (Ake Tangsupvattana 1999). Recently, authorities have denied that the proliferation of sex tourism contributed to the economy. They assert that tourists do not come to Thailand for sex tourism, but for the country's unique culture, so sex tourism is purportedly targeted for elimination (Reuters 2016). In contrast to this view the reality is that, after political turmoil took the country to the brink of economic recession in 2014, the suppression of sex tourism will actually damage the economy; a testament to its pervasiveness notwithstanding state proclamations. Although Thailand is a Buddhist kingdom, it is the home of an extensive commercial sex industry, especially for Thai men (Jeffreys 2009, 140). More essentially, this industry generates a lot of income. If this industry were eradicated, it is certain that Thailand will lose visitors and income (Reuters 2016). UNAIDS reports that there are about 123,530 sex workers in Thailand compared to 37,000 in Cambodia (cited in Reuters 2016), but this number should be multiplied because sex tourism pervades almost every kind of entertainment business in Thailand. Indeed, sex tourism has long led to portrayals of Thai society as promiscuous. Simultaneously, the perception of the economic significance of sex tourism has been serially undervalued. In the past, when Thailand was seriously affected by AIDS when the disease was first known about, the Thai state strove to conceal its spread because it feared it would damage the tourism industry (Ake Tangsupvattana 1999).

The tendency for the Thai state to pursue economic gain at the expense of environmental and cultural damages should now be increasingly clear. But there is more: for instance, in the Strategy of Thai Tourism 2015–2017 by the Ministry of Tourism and Sports, there is the intention to construct a foundation for development and promotion of tourism in order to make Thailand a high quality tourist destination with good balance and sustainability. In doing this, there are three stated missions: market promotion, goods and services development, and tourism management (Ministry of Tourism and Sports, 2015, 18). At the outset, we can see that the missions are one sided, favoring economic gains. Also, it seems to be blithely accepted that if a tourism management scheme is implemented well, balance and sustainability will follow.

Nevertheless, in the six key performance indicators (KPI) in this strategy, the only clear and quantifiable KPIs are the first three: income from tourism totaling THB 2.5 trillion in 2017; increasing number of provinces with income from tourism at more than THB 5 billion; increasing number of tourists during the low-season. The last three KPIs, the satisfaction of stakeholders of the Thai tourism situation, the determining carrying capacity in fragile tourist destinations, and the ranking of tourism competitiveness (especially in safety, environmental sustainability and health) (Ministry of Tourism and Sports, 2015, 19) are less so or even unquantifiable. Therefore, the third mission of tourism management seems to be the mission of management for economic gain, rather than sustainability.

Let us look briefly at the shifting tourism focus in Thailand. In 2012 thanks to the popularity of the Chinese movie *Lost in Thailand*, Thailand became the top Chinese tourist destination. Data from Table 7.3 show how high the economic power of Chinese tourists is in the GVC of Thailand's tourism.

Unfortunately, Chinese tourists in Asia have become notorious for their bad behavior. In Thailand there are myriad issues, including: fighting at 7-Eleven, scooping up extra food at the buffet and taking it to their hotel rooms, playing cards at the airport, washing feet in the sink of public restrooms in a national park, drying underwear openly at Bangkok's main airport, and using a canal in the old city area in Chiang Mai as a toilet (BBC 2015). Following local complaints, the Thai authority has listed some good behavior tips for Chinese tourists such as not touching paintings, avoiding using public property as lavatories, and encouraging safe driving (The Diplomat 2015).

There is, however, more to the question on Chinese tourists when we turn to the problem of where profits are captured in the tourism GVC. To profit from Chinese tourists in Thailand, Chinese tour operators set the consortium of nominee companies to return benefits to themselves. The majority of tourist facilities available to Chinese tourists, such as bus tours, restaurants, non-natural tourist attraction destinations, and some accommodation are owned by Chinese tour operators. Therefore, the real income from Chinese tourism goes to Chinese tour operators rather than Thai operators. The case is quite similar to Korean tours where the tour operators try to set their own facilities to bring the money back to Korea rather than to distribute to Thai local tourist businesses. In July 2016, police raided many companies that register as Thai tour companies, but actually are nominees of Chinese business-people (Isranews Agency 2016).

Instructively, Chinese tourism business practices in Thailand resemble business practices utilized in dealings with Thailand in the fruit business. Chinese

Table 7.3 Numbers of and revenue from Chinese tourists

	2011	*2012*	*2013*	*2014*	*2015*	*2016 Jan–May*
Number of Chinese tourists	1,721,247	2,786,860	4,609,717	4,631,981	7,934,791	4,184,071 (29.55% of total international tourists)
Revenue from Chinese tourists: billion THB	58,001.85	105,943.91	188,912.67	200,658.69	388,011.89	–

Source: Ministry of Tourism and Sports (2016)

companies control the market by directly buying fruits from the owners of fruit plants to export to China. In some cases, Chinese business-people directly purchase fruits from large fruit markets and then export them directly to China. We can see that in the context of GVC, Thai local business-people gain only a tiny piece of the pie. Some small farmers may gain, but big money goes to China.

The two cases: their critics and alternative strategies

It is really difficult to make sense of both the Sino-Thai high-speed rail saga and the new Chinese tourist phenomenon mentioned above. There are so many lingering questions that have yet to be clearly clarified by the promoters of both cases. We, however, attempt to critically review the two development cases in by addressing the issue from two complementary directions. First, we look at the process in which the cases were conceived, planned for, and developed (and implanted in the case of tourism) and the major deficiencies inherent in the process. We then turn to investigate the possibility that the cases will contribute to the long-term competitiveness of the country as promoted.

Deficiencies in the development process

In the case of rail development, three consecutive ruling governments involved in the project advanced the development of the project in a haphazard manner and failed to develop the project according to the standard framework of policy development and implementation. The present government had committed senseless "lock-ins" in at least three crucial component of the project. Specifically, strategic decisions concerning the selection of route, the choice of rail technology, and the viability of the project were prematurely finalized at the very early stage of development without supporting information from detailed and comprehensive research and analysis. The second lock-in lies in the selection of Chinese technology. There was no official report explaining why the junta-led government decided to lock itself in the early adoption of Chinese technology before securing Chinese's commitment to co-invest. Even after the government decided that the project will be wholly invested by Thailand, no international bid was called. The government still insisted on using Chinese technology and construction firms on the ground on the condition that Thailand must honor an earlier memorandum of understanding signed by the two countries when the central theme of the MoU on the co-investment was no longer applicable.

One explanation holds that the decision was made mostly out of political considerations. The military-led government desperately needed the strategic political support from China given that it has been under considerable pressure from the West regarding charges of human rights violation and democracy suppression. The Thai government also required diplomatic support from China in elevating Thailand's status in the international community given widespread disparaging of the coup. Moreover, the Sino-Thai train deal was struck at exactly the same moment as the rice and rubber deals. Evidently Thailand and China were set to engage in a peculiar barter trade, exchanging train systems for rice and rubber. The rice and rubber deals are particularly crucial for strengthening the political stability of the government because rice farmers and rubber planters were facing difficult times given recent low demand and falling prices of their products.

The third key lock-in is early faith in the viability of the project without strong support from any in-depth studies. The official figures about project viability were made public only after almost two years of negotiations had passed and Thailand decided to go ahead with the project on its own

In the case of tourism development relating to Chinese tourists and business-people, it also makes no sense to promote Thai tourism at the expense of cultural and environmental damages, particularly when the winners were the Chinese instead of Thais in the tourist business. Of course, the state's perception of tourism is simply a as a cash cow. Especially, in the time of economic stagnation, tourism's (and its relation to sex tourism) contribution to the economy increases its importance. Curbing commercial sex services would hurt a flagging economy that has struggled to recover after the political turmoil which brought on recession in 2014 (Reuters 2016). Economic determinants of tourism compelled the state to ignore its strategies to balance social and environmental impacts with economic income. In the implementation of the Ministry of Tourism and Sports' Strategy of Thai Tourism 2015–2017, there is a bias toward short-term economic payback rather than sustainability or other dimensions.

Another serial problem is that although the government originally wished to attract Chinese tourists to benefit from Thai tourist businesses both locally and nationally, there was an economic leakage to Chinese businesses in implementation. If we use the GVC framework presented in the first part of our chapter, we can see that Chinese tourist businesses can create "process upgrading" through improving the efficiency of internal processes, whether or not this upgrading is legal in Thailand. Furthermore, it seems to us that Chinese tourist businesses can trans-nationally produce "inter-chain upgrading". Namely Chinese firms can utilize the inherent capability of a new chain which allows them to capture greater gain going forward.

Deficiencies in achieving long-term competitiveness

In the case of rail, the recurrence of disruptive alterations to the fundamental features of the project such as the route and the investment model definitely indicates that the project has been promoted aggressively without clear national development vision or strategies. The dominant rationale for this project is to build the foundations for the long-term competitiveness through the position of Thailand as a regional logistics hub. Transportation connectivity and the resulting status as a regional logistics hub is a means not an end to the national economic and social development. To maximize benefits from costly transportation megaprojects, the project sponsors should work out in detail and in advance how the planned infrastructures and Thailand's position as a regional logistics hub can be exploited to deliver the greatest beneficial impacts to economic and social development. Official explanation has yet to be provided to thoroughly elaborate in which mode and to what extent the completion of the project will eventually lead to long-term competitiveness of the country. Also, one important issue is the continuous dispute about whether a 1meter gauge should be used instead of a 1.435 meter gauge. Instead of wasting valuable time and national scare resources to rush the implementation of high-speed rail, the government should rather divert effort and resources to ensure that the planned double tracking of 1-meter rail routes will be implemented in the most efficient and professional manner.

Thailand and China embarked on different strategies in advancing collaboration on the rail system. As mentioned above, China assumes a long-term development goal by viewing this project as a component of its grand strategic initiative. The OBOR, consisting of two main components, the land-based "Silk Road Economic Belt" (SREB) and ocean-based "Maritime Silk Road" (MSR), collectively provide comprehensive connectivity within Eurasia. Many geo-politics experts view the OBOR initiative as serving multifold strategic goals. In the immediate term, the planned massive investment in infrastructure offers an opportunity for China to export its excessive capacity in the construction industry. This is also supported by China's AIIB initiative. In the medium term, the Chinese support and investment in infrastructure will boost international standing of its currency. In the long term, it paves the way for China to exert economic and political influence over the countries along OBOR and to secure sustainable access to the world's key energy supplies.

In the case of tourism, although the Thai government has many tourism strategic plans, they are short-term strategies. Even though these plans wax lyrically on right balance and sustainability, implementation is another story. Thai tourism itself has advantages from natural beautiful resources and Thai people's hospitality. This is considered a perfect combination for tourism development anywhere in the world. With the influx of Chinese tourist and then revenue from them, it is difficult for the Thai state to negate the economic benefits. Unfortunately, the incredible numbers of Chinese tourists are beyond the carrying capacity of Thailand, both in the context of natural and cultural environments. This, in turn and in the long-run, will gradually sabotage tourism development in Thailand because tourist destinations are deteriorating from the flow of mass tourists. Therefore, in the strategic plans, sustainability must be equally perceived and adapted for economic profits. At the same time, in the implementation, sustainability must be seriously employed with a very clear KPI, not just lip-service to it.

From both cases here, the Thai government did not have a long-term strategic deployment plan but intended to remedy its immediate economic or political concerns. In the rail project, the government has failed to take a comprehensive look at the impacts and risks of the project on industry and logistics competitiveness of the country. The new rail link passing through Southern China, Laos, and Northeastern Thailand will provide better connectivity between Thailand and China which in turn stimulates trading between Thailand and China. There is no doubt that China with a population of over 1 billion and rising economic wealth has been considered the biggest market in the world. The Thai government is optimistic that the Thai-China rail link will lower transport costs of exports from Thailand to China, thereby providing a valuable opportunity for Thai products to penetrate into the huge markets in Southern China. However, the marketability of products does not hinge solely on lower logistics costs but rather on total transaction costs. The government has not been specific about the types of products that will become competitive in the Chinese market by using the Sino-Thai rail service or how the capability of Thai industry will be adequately pumped up to fully capitalize on this opportunity. Also, traffic always runs two ways. The new railway will not only facilitate the export of goods from Thailand but also imports from China. The rail service will undoubtedly lower logistics costs and time for the goods manufactured in and exported from China to Thailand. This could contribute to two potential but contradictory impacts on Thailand's economic well-being.

In order to grasp the benefits from tourism GVC, sustainable tourism development is very crucial. Tourist businesses depend on non-polluted natural beauty and hospitality. Without these, tourists will move away from Thailand, especially those with high spending. At the same time, the state has to challenge the tactical ploy of Chinese tourist businesses in order to create a real value from the tourism GVC for Thai business-people. If the Chinese business-people can successfully produce inter-chain upgrading by utilizing their inherent capability to a new chain in order to capture a greater gain, Thai local tourist businesses will lose their share in the GVC of tourism in their own country. Thailand will then have double negative impacts; the environmental and cultural externalities by Chinese tourists, and the loss of GVC in Thai tourism businesses to Chinese tourism businesses.

The question of middle-income trap leading to sick man of Asia and strategic alternatives

Government officials of all ranks recently announced that Thailand runs a risk of being caught up in the middle-income trap of slow economic growth over an unacceptable extended period, which may lead it to become a sick man of Asia. It is an indispensable necessity for Thailand to restructure its economy to drive the country out of the middle-income rank towards the high-income one. Over more than 30 years Thailand has been able to successfully leverage the advantage of low labor cost plus the development opportunities created with the establishment of the Eastern Seaboard Industrial Complex in transforming the country from being a low-income economy to now emerging as a middle-income economy. As the wage rate increases, the country will not be able to compete in the international market with other low-wage countries any more. To sustain high economic growth, Thailand must compete on a new playing field with innovation and high-value products as in the case of Sino-Thai rail, instead of relying on low-cost labor. The country also requires sustainable development rather than "easy money" from tourism. Thailand at the levels of firm, industry, and country must be prepared to face a new challenge through collectively developing a new set of competencies and policies. Thai enterprises especially the small and medium ones must seriously consider upgrading their capability to increase the likelihood of moving their positions in the GVCs up to new positions which enable them to earn more. Meanwhile the government should put in place all policy instruments necessary to accelerate the upgrading of firms' capability.

Different sets of factors are required for distinct modes of capability upgrading in each specific area. The provision of reliable basic infrastructure (transportation, telecommunications, information technology) such as rail, and the sustainable tourist destinations are mandatory for product and process upgrading.

In the case of Sino-Thai railway, key success factors for functional and chain upgrading include but are not limited to effective national innovation systems, R&D policies, and firms' absorptive capacity in high technology.[3] Thailand seems to fall victim to its past economic development success. In its endeavor to move out of the middle-income trap, Thailand still places all its bets on the development of basic infrastructure which used to be one of the effective instruments for uplifting the country's economic status from being a least-developed country to a developing country. At this stage of development, basic infrastructure is, unfortunately, no longer the sufficient condition for moving Thailand forward. The country should embrace a paradigm shift by redirecting its national focus to the provision of innovation and R&D infrastructure.

Both rail and tourism cases certainly reveal that all public talks about the government's stimulation in driving the country's innovation (of the former) and sustainable tourism (of the latter) is mostly lip-service. As far as the Sino-Thai railway was concerned, during the period of nearly two years of project development, the Thai side centered its negotiations with China solely on the issues of loan interest rate and mode of co-investment. The negotiation rarely touched on the skill transfer and when discussed the focus was only on the area of train operation while there was no serious discussion at all on the transfer of know-how and technology that would help Thailand become self-dependent in rail technology, leaving Thailand indefinitely relying on China for all the parts and components, and new technology for further renovation throughout the life of the system. The absolute lack of the government interest in building local capabilities in rail technology in conjunction with the provision of rail infrastructure is confirmed by the fact that in advancing the development of this high-speed rail system the Ministry of Transportation is the lone project champion while the involvement of ministries concerned with the development of the country's science and technology infrastructures including the Ministry of Science and Technology, Ministry of Industry, Ministry of Education has been minimal.

For tourism development in the context of the influx of Chinese tourists, Thai tourism GVC for Thai tourist business-people seems to be threatened by the Chinese's nominee companies. Without careful regulation of Chinese business-people' tactics, Chinese business-people may produce inter-chain upgrading that can control the stake in GVC of Chinese tourists coming to Thailand. Similar to the Sino-Thai railway case, product and process upgrading are essential for sustainability. This will elevate the quality of Thai tourism to attract higher spending tourists, promoting eco-tourism or cultural tourism, and will yield more value in GVC, especially, if this is coupled with soft power like what South Korea is using. The case of *Lost in Thailand*, mentioned above, is a very good reflection of using soft power to lure Chinese tourists to Thailand. However, the number of tourists must be balanced by carrying capacity.

As stated in the introduction the Thai government needs a long-term strategy to develop the country. Instead of formulating and implementing short-term strategies and policies (or without strategy and policies), for political and economic return, the government needs to use the dual development strategy in order to drive innovation and sustainability depending on required areas of development. From technological perspective, the case of Sino-Thai rail development represents the need to strategically think about innovation in infrastructural development. For a tourism development country that relies on natural and cultural environments, sustainability is the key.

Notes

1 http://data.worldbank.org/indicator/NE.EXP.GNFS.ZS?end=2014&locations=TH&start=2014&view=bar, accessed 10 July 2016.
2 Equivalent to about a total of 530 baht for a one-way trip between Bangkok and Nakhon Ratchasima.
3 Figure 4.36. UNCTAD. World Investment Report 2013 – Global Value Chains: Investment and Trade for Development.

References

Ake, Tangsupvattana. 1999. "Social Causality, Sex Tourism and Environmental Degradation in Thailand: An Application of the Philosophy of the Social Sciences to Relations between the Thai State and the Business of Tourism", Ph.D. Thesis, Department of Sociology, University of Essex.

Bangkok Post. 2015a. "Kirimaya Land 'Encroaches on Khao Yai Forest'", http://www.bangkokpost.com/print/544747/, accessed 4 July, 2016.

BBC. 2015. "Chinese Tourists Push Back against Rant about Poor Manners", http://www.bbc.com/news/blogs-trending-31928761, accessed 25 June, 2016.

Chandran, N., 2016. "G-20 Leadership to Strengthen China's International Profile, If It Can Overcome Reputational Issues", http://www.cnbc.com/2016/07/14/g-20-leadership-to-strengthen-chinas-international-profile-if-it-can-overcome-reputational-issues.html, accessed 19 July 2016.

Diplomat. 2015. "Thailand Tells Chinese Tourists How to Behave", http://thediplomat.com/2015/02/thailand-tells-chinese-tourists-how-to-behave/, accessed 25 June, 2016.

Dore, R. 2000. *Stock Market Capitalism: Welfare Capitalism* (Oxford: Oxford University Press).

Isranews Agency. 2016. http://www.isranews.org/isranews-news/item/48246-news_48246.html, accessed 7 July, 2016.

Jeffreys, S. 2009. *The Industrial Vagina: The Political Economy of the Global Sex Trade* (London: Routledge).

Ministry of Tourism and Sports. 2015. Strategy of Thai Tourism 2015–2017.

Ministry of Tourism and Sports. 2016. http://service.nso.go.th/nso/nso_center/project/search/ result_by_department-th.jsp, accessed 29 June, 2016.

The Nation. 2012. "Officials Checking Forest Encroachment on Samui" http://www.nationmultimedia.com/national/Officials-checking-forest-encroachment-on-Samui-30185808.html, accessed 4 July, 2016.

The Nation. 2014. "Phuket police target 80 sites in land-encroachment raids", http://www.nationmultimedia.com/national/Phuket-police-target-80-sites-in-land-encroachment-30242030.html, accessed 5 July 2016.

Reuters. 2016. "Thai Sex Industry under Fire from Tourism Minister, Police", http://www.channelnewsasia.com/news/asiapacific/thai-sex-industry-under/2963300.html, accessed 17 June, 2016.

Suttinee, Yuvejwattana. 2015. "Old Man Thailand Feels Pain of Economic Arthritis", http://www.bloomberg.com/news/articles/2015-03-17old-man-thailand-feels-pain-of-economic-arthritiss, accessed 15 June 2016.

Thai PBS. 2015a. "Bonanza Khao Yai Resort Faces Demolition for Encroachment of Khao Yai National Park", accessed 4 July 2016.

UNCTAD. 2013.World Investment Report 2013 – Global Value Chains: Investment and Trade for Development.

UNIDO. 2015. Global Value Chains and Development: UNIDO's Support towards Inclusive and Sustainable Industrial Development.

World Travel and Tourism Council. 2015. Travel and Tourism Economic Impact 2015 Thailand.

World Travel and Tourism Council. 2016.Travel and Tourism Economic Impact 2016 World.

World Travel and Tourism Council Data. 2016. https://knoema.com/WTTC2016/world-travel-and-tourism-council-data-2016, accessed 5 July 2016.

Xue, H. and Chan, A. 2013. "The Global Value Chain", *Critical Asian Studies*, 45, 55–77.

8 Turkey

A conventional peripheral agent of neoliberal globalization

Yonca Özdemir

Introduction

Beyond the BRICs, which are four of the largest economies in the world, there are some medium-sized economies, which are seen as recent economic risers in the world. Acting on their increasing size and importance in the global economy, these countries are seeking to acquire greater influence within regional and global affairs (vom Haua *et al.* 2012) Therefore, anyone who is interested in understanding the dynamics of the global political economy has to look beyond the original BRICs (i.e. Brazil, Russia, India and China) towards other countries that have become increasingly influential in the field of global development. Turkey is one of these countries, and thus, has been attracting widespread attention.

Among the emerging markets Turkey is considered an interesting one, but its development path has been rather conventional. Turkey has been an enthusiastic participant in neoliberal globalization since 1980, following the dictates of the international financial institutions. Not surprisingly it also has been suffering severely from its consequences. As the benefits of neoliberal policies become more dubious and many other enthusiastically neoliberal developing countries suffered from various economic crises in the 1990s, neoliberal policies came under serious attack. The successful case of China or other East Asian countries also made the benefits of the neoliberal development model increasingly suspect. As a result, many developing countries, especially the BRICs, have been following less orthodox paths to development. Nevertheless, curiously Turkey has been quite obstinate in applying neoliberalism.

Turkey's *neoliberal project* progressed in two phases which extended over more than three decades: first through the reforms in the 1980s, and then, through the reforms in the 2000s. Both of these phases commenced with a severe economic crisis, in 1980 and then in 2001. Economic crises have been quite common in Turkey, especially since the neoliberal reforms started. Indeed, in 1994, 1999, and 2001 Turkey experienced grave economic dislocations. The current tendency is to describe Turkey as a successful case of neoliberal restructuring and a good model for economic development. However, the reality is that the Turkish economy suffers from serious vulnerabilities, which became even more evident after the 2007–2008 global crisis. Today, Turkey is not only one of the most fragile emerging markets, but also politically it is an increasingly authoritarian state. Therefore, this chapter argues that the praise of Turkey by international economic circles is unfounded. In fact, neoliberalism has not brought economic stability. Looking at rising authoritarianism in Turkey, obviously neoliberalism has not brought democracy to Turkey either.

In this chapter, I will first give a brief account of Turkey's political economy until 1980 and then explicate how Turkey initiated and implemented the first round of neoliberal reforms in the 1980s. In the next section, I will explain how the economic and political conditions paved the way for the second-generation neoliberal reforms in Turkey in the 2000s. It will be argued that, although Turkey is widely praised for its neoliberal reforms, it has actually ended up with a vulnerable and unsustainable economic model, which will be referred as *speculative-led development*. With the 2007–2008 global economic crisis the Turkish economy has been rendered even more risky and fragile due to its increasing dependence on short-term capital flows. The politics of this process will also be pointed out, because it is quite puzzling that the Justice and Development Party (AKP) government, which has been relentlessly implementing the neoliberal project, has succeeded in establishing vast political support for these policies, and thus, consolidated neoliberalism both economically and politically.

The first phase of the neoliberal project

Founded in 1923 from the remnants of the Ottoman Empire, the Republic of Turkey shows some similarities to its counterparts, especially Latin American countries like Argentina and Brazil, when it comes to its economic development patterns. After the Great Depression, Turkey started to apply a closed economy model, known as *statism*, under one-party government until 1950. During that period the Turkish economy had significant growth, especially in the industrial sector. This was the highest growth period in Turkish history, although World War II interrupted this process of rapid industrialization.

As Turkey made a transition to democracy in 1950, the statist policies diminished, but after a military coup in 1960, which interrupted democracy for one and a half years, Turkey's official development strategy became *import substitution industrialization* (ISI), which again involved significant state intervention and protectionism in the economy. The main goals were to stimulate rapid industrialization and economic development and to have more economic independence. This period was also an impressive growth and rapid industrialization era for the Turkish economy with expanding social, economic, and political rights. The ISI strategy was adjusted more in favor of the capitalist groups with the 1971 military coup. However, the capitalist interests still suffered due to high labor activity.

As the world economy went into recession in the 1970s and as a result of rising oil prices and decreasing worker remittances and foreign aid, Turkey's economy began to face a severe foreign exchange shortage. This shortage led to high inflation and scarcities in the economy which soon culminated in a serious economic crisis by 1979. At the peak of the crisis, in January 1980, the existing government initiated a neoliberal stabilization program referred to as the *January 24 Decisions*. However, this program could not be implemented due to labor resistance and political instability. As a result, the Turkish military intervened again in September 1980 and then implemented the neoliberal economic reforms under the supervision of Turgut Özal, the economy bureaucrat who was the architect of these reforms.

The implementation of the "Washington Consensus"

The first phase of the neoliberal project in Turkey involved implementation of the *Washington Consensus* policies, or the so-called *first-generation neoliberal reforms*, beginning in 1980. The Washington Consensus entails an agenda of neoliberal economic reforms which include trade liberalization, fiscal discipline, reorientation of public expenditure, tax reform, financial liberalization, unified and competitive exchange rates, liberalization of FDI, privatization, deregulation of the economy in general, and secure property rights, as shown in Table 8.1 (Williamson 1990). As widely acknowledged, these reforms have been imposed on developing countries by the international institutions, especially by the IMF and the World Bank. The 1980s were the beginning of the neoliberal project for Turkey.

Basically the purpose of the 1980 stabilization program, which received wide support from the IMF, World Bank, and OECD, was to change the direction of the Turkish economy from inward-oriented ISI to a free-market based system. The initial goals of the program were balancing the payments and decreasing inflation (Öniş and Özmucur 1990). Yet, the 1980 economic reforms aimed not

Table 8.1 Washington Consensus and Augmented Washington Consensus policies

Original Washington Consensus	*Augmented Washington Consensus the previous 10 items, plus:*
1. Fiscal discipline	11. Corporate governance
2. Reorientation of public expenditures	12. Anti-corruption
3. Tax reform	13. Flexible labor markets
4. Financial liberalization	14. WTO agreements
5. Unified and competitive exchange rates	15. Financial codes and standards
6. Trade liberalization	16. "Prudent" capital-account opening
7. Openness to FDI	17. Non-intermediate exchange rate regimes
8. Privatization	18. Independent central banks/inflation targeting
9. Deregulation	19. Social safety nets
10. Secure Property Rights	20. Targeted poverty reduction

Source: Rodrik (2006, 978)

only stabilization, but also structural adjustment in Washington Consensus style. Therefore, they could be considered as a *shock therapy* for the Turkish economy, and in that respect, they were neither original nor unique to Turkey. They involved making prices flexible, whether they were exchange rates, interest rates, or prices of state owned enterprise products, and removing controls on the economy in general. Therefore, the public sector started to withdraw from manufacturing, import quotas eliminated, and restrictions on foreign exchange and foreign investments removed. All these meant reducing direct state participation in the economy and integration with the international capital. They were also highly anti-labor in nature as real wages declined and labor activities were severely restricted. These policies even exceeded what the IMF and WB had expected.

The reform program was declared "successful" by the international financial institutions, as it achieved its balance of payments objective and brought economic growth. However, it failed to decrease inflation to single-digit levels, despite all the measures taken. Aside from rising inflation, developments in the Turkish economy in the 1980s were perceived as impressive. The Turkish economy grew 4.9 percent on average between 1981 and 1985 and the growth rate reached to 7 percent in 1986. The share of exports in GNP also grew from 5.2 percent in 1980 to 15 percent in 1985 (Öniş and Özmucur 1990). However, economic growth was volatile and there were major macroeconomic instabilities (see Figure 8.1). As early as 1982, there was a bankers' crisis thanks to the immature financial liberalization. Moreover, the February 1988 disinflationary program soon proved unsuccessful due to political instability and the inflation increased further (Alper and Üçer 1998). There were also complaints that tight monetary policies worsened income distribution and decreased economic growth and investment (Hershlag 1988).

As mentioned, a very important element of the new neoliberal economic agenda was financial liberalization. Thus, the foreign exchange regime was liberalized in

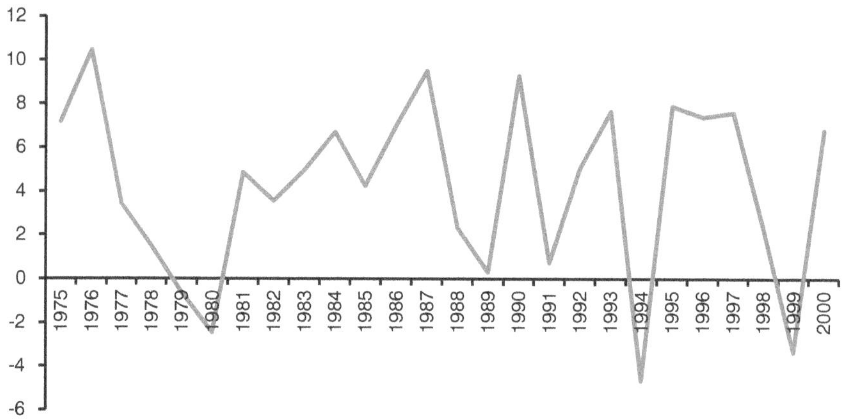

Figure 8.1 GDP growth rates (%), 1975–2000

Source: World Bank, World Development Indicators database, accessed on 24 June 2016 (http://databank.worldbank.org/data/reports.aspx?source=world-development-indicators).

1984. Some measures were also taken to increase Central Bank independence after 1986. Moreover, in the second half of the 1980s, the government changed the deficit financing method from monetization, which was the most inflationary way, to bond financing and tried to stabilize the exchange rate to control inflation (Dibooğlu and Kibritcioğlu 2001). However, the most important turning point was the capital account liberalization in August 1989, which not only fully liberalized inflow and outflow of all kinds of capital but also made the Turkish lira (TL) convertible. This was a very immature move, because inflation and budget deficits were still not under control and foreign and domestic debt was high.

On the political front, Turkey made a transition to controlled democracy in 1983 when the first elections after the 1980 coup were held. Later in 1987 there was further democratization of politics through constitutional changes. From that point on the pace of neoliberal reforms slowed down. After the strict belt tightening of the early 1980s, the long-term negative effects of the neoliberal policies were felt more by the mid-1980s and the different sections of the society began to demand compensation for their losses. As the popular pressures rose, the neoliberal reforms almost halted and Özal, who was the prime minister at that time, started to resort to traditional populist policies. Thus, especially from 1987 on, there was some retreat from the reforms, especially regarding public spending and budget deficit. The enthusiasm for privatization and deregulation of the prices and agricultural markets was also lost.

In short, in the first phase of neoliberalism, the liberalization of the economy was fast in the beginning, but could only be partially completed due to popular pressures rising under the democratizing Turkish polity which could be controlled through traditional populist and clientelist policies. These populist and clientelist policies required side payments to certain sections of society, such as subsidies to businessmen and farmers. Therefore, coupled with insufficient tax revenues, fiscal indiscipline was lost and budget deficits increased, causing high debt and chronic inflation.

The stagnation of the Washington Consensus

Although the Turkish economy changed from an inward-oriented one to a market-oriented one in the 1980s, not all reforms could be effectively implemented. Eventually ANAP fell from the government with the 1991 elections and a coalition government came to power. The new government could be called the *coalition of the losers* as the two parties in coalition represented mostly the groups who had suffered from the negative effects of the first-generation neoliberal reforms, i.e. labor, farmers, small and medium entrepreneurs, civil servants, and retired people. Therefore, the new government immediately raised wages, salaries, and subsidies in order to appease the rising discontent.

The 1990s are considered as the *lost decade* for Turkey as those years were marked with volatile growth, high inflation, and unstable governments. Despite the fact that they were unevenly and incompletely applied, Özal's neoliberal reforms survived in the 1990s, but there were some serious lags as well. Also, the problems created by these reforms continued and deepened. The coalition governments of the 1990s tried to complete the implementation of the reforms, especially privatization, but they were too weak to go on with such controversial policies and instead chose just to save the day. Moreover, a series of crises emerged and unstable coalition governments were not able to stabilize the economy.

Probably the most damaging of Özal's neoliberal reforms was the capital account liberalization. The successive governments of the 1990s continued with economic expansion and spending which led to growing public expenditure in order to appease the distributional conflicts. Those expenditures were financed through foreign capital flows, which could be sustained through high interest rates. No fiscal stabilization or regulation of the banking sector occurred until 1999 and the banks' main source of profit became financing the public sector deficits. Commercial banks were financing public deficits through short positions (short-term dollar debt vs. long-term Turkish government bonds) (Akat 2000). This process caused the TL to appreciate, and thus, increased trade and current account deficits. In the meantime high inflation continued, leading to dollarization of the economy. Therefore, the economy became extremely fragile. A crisis erupted in 1994 when Turkey faced a sudden and massive capital outflow. However, soon capital inflows and economic growth resumed, thanks to an IMF deal and the following high consumption.

Towards the end of the 1990s, economic volatility increased further due to some unfortunate events. In 1998, Russia, the most important trade partner of Turkey, had an economic crisis. Then, in 1999 a strong earthquake hit the most industrialized region of Turkey. Eventually, the Turkish economy looked quite shaky and the government agreed a Staff Monitoring Program with the IMF in July 1998 and then a stand-by agreement was signed in December 1999 with the purpose of bringing inflation to single-digit levels by 2002. According to the new program, inflation was to be controlled through a pre-announced exchange rate policy. This program also involved tight fiscal policy, incomes policy, tight monetary and exchange rate policies, tax reform, privatization, banking regulation, and reform of agricultural support. This program was the first indication that Turkey was about to apply the second generation of neoliberal reforms.

Suddenly a banking crisis erupted in November 2000. This crisis was triggered by the rapid drop in interest rates due to the IMF program in effect, which caused a consumption boom and a surge in imports, deteriorating the current account deficit further. In addition to that, low-interest rates applied in Turkey and instabilities in other emerging markets started to trigger capital outflows, eventually leading to crisis. Despite a quick IMF bailout, a much more severe crisis in February 2001 erupted, and this became an extremely important turning point for the neoliberal project in Turkey.

In short, the first phase of the neoliberal project in Turkey, i.e. implementation of the Washington Consensus policies, was effective but implemented only partially. Among ten policies listed under Washington Consensus, the Turkish governments clearly failed in fiscal discipline. There was also limited implementation of privatization. Also, although the TL was devalued in 1980, the competitiveness of the exchange rate gradually deteriorated with capital account liberalization. When it came to deregulation of the economy, there was also partial success.

Turkey was not the only country which could not implement the first-generation neoliberal reforms evenly and fully. However, as widely known, even successful implementation elsewhere did not bring the expected positive results. Neoliberal reforms had adverse effects on the implementing economies, such as sluggish growth, rising external imbalances, periodic crises, and rising inequality. These negative effects were presented by the IMF as an outcome of insufficient implementation. Thus, the IMF argued that deeper and further reforms were needed (Singh *et al.* 2005). Also needed were deep-seated institutional changes to support these reforms (Krueger 2004). Consequently, the original Washington Consensus list of reforms was augmented by a list of *second-generation reforms* and again imposed over the developing countries (Rodrik 2006). *Augmented Washington Consensus* includes an additional set of neoliberal reforms that complement the first-generation reforms of the Washington Consensus plus the institutions that consolidate and reinforce them (see Table 8.1).

Especially with the increasing economic instabilities faced in the 1990s, it had become obvious that Turkey had exhausted the limits of the first phase of neoliberalism, and thus, needed to get underway the more advanced phase. While many similar countries had already started to implement the second generation neoliberal reforms, it took the financial crisis of 2001 for Turkey to move to the more advanced phase, which corresponds to Augmented Washington Consensus.

The second phase of the neoliberal project

Despite the neoliberal reforms initiated from 1980 on, Turkey had not really been a totally liberal economy by the end of the twentieth century. About 50 percent of all land and about 60 percent of the industrial sector still belonged to the state. The state also ran three state banks that dominated about 50 percent of the market. One of these banks helped the agricultural sector and the other assisted to small-business owners through subsidized loans. (Gorvett 2001) Therefore, state still had a significant role in the economy. Despite the corruption and clientelism involved in that system, subsidies to merchants and farmers had wide support within the society. However, as the crisis manifested itself, the Turkish government was no longer able to sustain this system. Thus, the semi-liberal Turkish economic system could persist only until the 2001 financial crisis. After this point Turkey fully embraced neoliberalism and started to deeply integrate with the global economy through second generation neoliberal reforms of the Augmented Washington Consensus.

The 2001 crisis: the breaking point

The 2001 financial crisis proved to be the most severe crisis in Turkey's economic history since World War II. The second phase of the neoliberal reforms in Turkey had started even before the 2001 crisis, with the 1999 IMF deal. However, the implementation of most of these reforms could be possible only after the 2001 crisis. It was with this crisis the completion of the neoliberal project became possible.

The 2001 crisis aggravated an already unstable economic situation in Turkey. On February 22 the government had to abandon the crawling peg foreign exchange regime and the TL lost about 40 percent of its value against US dollar in just few days. At the same time, interbank interest rates rose to as high as 7,000 percent and about $7.5 billion fled Turkey in just two days following the crisis (Yeşilada 2002). Turkey, urgently in need of funds to overcome the crisis, was pressed to restore confidence of the investors, and thus, brought a senior World Bank economist, Kemal Derviş, to gain credibility in the domestic and international markets. Derviş became the technocratic Economy Minister of Turkey. Through his economic program, he succeeded not only in guaranteeing international funds for stabilization, but also initiating the more advanced phase of neoliberalism in Turkey.

As early as April 2001, Turkey made another agreement with the IMF which promised a $10 billion loan. The new agreement with the IMF imposed stricter conditions on Turkey. For example, Derviş had to secure all the new legislation required by the IMF to obtain the assistance in mid-May. The Turkish parliament had to pass the bulk of the 15 priority new laws. In general, these reforms targeted liberalization of state-dominated markets and the elimination of government price subsidies, particularly in the agricultural sector. On March 15, 2002, the Turkish government announced price hikes in some public products, including a 20 percent increase in electricity, fuel, phone and bread prices. The IMF also required tighter supervision of the Turkish banking sector and fiscal discipline.

In May 2001 $8 billion in new loans was pledged for Turkey by the IMF. This brought the IMF credit available to the country to $19 billion, making Turkey the largest debtor of the IMF. Then, in January 2002, the IMF and the World Bank promised a further $10 billion rescue package in addition to the funds already agreed to reward an increase in the speed of reforms and to eliminate worries about Turkey's ability to service its large domestic debt. The condition was that "this time Turkey get real" for dismantling its semi-liberal economic system to replace it with a truly liberal one (Friedman 2001). In fact, the money was released only after the Turkish government started legislating the required structural reforms.

The crisis not only affected the financial markets and investors but also the lives of the Turkish people. According to *Turkish Daily News* (April 8, 2001), it was estimated that about 500,000 jobs were lost in Turkey just within the first 45 days after the crisis, increasing the unemployment rate to its highest point in the last 20 years. A lot of businesses went bankrupt and the economy contracted about 5.7 percent in 2001 (see Table 8.2). The GDP per capita recorded a 27.5 percent fall, from $4,215 in 2000 to $3,054 in 2001.[1] What was perhaps most dangerous about Derviş's program was its impact on the agricultural sector, which sustained almost 45 percent of the Turkish population. Farmers were losing not only their price supports, but also the subsidized loans provided by the state bank. At the same time, public employees were losing through forced layoffs, forced retirement plans, and limits on wage rises. However, the Turkish government's

Table 8.2 Annual GDP growth rates of Turkey, 2000–2015

2000	*2001*	*2002*	*2003*	*2004*	*2005*	*2006*	*2007*	*2008*	*2009*	*2010*	*2011*	*2012*	*2013*	*2014*	*2015*
6.8	−5.7	6.2	5.3	9.4	8.4	6.9	4.7	0.7	−4.8	9.2	8.8	2.1	4.2	2.9	4.0

Source: World Bank, World Development Indicators

commitment to economic reforms and the IMF support increased confidence of the international investors and financial flows returned (Öniş 2006). As a result, although the effects of the crisis were still prevalent, the economy started to recover in 2002.

In conclusion, although the economic liberalization process in Turkey had started in 1980, it could be completed thanks to the 2001 crisis. After this crisis, not only the incomplete first-generation reforms, such as privatization and fiscal discipline, were implemented effectively, but also the missing second-generation reforms could be initiated. Indeed, the reforms proposed and pursued by Derviş were designed to eliminate the remaining state interventions in the economy through long-promised structural measures, which meant dismantling the last impediments to the completion of the neoliberal project. Hence, if the reforms of 1980 were the implementation of the Washington Consensus in Turkey, 2001 was the outset of the Augmented Washington Consensus. Derviş effected this launch, but definitely these policies were consolidated and deepened under a AKP government.

Neoliberalism under AKP: the last phase of the neoliberal project

As mentioned, the Turkish economy had started to recover by 2002. However, this did not prevent the resounding defeat of the coalition government in power in the November 2002 elections. The lack of confidence in the government, due to the 2001 crisis and the subsequent austerity program, was demonstrated in the November 2002 elections when all the governing parties were swept from the parliament and the AKP (Justice and Development Party), a party which was established just 14 months before the elections, came to power by winning an unexpected majority of the seats in the legislature.

The AKP and its definitive leader Erdoğan saw the neoliberal program initiated by Derviş as a ready-made recipe. Since the short-term negative effects of the existing stabilization program were over and the economy had started to grow, the AKP just continued with the same program. Despite strong signs of recovery, the AKP government signed another four-year stand-by agreement with the IMF in 2004 which assured the investors that further liberalization process of the Turkish economy would continue until 2008.

The AKP's economic policies can be summarized as the extension and consolidation of neoliberalism in the style of the Augmented Washington Consensus (Rodrik 2006). Some of the Augmented Washington Consensus reforms were already completed by 2002. For instance, capital account liberalization was already fulfilled in 1989, though not prudently. WTO agreements were already in place before the crisis and even a Customs Union with the EU was realized by 1996. Financial codes and standards were tightened during 1999–2001 through the banking reforms. A free floating exchange rate system also became effective just after the 2001 crisis. Besides, the Central Bank became more independent and adopted inflation targeting monetary regime right after the crisis. The AKP government maintained and even deepened these policies. In addition, they committed themselves to the previously partial reforms, such as privatization and fiscal discipline. Price stability became the central goal of economic policy, and as a result of that, the primary budget surplus was kept at 6.5 percent. In addition, the AKP undertook flexibilization of labor markets. Last but not least important, the AKP focused on social safety nets and targeted poverty reduction, which were very crucial to raise political support for this profoundly neoliberal agenda. The only missing item from the Augmented Washington Consensus list was the anti-corruption reforms.

In the first five years of the AKP government (2003–2007), the Turkish economy grew rapidly, with an annual rate of approximately 7 percent (see Table 8.2). Fiscal adjustment was accomplished and inflation dropped to around 10 percent by 2004, causing some economists to call it a very successful example of neoliberal transformation.[2] Nevertheless, as will be explained, this has been a *speculative-led model* of development since it is contingent on huge volumes of foreign capital inflows which are badly needed to finance domestic consumption and chronic current account deficit. On the other hand, savings and fixed-capital investments, which are essential for long-term growth, have remained low. Besides, there was no improvement in unemployment rates.

The reason why economic stability has been illusionary rather than real is that economic growth itself has not been as stable as claimed. For instance, as can be seen in Table 8.2, while the growth reached to 8–9 percent in 2004 and 2005, it already dropped to below 5 percent by 2007. Not surprisingly things got even worse with the 2007–2008 global crisis which caused a serious contraction in the economy. After two years of high growth in 2010 and 2011, growth stayed at modest rates. Since 2011, growth has not exceeded 5 percent and it is not expected to go above this rate sometime in near future. In fact, in its "Global Prospects and Policy Challenges" report, the IMF (2016b) forecasted that Turkey would grow by 3.2 percent in 2016 and 3.6 percent in 2017, mostly through domestic demand and with higher inflation. Yet, the problem is less the rate of growth but the nature of this growth. As also indicated by the IMF (2016a, par. 4) itself, there are serious structural problems in the Turkish economy:

> Monetary tightening was insufficient to reduce inflationary pressures, amid sharp lira depreciation ... [E]xternal imbalances persist ... The current domestic demand-based growth does not help rebalancing and the low private saving rate, if unaddressed, will perpetuate accumulation of external imbalances. Moreover, financing of the deficit remains a concern with some of it coming from reserves.

The irony is that, the Turkish economy is in this fragile position because of the very policies that the IMF had prescribed to Turkey. The implementation of the neoliberal project in Turkey through the Washington Consensus and the Augmented Washington Consensus policies has created an economy which does not grow through production but consumption, and the deficits created by domestic consumption are financed through volatile foreign capital flows. Still, the Turkish case is regarded as an exemplary neoliberal transformation among the emerging markets.

To start with, open capital account has become an important deadlock for the Turkish economy. Intensified foreign capital inflows have been rendering the Turkish economy more crisis-prone. Foreign capital flows attracted to Turkey with high interest rates have a quite negative influence through their effect on trade. They cause the TL to appreciate, and thus, weaken the export and investment levels.[3] Consequently, overvalued currency swells the current account deficit (almost 10 percent of the GDP by 2011), increasing the fragility of the Turkish economy (see Figure 8.2). Between 2002 and 2007 exports grew, especially in medium-low and medium-high technology (though not high value-added) products, thanks to developments in the euro-dollar parity, low wages, and the global economic boom. However, due to the overvalued TL, imports have grown even faster. Because of abundant and cheap foreign currency, more and more intermediate goods are imported, so even rising exports in Turkey (especially automotive and durable consumption goods) are not enough to decrease the current account deficit and unemployment. In fact, Turkish exports contain 80–85 percent imported materials and imported goods (Rodrik 2012). As a result, the Turkish economy has been in a chronic current account deficit and the level of this deficit is beyond acceptable levels (see Figure 8.2).

Another weakness of the Turkish economy is that there has been no improvement in the unemployment rate, even in very high growth years (see Figure 8.3), so this has been called *jobless growth* (Yeldan 2007), which is also an outcome of

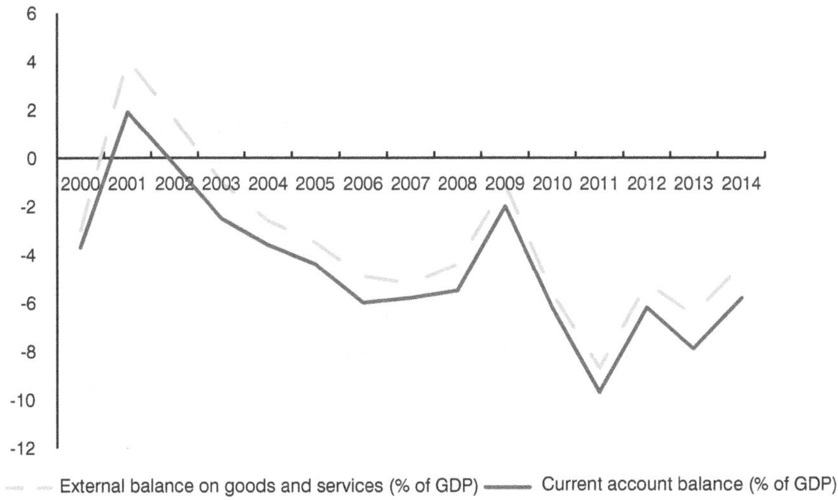

Figure 8.2 External balance of Turkey, 2000–2014

Source: World Bank, World Development Indicators

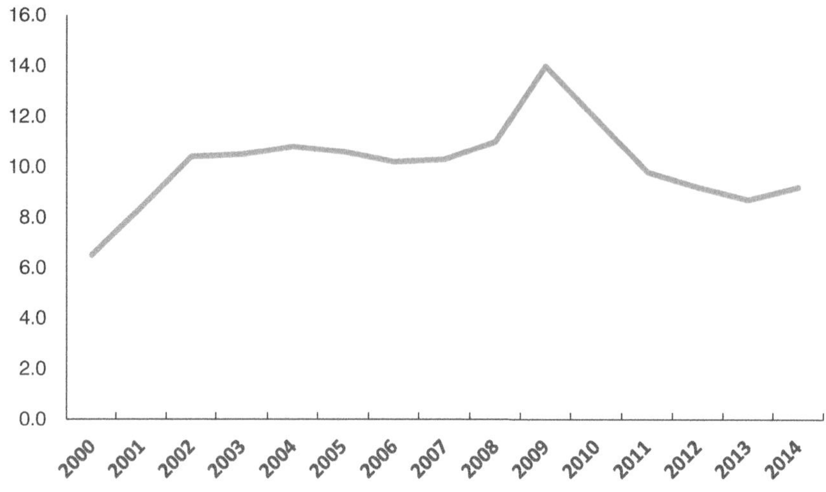

Figure 8.3 Unemployment rate in Turkey (%), 2000–2014

Source: World Bank, World Development Indicators

the speculative-led development model. Unemployment in Turkey was below 6 percent in 2000, but then increased to over 10 percent by 2002. Even after the recovery from the crisis, unemployment got stuck around the 10 percent level. It can be argued that, the neoliberal policies followed after the 2001 economic crisis have made unemployment chronic in Turkey.

Growth does not create much employment in Turkey, because the economic policies followed by the government make the currency appreciate and the overvalued currency decreases the chances of labor intensive sectors to compete in international markets. With overvalued TL, it is only the capital intensive sectors which succeed in the international markets (Yeldan 2010). The intermediate goods that these sectors need are largely imported through foreign capital flows. Therefore, even the growth of these sectors and growth in their exports increase the current account deficit, and thus, foreign debt. According to Yeldan (2010), falling export competitiveness has another negative effect. In order to compensate for their decreased competitiveness, exporters are trying to push wages down and create a poor quality and insecure labor market so that production costs are lower. Thus, even when workers do not lose their jobs, they are forced to work under worse conditions. In fact, as will be explained later, labor conditions worsened both legally and in practice during the AKP government.

Since everything is left to the markets, there is no significant industrial policy nor enough fixed-capital investment that would compensate for the structural weaknesses of the economy, such as chronic trade deficit and unemployment. Another major problem in the Turkish economy is low levels of savings, which also affects investment rates. In 1998 the savings rate in Turkey was above 24 percent of the GDP. But this rate dropped to 17.8 percent in 2000 and has not increased much since then (see Table 8.3). The savings rate is around 15 percent of the GDP, well below average compared to other upper middle income countries. Besides, contrary to other countries, the savings rate is in decline (IMF 2016c). We can say that this is the biggest impediment to future economic growth (Rodrik 2012). However, the reason for the low level of savings is the speculative-led development model created by neoliberal policies, because this kind of a development model fuels consumption rather than savings. Since high consumption fuels imports, this also has a negative effect on the current account balance. As current account deficit is financed by short-term foreign capital flows, the Turkish economy is trapped in a vicious circle and cannot break its dependence on external capital flows.

The impact of the 2007–2008 global crisis

The more advanced phase of Turkey's neoliberal development was first put into test with the 2007–2008 global economic crisis. Actually the global crisis revealed the Turkish economy's existing vulnerabilities and how unsustainable this economic model was, especially under unfavorable global economic conditions. The countries most affected by the global crisis were the ones which heavily relied on external capital flows because of large current account deficits (Lane & Milesi-Ferretti 2011). Turkey was especially vulnerable with a current account deficit of 5.9 percent of its GDP by 2007.

The Turkish economy deteriorated rapidly with the global crisis. The economy grew only 0.7 percent in 2008 and contracted 4.8 percent in 2009 (see Figure 8.3). According to a study conducted by Blanchard, Das and Faruquee (2010), Turkey was one of the economies which were most adversely affected by the global crisis along with Lithuania, Latvia, Estonia, and Russia. By March 2009 industrial capacity utilization rate was only 64.7 percent. The difference between the actual and expected growth rate between the third quarter of 2008 and first quarter of 2009 in Turkey was more than 20 percentage points (Blanchard, Das and Faruquee 2010). Unemployment peaked to 14 percent (see Figure 8.2). This indicated that not only Turkey had high unemployment, but also its unemployment increased rapidly with external shocks.

The global crisis also had a negative impact on the debt position of Turkey. Total debt service ratio increased from 7.7 percent of gross national income (GNI) in 2007 to 10.3 percent in 2009. Public debt was more under control thanks to the tight fiscal policies of the post-2001 crisis period. However, this time indebtedness in the private sector increased, growing to be the factor that contributed most to Turkish foreign debt, especially short-term debt (Uçkun and Doerr 2010). Private debt service increased from \$30.2 billion in 2007 to \$48.8 billion in 2009. Total short-term debt increased from 56.4 percent of Turkey's reserves in 2007 to 89.9 percent in 2010 and then to 104.3 percent in 2014.[4] Therefore, the crisis worsened the debt position of Turkey which left the economy more vulnerable.

In short, before the crisis international economic circles were highly praising Turkey for following strictly neoliberal prescriptions and thus further liberalizing its economy. However, Turkey was quite adversely affected by the global

Table 8.3 Turkey's savings and fixed investment (% GDP), 2000–2014

	2000	2001	2002	2003	2004	2005	2006	2007	2008	2009	2010	2011	2012	2013	2014
Gross domestic savings	17.8	19.2	19.2	16.6	16.8	16.5	17.1	15.9	17.3	13.8	14.0	14.9	15.0	14.1	15.8
Gross fixed capital formation	20.4	15.9	16.7	17.0	20.3	21.0	22.3	21.4	19.9	16.9	18.9	21.8	20.3	20.3	20.1

Source: World Bank, World Development Indicators

economic crisis. With record level chronic current deficit, dependency on hot money flows to cover that deficit, low savings, low fixed-capital investment, high unemployment, and high private sector indebtedness the Turkish economy was already quite vulnerable before the crisis. The crisis just made this vulnerability more visible (Uçkun and Doerr 2010). Therefore, even the banking sector which was strengthened through reforms was not sufficient to prevent the negative impact of the crisis.

Then, how could the Turkish economy return to growth rapidly? The main factor was again foreign capital flows. The return of foreign capital was faster this time compared to the 2001 crisis. The emerging economies which offer high interest rates, like Turkey, became attractive targets for international hot money because of the instability and low-interest rate policy in the advanced economies. Under these conditions from 2009 onward, Turkey's current account deficit began to be financed mainly by short-term capital flows coming from the advanced countries, while it was mostly financed by tourism, FDI and long-term credits before the crisis (Rohn *et al.* 2012).

The socio-economic impact of the neoliberal project and political support for the AKP

The neoliberal project implemented by the AKP had serious adverse effects on different sections of the society. Highly dependent on foreign capital and keen to make the Turkish economy grow, AKP's policies caused the dissolution of the peasantry, extreme marginalization of labor, and commodification of all kinds of natural and human resources. AKP reduced the rights of the formal employees by modifying the labor laws. In fact, new changes in labor law proved to be detrimental for the formal workers. With the new Labor Law no. 4857 enacted in 2003, various flexible and insecure forms of employment became legalized. The AKP government also modified the Labor Security Law no. 4773 enacted by the previous government by decreasing its coverage and enforcement (Koç 2012).

Consequently, the AKP period saw the fastest erosion of workers' rights in Turkey. Unionization rate decreased from 10 percent in 2000 to 5.7 percent in 2010. This is not only the lowest rate of unionization among OECD countries but also the lowest rate for Turkey since the 1950s (Çelik 2010). Also, extensive privatization during the AKP period caused many workers to be laid off or lose benefits (Koç 2012).

Many find it paradoxical that AKP committed itself to neoliberal reforms and policies, although AKP constituents, who are mostly from the lower echelons of society, were looking for social justice (Öniş and Keyman 2003). Although AKP defined itself as a conservative liberal party and pledged to please the international financial institutions right from the beginning (Özbudun 2006; Öniş 2012), it also proved to be increasingly popular among the working classes and the poor. How was that possible? There are basically three reasons: the imaginary economic stability, consumption boom, and social policies. All these factors caused the neoliberal project under AKP to face no serious resistance and even receive wide political support.

With Turkey's quick recovery from the 2001 crisis, many people appreciated the return of high growth rates, perceived this as economic success, and basked in the illusion of economic stability. As the presumed economic stability was restored, the memory of the inflationary years and the 2001 crisis seemed to overshadow the costs of AKP's neoliberal policies. The public fear of the return of inflation and crises was manipulated successfully by Erdoğan to claim that AKP's neoliberal policies were the only possible alternative and guarantee for economic stability in Turkey. Also, the absence of a real political alternative to the neoliberal project, and the weakness of the opposition in that respect, contributed to the wide acceptance of neoliberal policies in Turkey despite their detrimental effects (Y. Özdemir 2015).

Perhaps the most important reason for the AKP paradox is the consumption boom generated by the speculative-led development model (Bağımsız Sosyal Bilimciler 2008). Despite high unemployment and economic strains on people due to neoliberal policies, consumption increased in Turkey. As an economy where savings and investment rates are low, economic growth inevitably relies on domestic consumption. There are also political effects of this situation. The AKP exploits certain economic processes to boost domestic consumption and domestic consumption boosts the political popularity of AKP.

Consumption in Turkey is fueled by the rise in the availability of credit. As mentioned, inflation dropped thanks to the tight fiscal and monetary policies and the economy boomed during 2002–2007. This resulted in better credit terms, i.e. decline in interest rates and extension of credit maturities, which made it easier to borrow money on the part of consumers. As a result, the volume of consumer loans and credit card debt increased from 1.8 percent of GDP in 2002 to 18.7 percent in 2012 and household debt reached to about 50 percent of disposable personal income in 2012 from 7.5 percent in 2003. The share of interest payment in disposable household income also increased, from 2.1 percent in 2003 to 4.9 percent in 2012 (Ergüneş 2009; Karaçimen 2014, 163–164). The number of credit cards in use was 20 million in 2003, but increased to about 78 million by 2011. The volume of credit card transactions increased from 36 billion TL in 2003 to 215 billion TL in 2010. Also spending with credit cards as a share of total spending per person increased from 8 percent in 2003 to 20 percent in 2010. Hence, Turkey has been experiencing a real credit card boom (Bahçe 2012). In fact, the growth in consumption has been fueled by this credit boom, especially consumer credits and credit purchases.

The recent rise in consumer debt is historically unique in Turkey (Karaçimen 2014). However, the growth of household credit is not unique to Turkey. It has been happening in many developing countries in the last decades thanks to financial liberalization reforms promoted by the Washington Consensus and its augmented version. Liberals also argue that, in cases like Turkey, decreased inflation rates, and thus decreased interest rates, have also contributed to this process. Yet, critical scholars see this as an outcome of financialization of personal income (Bryan *et al.* 2009; Dymski 2009; Lapavitsas 2013).

The IMF programs adopted after the 2001 crisis forced Turkey to decrease its public debt and inflation. As mentioned, Turkey was forced to maintain a

6.5 percent primary surplus. The 2001 crisis also caused some banks to become insolvent and the market was cleared from fragile banks. The new banking laws and supervision mechanisms adopted made sure that the banking sector got stronger. With the privatization of some banks and increased liberalization of the sector, foreign banks entered into the market and their share in the market reached to 39.7 percent by 2007 (Ergüneş 2009). These banks have aggressively sought to expand themselves in the consumer credit market. What is more, Turkish companies had increased opportunities to find loans abroad and the banks in Turkey had increased their ability to raise funds internationally. All these factors increased competition in the banking sector. Having lost their easy source of revenue (public debt) due to the tight fiscal policies pushed by the IMF and because of increased competition in the market, the Turkish banks shifted their attention to consumer lending, and thus, the supply of consumer credits increased rapidly (Ergüneş 2009; Karaçimen 2014).

However, the growth of consumer credits cannot be simply attributed to competition among and advertisement by the banks. The full transition to neoliberalism in the post-2001 period actually increased the need for people to borrow because of reduced wages, increased flexibility in the job markets, and increased unemployment. According to Karaçimen (2014), the post-2001 economic policies increased the use of debt so that people could maintain and even increase their living standards. As Köse and Bahçe (2009) suggest, this is an outcome of more and more people not being able to make ends meet. According to a study, 44.7 percent of Turkish population has less income then their consumption. This rate is 51.6 percent for farmers with property, 54.1 percent for labor without property, 52.3 percent for retired people, 66.9 percent for the urban unemployed, 69.7 percent for agricultural labor, and 75 percent for the rural unemployed. It has to be noted that over 70 percent of the consumption of these groups of people is basic necessities, such as food, clothing, housing, and transportation (Bahçe 2012). Therefore, it is not surprising that especially credits to low-income households and wage earners have increased. In fact, about 42 percent of consumer borrowers in Turkey are people who earn less than 1000TL[5] per month (Karaçimen 2014). Thus, even if people do not have enough income, they can get credit and continue to consume even their daily needs through credit. In other words, rising household indebtedness helps people live better than they normally would do merely with their income.

All these processes contribute to AKP's political popularity for the following reasons. First of all, falling inflation rates and the resultant ease of finding bank loans was credited to the AKP government, although inflation and public debt were decreased due to the IMF program initiated by the previous government. Besides, through consumer debt many people got involved with the financial system and began to have a stake in financial stability. AKP and international institutions were quite successful in associating financial stability with the AKP government. Thus, people were made to believe that financial chaos would return if AKP is removed from the government. Also, rising consumption levels increased life standards of many people. As Özkan (2014, 18) states,

> Under the AKP government, a new kind of citizenry has been created, one which has increased its levels of consumption while becoming dependent on bank loans; in return, it unquestioningly accepts the life and working conditions imposed by the current system.

In short, by both allowing people to live better than what their income permits and also by linking people's economic prospects further to the whims of financial markets and making them believe that financial stability can only be sustained with the AKP in power, booming consumer credit became an important factor that made the neoliberal development model under the AKP politically popular, despite its detrimental effects on the working classes.

New social policies are another factor that boosts political support for the AKP. In fact, social policies went through a major transformation in Turkey during the AKP period. Despite the fact that this transformation expanded social aid to the poorest sections of the society, in general it reduced social policy to *charity*. As opposed to the rights-based welfare state social policies, the AKP adopted neoliberal forms of policies, i.e. social safety nets and targeted poverty reduction. These new models of social assistance provided the AKP with significant tools of populism and vast opportunities to extend patrimony. Instead of securing workers' social rights, public resources were used to feed social safety nets and targeted assistance programs that looked as if they were a personal gift from the AKP.

The AKP's social policies did, however, offer compensation to those who suffered most under neoliberalism. The new social assistance programs gave long-neglected sectors of the population, especially the unorganized urban and rural poor, significant access to material benefits. However, the expansion of social assistance has entailed an extraordinary concentration of power and resources in the hands of the governing party and a further weakening of intermediary social and political institutions, because they created personal loyalty to AKP. The unorganized and depoliticized masses are now mobilized with neoliberalism's *charitable solidarity* under the authoritarian AKP government (Yıldırım 2009).

What is also significant about these new kinds of social aid is that their sources are sometimes questionable and they are the fundamental source of new forms of clientelism and corruption in Turkey. Social aid in the form of charity is intertwined with bribery, or at least carried out in conformity with the AKP's political interests in such a way as to maximize its chances of re-election. Some other scholars have also indicated that there have been some semi-official negotiations between the municipalities and individuals and/or entities seeking urban rents and urban policies were arranged in a way that would raise capital for the pro-AKP businessmen[6] (A.M. Özdemir and Yücesan-Özdemir 2008). Not surprisingly, anti-corruption reforms remain as the only missing part of the Augmented Washington Consensus. Certainly, this new model of social policy has not solved the social problems of Turkey, such as inequality, poverty, and unemployment, but it has been very effective in terms of raising support for the neoliberal project in Turkey.

Conclusion

Is Turkey really a "good model" for other emerging economies? After discussing the economic developments in Turkey since 1980 in detail, the obvious answer to this question is "no." As the story of Turkey in the period of 1980–2015 tells us, Turkey has become a conventional peripheral actor in the global economy, which can be labeled as a "poster child" of neoliberal development model.

Turkey implemented the neoliberal project in two phases, first in the 1980s and then in the 2000s, but quite full heartedly and also relentlessly. As a result, Turkey has faced many of the problems associated with the neoliberal policies, such as volatile growth, vulnerability to crises, high unemployment, poverty, inequality, and serious external imbalances, which still continue today. Although Turkey's high growth rates in the 2000s were highly praised by the international economic circles, the reality is that the Turkish economy is quite fragile and it largely depends on short-term foreign capital flows for growth. Rather than a successful model, Turkey's development pattern is highly unsustainable. Even the last IMF report on Turkey states that "These trends point to the external vulnerability of the Turkish economy and may ultimately prove unsustainable" (IMF 2016c, 4).

For the countries which lack the capital they need for their economic growth, all kinds of liberal policies are prescribed as solutions. However, such solutions have not brought any real solution to development needs of these countries. In fact, as demonstrated in the Turkish case, especially capital account liberalization makes developing countries rely on volatile foreign capital flows which can be detrimental (Öniş and Aysan 2000; Ghosh 2005; Cordero and Montecino 2010). Markedly when there is a disruption in the global financial markets, like in the example of the 2007–2008 reversal of capital flows, these economies are left quite vulnerable. Another problem is that foreign capital flows also lead to appreciation of local currency, creating a serious disadvantage for these countries in trade (Ghosh 2005; Rodrik and Subramanian 2009). Turkey is caught up in such a vicious circle. On the one hand, Turkey is dependent on foreign capital flows. On the other hand, because of these capital flows, it becomes more and more dependent on foreign capital flows. In the end, with lack of savings and investment, and deprived of the opportunity to have a trade surplus, the Turkish economy is destined to grow only through domestic consumption and speculation, and thus, continuously suffers from external deficits and debt. Therefore, Turkey is not just a conventional peripheral agent in the global economy, but also it is a textbook case for its shaky economic bases structured by neoliberal practices.

It is not possible to explain what is going on Turkey without putting it in the context of transformations in the global economy, such as increased liberalization, increased mobility of capital, and financialization. Yet, we also have to consider the unique characteristics of Turkey in terms of how the AKP managed to complete the neoliberal transformation of Turkey to become an outmost agent of neoliberal globalization. As a peripheral economy in the global system, Turkey is liberalized, privatized, and marketized and labor is rendered more flexible and insecure in the 2000s and 2010s. At the same time, Turkey is also one of the countries where poverty alleviation is connected to neoliberalism through new populist social transfers which serve to strengthen the power of the hegemonic classes. This situation deepens and consolidates neoliberalism further. Interestingly, although the neoliberal development model has come under strong criticism because of various crises (i.e. the 1997 Asian crisis, the 2001 Argentine crisis, and lastly the 2007–2008 global economic crisis), and many developing countries have gradually started to look for more independent paths and heterodox solutions, Turkey still has not sought any alternative. It is highly possible that Turkey soon faces another severe crisis, which may eventually create an urge to adopt a more sustainable, more heterodox, and more independent development model.

Notes

1 World Bank, World Development Indicators, accessed on 24 June 2016. http://databank.worldbank.org/data/reports.aspx?source=world-development-indicators.
2 However, one should not forget that that same period was a period of high growth for almost all economies as 2003–2007 was the global economic boom period.
3 According to Rohn *et al.* (2012), the TL gained 40–45 percent value from the beginning of 2003 to the end of 2010, and then lost 15–20 percent value until the second half of 2011, but then again started to appreciate.
4 World Bank, *World Development Indicators*.
5 This corresponds to approximately $472 by mid-2014.
6 The most common way for the AKP municipalities to raise charity funds was to favor pro-AKP businessmen in public bids and in the privatization of publicly owned companies in exchange for donations to their charity funds.

References

Akat, A. S. 2000. "The Political Economy of Inflation in Turkey." *Journal of International Affairs* 54(1): 265–282.

Alper, E. and M. Üçer. 1998. "Some Observations on Turkish Inflation: A 'Random Walk' Down the Past Decade." *Boğaziçi Journal* 12(1): 7–38.

Bağımsız Sosyal Bilimciler. 2008. *2008 Kavşağında Türkiye: Siyaset, İktisat ve Toplum.* (İstanbul: Bağımsız Sosyal Bilimciler).

Bahçe, S. 2012. "Borçlanma ve Kredi Kartları: 'Homo Consumens'in Esareti." *Birikim* 278–279: 124–130.

Blanchard, L. J., M. Das, and H. Faruquee. 2010. "The Initial Impact of the Crisis on Emerging Market Countries." *Brookings Papers on Economic Activity* (Spring): 263–323.

Bryan, D., R. Martin, and M. Rafferty. 2009. "Financialization and Marx: Giving Labor and Capital a Financial Makeover." *Review of Radical Political Economics* 41(4): 458–472.

Cordero, J. A., and J. A. Montecino. 2010. *Capital Controls and Monetary Policy in Developing Countries*. Washington, DC: Centre for Economic and Policy Research, April.

Çelik, A. 2010. "Muhafazakar Sosyal Politika Yönelimi: Hak Yerine Yardım-Yükümlülük Yerine Hayırseverlik." *İstanbul Üniversitesi Siyasal Bilgiler Fakültesi Dergisi* 42: 63–82.

Dibooğlu, S. and A. Kibritcioğlu. 2001. *Inflation, Output, and Stabilization in a High Inflation Economy: Turkey, 1980–2000.* Office of Research, No. 01-0112. University of Illinois, Urbana-Champaign.

Dymski, G. A. 2009. "Financial Risk and Governance in the Neoliberal Era." In *Managing Financial Risks: From Global to Local*, edited by G. L. Clark, A. D. Dixon, and A. H. B. Monk (Oxford: Oxford University Press): 48–68.

Ergüneş, N. 2009. "Global Integration of the Turkish Economy in the Era of Financialization." *Discussion Paper* No. 8, Research on Money and Finance.

Friedman, T. 2001. "Turkey's Moment of Truth." *The New York Times*, June 5.

Ghosh, J. 2005. "The Economic and Social Effects of Financial Liberalization: A Primer For Developing Countries," *DESA Working Paper* No. 4. http://www.un.org/esa/wp4_2005.pdf.

Gorvett, J. 2001. "IMF-Backed Reforms Separate Economy from Politics, Face Opposition of Turkey's Ruling Elites." *The Washington Report on Middle East Affairs* 20(5): 31.

Hershlag, Z. Y. 1988. *The Contemporary Turkish Economy* (London: Routledge).

IMF. 2016a. "Turkey: Concluding Statement of the 2016 Article IV Mission," February 2. https://www.imf.org/external/np/ms/2016/020216.htm.

IMF. 2016b. *Global Prospects and Policy Challenges*, G-20 Finance Ministers and Central Bank Governors' Meetings February 26–27, 2016, Shanghai, China. https://www.imf.org/external/np/g20/pdf/2016/022616.pdf.

IMF. 2016c. "Turkey Selected Issues," *IMF Country Report* No. 16/105, April, Washington DC. https://www.imf.org/external/pubs/ft/scr/2016/cr16105.pdf.

Karaçimen, E. 2014. "Financialization in Turkey: The Case of Consumer Debt." *Journal of Balkan and Near Eastern Studies* 16(2): 161–180.

Koç, Y. 2012. *AKP ve Emekçiler 2002–2012* (Ankara: Epos).

Köse, A. H., and S. Bahçe. 2009. "Hayırsever Devletin Yükselişi: AKP Yönetiminde Gelir Dağılımı ve Yoksulluk." In *AKP Kitabı: Bir Dönüşümün Bilançosu*, edited by İ. Uzgel and B. Duru (Ankara: Phoenix Yayinevi): 492–509.

Krueger, A. O. 2004. "Meant Well, Tried Little, Failed Much: Policy Reforms in Emerging Market Economies," remarks at the Roundtable Lecture at the Economic Honors Society. New York University, March 23.

Lane, P. R. and G. M. Milesi-Ferretti. 2011. "The Cross-country Incidence of the Global Crisis." *IMF Economic Review* 59(1): 77–110.

Lapavitsas, C. 2013. "The Financialization of Capitalism: 'Profiting without Producing'." *City* 17(6): 792–805.

Murphy, Emma, 1999, *Economic and Political Change in Tunisia*, London: Palgrave Macmillan.

Öniş, Z. 2006. "Varieties and Crises of Neoliberal Globalisation: Argentina, Turkey and the IMF. *Third World Quarterly* 27(2): 239–263.

Öniş, Z. 2012. "The Triumph of Conservative Globalism: The Political Economy of the AKP Era." *Turkish Studies* 13(2): 135–152.

Öniş, Z. and A. F. Aysan. 2000. "Neoliberal Globalisation, the Nation-State and Financial Crises in the Semi-Periphery: A Comparative Analysis." *Third World Quarterly* 21(1): 119–139.

Öniş, Z. and S. Özmucur. 1990. "Exchange Rates, Inflation and Money Supply in Turkey: Testing the Vicious Circle Hypothesis." *Journal of Development Economics* 32(January): 133–154.

Öniş, Z. and E. F. Keyman. 2003. "A New Path Emerges." *Journal of Democracy* 14(2): 95–107.

Özbudun, E. 2006. "From Political Islam to Conservative Democracy: The Case of the Justice and Development Party in Turkey." *South European Society & Politics* 11(3–4): 543–557.

Özdemir, A. M. and G. Yücesan-Özdemir. 2008. "Opening Pandora's Box: Social Security Reform in Turkey in the Time of the AKP." *SEER-South-East Europe Review for Labour and Social Affairs* 4: 469–483.

Özdemir, Y. 2015. "Turkey's Justice and Development Party An Utmost Case of Neoliberal Populism." Paper presented at the ECPR's General Conference, Montreal, Canada, August 26–29.

Özkan, B. 2014. "Turkey: Nearing the End of its 'Winter Sleep'." *Research Turkey* III(6): 13–20.

Rodrik, D. 2006. "Goodbye Washington Consensus, Hello Washington Confusion? A Review of the World Bank's Economic Growth in the 1990s: Learning From a Decade of Reform." *Journal of Economic Literature* 44(4): 973–987.

Rodrik, D. 2012. "The Turkish Economy After the Global Financial Crisis." *Ekonomi-tek* 1(1): 41–61.

Rodrik, D. and A. Subramanian. 2009. "Why did Financial Globalization Disappoint?" *IMF Staff Papers* 56(1): 112–138.

Rohn, O., R. Gönenç, V. Koen and R. Karaşahin. 2012. "Tackling Turkey's External and Domestic Macroeconomic Imbalances." *OECD Economics Department Working Papers* No. 986, September 13.

Singh, A., A. Belaisch, C. Collyns, P. De Masi, R. Krieger, G. Meredith, and R. Rennhack. 2005. "Stabilization and Reform in Latin America: A Macroeconomic Perspective of the Experience since the 1990s." *IMF Occasional Papers* No. 238. International Monetary Fund, Washington, DC.

Uçkun, D. and M. Doerr. 2010. "Emerging Markets: Theory and Practice/Turkey's Reforms Post 2001 Crisis." *Journal of Global Analysis* 1(1): 51–74.

Vom Haua, M., J. Scott and D. Hulmeb. 2012. "Beyond the BRICs: Alternative Strategies of Influence in the Global Politics of Development." *European Journal of Development Research* 24(2): 187–204.

Williamson, J. 1990. "What Washington Means by Policy Reforms." In *Latin American Adjustment: How Much Has happened*? Edited by J. Williamson (Washington: The Institute for International Economics): 5–24.

Yeldan, E. 2007. "Patterns of Adjustment under the Age of Finance: The Case of Turkey as a Peripheral Agent of Neoliberal Globalization." *PERI Working Paper Series* no. 126, University of Massachusetts, Amherst, MA.

Yeldan, E. 2010. "Global Crisis and Turkey: A Macroeconomic Assessment of the Effects of Fiscal Stimulus Measures on Employment and Labour Markets." In *Crisis and Turkey: Impact Analysis of Crisis Response Measures*, edited by H. Ercan, E. Taymaz, and E. Yeldan (Ankara: ILO): 9–40.

Yeşilada, B. 2002. "Financial Crisis in Turkey: A Wakeup Call for Economic and Political Reforms." Paper presented at the Annual Conference of the International Studies Association, New Orleans, Louisiana, March 22–28.

Yıldırım, D. 2009. "AKP ve Neoliberal Popülizm." In *AKP Kitabı: Bir Dönüşümün Bilançosu*, edited by İ. Uzgel and B. Duru (Ankara: Phoenix Yayinevi): 66–107.

9 The persistence of neoliberalism since the Arab uprisings

The cases of Egypt and Tunisia

Angela Joya

Introduction

In late 2010 and early 2011, millions of people in Tunisia and Egypt took to the streets rejecting not only authoritarianism but also the neoliberal model of development that resulted in declining living standards, high unemployment, and rising poverty. The initial post-revolutionary transition period was full of promises and potential for a new socio-economic order. Movements campaigned to "Drop the Debt" and revisit corrupt economic deals that took place under the old regimes (Gamal 2011, Ben Rouine 2013). At first glance, Tunisia and Egypt may appear to be on divergent paths: the former on the path to democracy and the latter reverting to authoritarian rule. Tunisia has been described as the "success case of democracy", a model for the rest of the Arab world (Bellin 2014). In contrast, Egypt, with a former military general as its current president, is seen as a place where democracy has failed, and revolution has been aborted. There is ample reason for such claims; Tunisia has had a peaceful transfer of political power; its military has remained out of politics and its unions and social movements have paved the way for an active and vibrant civil society. Egypt, on the other hand, experienced a military coup against an elected government, resulting in the pervasive influence of the military in Egypt's political and economic affairs. Despite these differences, I argue that there is a significant degree of convergence in the political economy of the two countries that has been missed by scholars who focus solely at the political level.

Five years after the uprisings, the two countries are not so far apart when assessed through the lens of critical political economy. By late 2015, both Tunisia and Egypt faced the same socio-economic challenges that existed before the uprisings of 2010–2011; both countries have turned to the international financial institutions (IFIs) for market-led solutions to these challenges. In this context, the inability of transitional governments to offer effective responses to the pressing needs for employment and sustainable livelihoods may increase the degree of political violence in both countries. Despite a relatively peaceful political transition, Tunisia suffers from a lack of sustainable economic development, high levels of unemployment, regional disparities making the country increasingly prone to attacks by militant Islamist groups who recruit from the ranks of the unemployed youth. Under Abdel Fattah el-Sisi, Egypt presents an image of stability and economic vibrancy, reflected in the development of massive infrastructural projects. However, the country continues to suffer from high levels of unemployment, rising inequality and poverty levels, and increasing social tensions as the government has adopted punitive measures against civil society actors and trade unions (Barakat 2016; Trofimov 2016; Amnesty International 2016, 19).[1]

This chapter argues that, after five years of revolution, neoliberalism persists in both Egypt and Tunisia due to both a realignment of domestic and regional political forces and sustained pressure from international financial institutions (IFIs) such as the International Monetary Fund (IMF) and the World Bank. Section 1 examines the historical context of economic development while Section 2 looks at the neoliberal experiment in Tunisia and Egypt. Section 3 discusses developments in Tunisia and Egypt's political economy since the uprisings. The chapter concludes with an assessment of socio-economic developments over the past five years and the implications for social justice and democratic development in both countries.

Tunisia and Egypt: a brief historical overview

Tunisia and Egypt lend themselves to a comparative study; both countries experienced a similar trajectory in their economic development during the post-World War II period. Both embarked on state-led nationalization and modernization in the post-independence period of the 1950s and 1960s, only to shift to limited economic liberalization in the 1970s. The economic crisis of the 1980s resulted in the breakdown of the statist model and the pursuit of economic liberalization.

Independence to infitah

After gaining independence from France in 1956, Tunisia launched a modernization program initiating industrialization, capital-intensive agriculture, land reform and nationalization. Habib Bourguiba, Tunisia's first post-independence president, adopted a populist authoritarian model by forging links between workers, peasants and the state. The most notable period of statism in Tunisia was between 1961–1969 when a relatively successful policy of Import Substitute Industrialization (ISI) was carried out. However, the lingering power of the landed classes hampered its progress and, in 1969, the World Bank threatened to revoke its financial aid if Tunisia did not adopt a market-friendly approach to development. Rural notables and the commercial bourgeoisie supported the push for economic liberalization, and under pressure by the Bank and by these internal political forces, Tunisia moved away from ISI, embracing a policy of economic liberalization, or *infitah*, in the 1970s (Murphy 1999).

The *infitah* policies offered an opening for the landed classes to diversify their economic activities by moving to urban centers and engaging in commercial activities such as transport, construction and hotel management. This period saw the consolidation of power of Tunisia's commercial bourgeoisie, which became an important pillar of the Tunisian state and economy until the end of 2010. By

1991, the state sought to achieve growth through the full or partial privatization of sectors such as textiles, industry, hotels, and fishing companies (Saghir 1993, 3). The Tunisian state under Zein al Abidine Ben Ali, Bourguiba's successor, became heavily involved in the privatization process subsidizing the risks taken by the private sector.

Following a similar trajectory, Egypt embarked on a populist statist model of economic development after the end of the British Protectorate in 1952. Under Gamal Abdel Nasser, the pursuit of industrialization was accompanied by land reform. To enable the success of this program, the state gave workers and peasants a stake in economic development. However, the landed classes' power remained unbroken, resulting in pushback against land reform and nationalization from 1969 onward, resulting in the decline of the statist model. In 1974, Anwar Sadat launched a program of economic liberalization that pursued development goals by combining Gulf capital with Egyptian labor and western technology. The track record of *infitah,* however, was lackluster as the primary beneficiaries were the commercial bourgeoisie and the landlords. Prices of basic commodities rose at the same time that the government announced cuts in bread subsidies: This led to the famous bread riots in the late 1970s which extended beyond Egypt to other countries in the region (Walton and Seddon 1994).

The neoliberal experiment

The neoliberal experiment unfolded in the context of a region-wide economic crisis in the 1980s. Countries in the Middle East and North Africa (MENA) faced economic crises, forcing governments to increase external borrowing to sustain the public sector. Declining economic growth soon resulted in the liberalization of various economic sectors as elite strategies for accumulation reoriented towards the global economy. Although the neoliberal experiment in Tunisia and Egypt followed different timelines, the process produced similar dramatic socio-economic transformations.

Tunisia in the mid-1980s reached agreements with the IMF and the World Bank for a stabilization package, resulting in structural reforms. Between 1987 and 2010, Tunisia implemented market reforms spanning five different National Development Plans.[2] While the immediate goals of the reforms were to bring inflation under control and enable Tunisia to repay its external debt, the long-term goals were to move the country away from the statist model towards a "free" market model (World Bank 2008). Under Ben Ali, structural adjustment policies deepened Tunisia's economic vulnerability within the global economy. Throughout the 1990s, the participation of private investors increased in the service, tourism, infrastructure, agriculture and manufacturing sectors, largely through the privatization of state enterprises (King 2003). Further deepening Tunisia's global economic integration, the ratification of the General Agreement on Tariffs and Trade (GATT, later the World Trade Organization, or WTO) allowed Tunisia to negotiate multilateral deals with global investors and the European Union (EU). Tunisia has since enjoyed access to EU markets where 80 percent of its goods are exported (Hoddouk 2016). By the end of 2002, the government partially or totally privatized 140 state-owned enterprises, which became the basis of Tunisia's 5.7 percent growth rate in the early 2000s (Pfeifer 1999). The subsequent Development Plans (2002–2006) encouraged investment in the knowledge economy with the hope of generating much-needed employment.

Despite these reforms, the Tunisian state retained significant control over various sectors of the economy, including telecommunications, energy, transportation, banking, fertilizers, mining, and construction materials. In essence, the state subsidized the privatization process, allowing for the private accumulation of wealth for businessmen close to Ben Ali. Between 1994 and 2007, state incentives accounted for 40 percent of the investment cost of projects qualified for privatization. Despite such state support for the private sector, the latter's performance remained unimpressive with regard to capital investment. Overall, the share of private investment in Tunisia was just over 60 percent in 2008, which was lower than Egypt (over 70 percent) and Morocco (close to 80 percent). Similarly, private investment's share of Tunisia's GDP declined from 15.3 percent in 2000 to 12.5 percent in 2004 and stagnated at 14 percent between 2006 and 2011 (Achy 2011).

Although liberalization stimulated growth in the service sector and brought deficits and inflation under control in Tunisia, unemployment continued to rise – from 13.1 percent in 1984 to 16.1 percent in 1993 (King 2003, 39). Between 1998 and 2006, 19,000 jobs were created in the public sector; between 2007 and 2010 less than 10,000 were created (Achy 2011). The private sector failed to create the much-needed employment in Tunisia. While World Bank data indicates a decline in the rate of unemployment from 17 percent in the late 1990s to 12 percent in 2008, scholars have pointed out that underlying this perceived decline in unemployment was a rise in the informal sector (Pfeifer 2016, 18, 20). Moreover, the types of jobs that were created were considered low-paid relative to the public sector and with temporary contracts. Thus, productivity gains of the 2000s were mainly captured by the employers and corporations and not shared with the workers (ibid.).

Market liberalization worsened uneven geographic development in Tunisia; government redistribution and public spending, as well private investment patterns reinforced regional disparities, leaving the South and West of the country neglected. Ninety percent of public spending managed by the central government was channeled primarily to the richer regions while regional governments were left with 7 percent of the budget for services. Meanwhile, the privatization program resulted in the rise of crony capitalism, enriching businessmen from the North and Northeast while depriving underdeveloped parts of the country. Rather than increasing pluralist democracy by opening up the political process to other social and political actors, market liberalization led to "the hardening of authoritarianism" (King 2003) and the consolidation of power by the landed and commercial classes.

Tunisia continues to struggle to meet social justice goals in at least four areas: taxation, jobs, social spending and regional development. On average only one-third of Tunisia's tax revenue is from direct taxes; the rest is indirect, which means the poor carry a higher share of taxes given that they consume all their income, whereas a significant portion of the income of the rich is shielded from indirect taxes (Achy 2011). This further exacerbates the gap between the rich and the poor, which had increased between 2005 and 2010 (Achy 2011, 16–17). By 2010, there was a huge discrepancy between individuals and corporate tax levels, where the latter paid only 35 percent taxes and the former 65 percent in taxes. Of the taxes collected, Tunisia only spent 4 percent and 5 percent of GDP in transfers and subsidies yearly: 2.5 percent on food and 4 percent on fuel (Achy 2011).

Similarly, between 2004 and 2010, according to the African Development Bank (AFDB), the marginalized regions experienced a disproportionate rise in poverty ratio (AFDB 2015; also see Pfeifer 2016, 13–14 on how both Egypt and Tunisian official statistics on poverty masked real levels of poverty in these countries). Poverty rates in Greater Tunis, northeast and center rose from 2 percent to 2.5 percent between 2004 and 2010; in contrast in the northwest, center-west and southwest, they rose from 9 percent to 15 percent between 2004 and 2010 (Achy 2011).[3] The Greater Tunis, northeast and center which is home to 60 percent of Tunisia's population, was home to 90 percent of formal enterprises. In contrast, the northwest, center-west and southwest, which collectively had 30 percent of the population, only had 8 percent of the formal enterprises. Uneven regional developments will remain a major challenge for the Tunisian government in the coming years.

Egypt pursued market liberalization after facing a serious economic crisis in the mid-1980s. The oil shocks of the 1980s resulted in a decline in Egyptian workers' remittances from the Gulf States and an increase of foreign debt ($36 billion in 1986). Debt service obligations consumed 40 percent of Egypt's foreign exchange earnings, putting pressure on food imports. Unemployment and inflation increased as wages stagnated. As government revenues declined, Egypt was forced to look for external loans. To qualify for such loans, Hosni Mubarak agreed to implement IMF reforms starting in the 1980s; full-scale market liberalization followed in the 1990s. In the context of a new investment law (230/1989) market reforms aimed to cut the budget deficit by cutting government public expenditures. After the signing of the Economic Reform and Structural Adjustment Program (ERSAP) in 1991, the government privatized state-owned enterprises, liberalized the agricultural sector and launched special economic zones to attract private investment. These reforms expanded market opportunities for the private sector in agriculture, insurance, industry, real estate construction, and tourism.

After a decade of reforms, macroeconomic indicators were not promising for Egypt's economy; as one scholar noted, "private-sector investment stayed virtually unchanged – it reached only 15.7 percent of GDP by 1997. ...The government had cut its total investment in the economy from 12 percent of GDP in 1987 to 6 percent in 1994 – in nominal terms – this was a decline of roughly 5.6 billion Egyptian pounds" (Rutherford 2008, 204). At the same time, public sector banks had accumulated EGP 95.2 billion worth of bad debts to the private sector by 1999 (Wahish 2000). Notwithstanding these developments, by the end of the 1990s, the reforms gave birth to a new class of neoliberal businessmen based in the ruling New Democratic Party of Hosni Mubarak. These businessmen were the beneficiaries of privatization policy, which transferred control of various economic sectors, often at below the market price. Parallel to this development, in rural Egypt, landed classes increased their landholdings through the privatization of cooperatives, state-owned lands and communal lands.

A decade after market liberalization, it was clear that workers and ordinary citizens had a very different experience with neoliberalism. Workers increasingly struggled with a liberalized rental market, rising food prices and stagnant wages. Peasants faced rising land rents, dispossession and increasing levels of violence at the hands of state security forces. Students faced increasing unemployment as a result of years of cuts to public sector employment. By this time, neoliberalization increasingly became associated with corruption, embezzlement and the theft of public resources. In this context, Egypt witnessed rising levels of worker actions, protests and unrest – university graduates, unable to find public sector employment, mobilized. By the end of the decade, protests became increasingly oriented to domestic social, economic and political issues (Beinin 2016).

In both Tunisia and Egypt, neoliberal reforms strengthened the power of existing elites while also giving rise to new business elites who profited from a clientelistic relationship with the ruling parties. In Tunisia, privatization granted private investors access to cheap credit and technological assistance, as well as property rights to former state lands. In both countries, the dismantling of agricultural cooperatives revived clientelistic networks of landlords and village *umdas* (King 2003, 26; Ayeb and Bush 2014). Cuts to state subsidies – part of Tunisia's Fifth Five-Year Plan between 1977 and 1981 – subjected peasants and small farmers to deregulation of agricultural inputs prices (Ayeb and Bush 2014). Privatization of the agricultural sector actually reduced the sector's contribution to Tunisia's GDP, from 13 percent in the 1990s to 8 percent by late 2000s, resulting in the concentration of economic and political power in the hands of landed classes (Achy 2011, 4–5). In turn, the unequal redistribution of wealth in rural areas intensified poverty levels increasing small farmers' debt and resulting in food and water insecurity. In Egypt, Law 96 (1992) dispossessed over a million peasants and small farmers (Ayeb and Bush 2014).

Privatization increased informality in the labor market as market reforms undermined the bargaining power of trade unions in the 1990s and 2000s (Beinin 2015).[4] During the privatization of state enterprises, both Tunisia's and Egypt's official trade unions sided with the state and demanded the acceptance of austerity from their memberships (King 2003). In the process, labor rights were watered down, and constitutional guarantees were no longer respected by the state. In both countries, the informal sector became the destination for many who could not find work in the formal labor market (Achy 2011; Assaad 2014).

In 2003, Tunisia experienced a proliferation of "irregular and poorly paid jobs in the formal sector"; 40 percent of the non-agricultural jobs were found in the informal sector (King 2003; Achy 2011). In tourism, which constitutes 14 percent of Tunisia's gross domestic product, hiring 400,000 workers, only 35 percent of jobs are permanent while 53 percent are temporary jobs. The remaining 12 percent are apprenticeships. In the textile sector, 44 percent of jobs are non-permanent, 45 percent permanent and 11 percent apprenticeships – Achy concludes that, during the neoliberal period of the 1990s and 2000s (in the textile and tourism sectors at least) "Tunisia's competitiveness [was] largely the result of poor working conditions and low wages" (2011, 15).

The contribution of most export-oriented sectors to economic growth has been limited due to their low-value-added character and their weak integration with the rest of the economy. In Egypt, between 1984 and 1991, 24 percent of the workforce was found in the informal sector; by 2006, this percentage had reached 60 percent of the workforce (UNDP 2010, 22).

Neoliberal policies produced high levels of unemployment, declining living standards, insecure job conditions, income inequality and increasing levels of police brutality (El-Said and Harrigan 2014) (see Table 9.1). In Tunisia, the wealthiest 20 percent of the population increased their share of income from 42 percent in 1970/1975 to 46.3 percent in 1990, while the bottom 20 percent saw its income share remain static: from 6.0 percent in 1970/75 to 5.9 percent in 1990 (King 2003, 39). While the GINI coefficient declined between 2000 and 2005, it increased to 40 percent by the end of the 2000s (Achy 2011, figure 7). By 2011, Egypt had become the ninetieth most unequal country with the GINI coefficient of 34.4.The angst among the educated unemployed youth who constituted the majority of the unemployed in both countries had reached potent levels by 2010 in both countries (see Table 9.2). More than two decades of neoliberal reforms (1991–2010) thus coincided with a crisis of the legitimacy of the state and ruling elites (El-Said and Harrigan 2014).

Despite this increasing social polarization, the World Bank praised Tunisia's 20-year annual average growth of 5 percent, placing the country among "the best performers in the region and in emerging countries" (World Bank 2008). Similar praise was bestowed upon Egypt by the International Monetary Fund (IMF) (Pfeifer 1999). Positive growth rates, however, masked the underlying inequality that liberalization had fostered in both countries. While the World Bank continues to downplay the role of inequality in triggering the revolution (Verme 2013), they admit that perhaps the *perception* of inequality more than *actual* inequality played a bigger role in the uprisings. Scholars such as Schielke (2015) have captured the

Table 9.1 Unemployment rate, Egypt, age group 15–24 years, 1998–2007

	1998	*2007*
Male	15.8 percent	17.2 percent
Female	42.8 percent	47.9 percent

Source: United Nations Human Development Report (2015)

Table 9.2 Unemployment rate, Tunisia, age group 15–24 years, 1997–2011

	1997	*2011*
Male	33.3	43.2
Female	29.0	18.0

Source: United Nations Human Development Report (2015)

way people's day-to-day lives underwent dramatic transformation in places like urban Egypt, under the auspices of impersonal forces of the "free" market.

The uprisings

On the back of decades of grievances and rising social tensions, a series of uprisings engulfed the Arab world in the winter of 2010–2011. In Tunisia, the immolation of 26-year old Mohammed Bouazizi, on December 17, 2010, became the spark that ignited mass protests. The case of Bouazizi reveals a lot about the anxieties and insecurities experienced by the younger generation in the Middle East and North Africa. Bouazizi precariously earned his living by working a fruit cart. After numerous attempts, he was denied a license for his cart, making him vulnerable to police extortion. Bouazizi set himself on fire after police confiscated his scales. The sense of powerlessness over his life and work drove him to take his life in protest, overlooking the provincial headquarters.[5] The protests that followed forced Ben Ali's regime out of power on January 14, 2011.

The uprisings were the culmination of increasing social protests; in 2008, Tunisia experienced the longest and largest protests the country had seen in decades (Beinin 2015). The protests began in January 2008 at the *Compagnie des Phosphates de Gafsa* (CPG) in the Gafsa region, over the nepotistic hiring practices of the company. Workers of the Union Generale Tunisienne du Travail (UGTT) were central to the mobilization efforts. The case of Gafsa revealed that Tunisia's economic growth failed to reach most Tunisians (Allal 2010).

After the collapse of the regime, a political struggle ensued between powerful remnants from the Ben Ali period, the Islamist Ennahda Party and secular forces aligned with the workers' movement. Tunisia successfully adopted a new constitution on January 26, 2014, transferred power through peaceful elections in October of 2014, witnessed the growth of over 100 political parties, and experienced the participation of civil society organizations and trade unions in both social and political arenas. Indeed, what makes Tunisia unique is the existence of a vast number of civil society organizations and trade unions, allowing space for public mobilization. Dating back to the 1980s, the strong, independent and politically oriented trade union movement has been able to win a considerable degree of democratic demands in Tunisia. As a result, a number of scholars, think tanks and Western governments share the view that Tunisia has experienced a successful transition to democracy (Marzouki and Madeeb 2015).

Over the past three years, however, tensions have sharpened between the Islamists and secular forces – especially after the assassination of two secular political leaders allegedly at the hands of Islamist extremists. The UGTT nonetheless has played a central role in facilitating a "national dialogue" between opposing forces along the political spectrum. The UGTT was also instrumental in mobilizing and demanding an elected National Constituent Assembly in October of 2011, which wrote the new constitution.

Inspired by mass protests in Tunisia, millions of Egyptians ousted President Mubarak on January 25, 2011. Their revolutionary slogans decried the poverty, unemployment, corruption and police brutality associated with Mubarak's regime. Since 1998, strikes and protests had been occurring with increasing frequency in various parts of the country. Estimates indicate that between 1998 and 2010, a total of 3,426 strikes, protests and occupations took place across Egypt (Beinin 2016, Table 3.1). Workers demanded back wages, wage increases, affordable food and housing, the right to adequate health care and a better education system.

Like Tunisia, Egypt had experienced rising levels of social tension and income inequality that alienated many Egyptians from the ruling class. The polarization of wealth was visible in the proliferation of luxury villas and gated communities catering to a minority elite while the rest of the country struggled to afford the rising costs of food, rent, education and health care at a time when unemployment levels remained high. Other Egyptians began to mobilize around issues of social justice since the early 2000s, culminating in the outcry for bread, freedom, social justice and human dignity (*aish, hurriya, adaala Igtima'iyya, karama insaniyya*) during the revolutionary movement in 2011.

After Mubarak's removal from power, struggles broke out between Islamists, the military and Mubarak-era capitalists, workers and activists. Fearful of the return of the regime, activists joined with the Muslim Brotherhood and demanded an end to the transitional military rule of the Supreme Council of the Armed Forces (SCAF). Post-uprising Egypt was shaped by both inter-elite rivalries and by struggles from below. After the successes of the Brotherhood in the parliamentary (2011–2012) and 2012 presidential elections, a new set of struggles broke out between the military and the Brotherhood. By mid-2013, a new alliance between the military, secular forces and secular activists brought the Brotherhood's rule to an end through a bloodless coup. Inter-elite struggles directly affected the space within which popular struggles were taking place. Both the Brotherhood's Freedom and Justice Party and the military rulers implemented laws that restricted freedom of assembly, speech and organization. This restricted the ability of civil society activists and workers to press for their demands.

In both Tunisia and Egypt, new political parties and social movements organized around social justice and democracy. The ruling elite initially remained in disarray, further emboldening the democratic movements spearheading the uprisings. However, this honeymoon period did not last long as the forces of reaction pushed back. In both countries these forces included the Islamists who felt marginalized under decades of authoritarian rule. Thus while workers, students and activists initiated the uprisings and brought down the regimes in both countries, they were marginalized from the political process, leaving little room for them to affect legislative change. Over the next four years, multiple struggles continued among political elites, workers, activists, students and the unemployed.

Five years after the uprisings

The five years following the uprisings witnessed a series of uneven reforms in both countries. Initially, governments expressed a willingness to respond to the public's calls for social justice by increasing public expenditure and regulating prices. However, this did not last long. On-going protests and strikes by workers, students, activists and the unemployed demanded radical changes to meet their revolutionary demands. Macroeconomic constraints have limited governments' ability to effectively respond to popular demands for change. In the ensuing policy vacuum, IFIs intervened with the goal of ensuring the continuity of the neoliberal policy paradigm.

Tunisia

After the revolution, the Tunisian economy took a serious hit as private investors left the country, leaving Tunisia to return to the IMF for loans amidst on-going mass protests and strikes (Marzouki and Meddeeb 2015). The tourism sector was the hardest hit, suffering from both capital flight and the fallout from terrorist attacks. Travel and tourism sectors have traditionally absorbed close to 400,000 workers (directly and indirectly), contributing between 9–10 percent to Tunisia's GDP between 2005 and 2010 (Turner 2015, 3). By spring of 2016, Tunisia had lost millions of dollars in tourism revenue (Reuters 2016). By 2014, Tunisia's agricultural sector absorbed 20 percent of the workforce, but only contributed 14 percent to the country's GDP, constituting 14 percent of exports. Since the revolution, trade unions and civil society groups have demanded new constitutional arrangements that guarantee individual rights and justice as well as higher wages, secure jobs and a new labor law (Hartshorn 2015). The on-going protests and strikes indicate that these demands continue to shape the meaning of democratic transition for workers and activists, and have been met with lackluster action by governments and capital.

Policy responses to socio-economic challenges under public pressure have been fraught with problems (*The Economist* 2015). In April of 2011, in response to popular pressure, the transitional government of Gannouchi adopted a public spending measure to meet the immediate needs of the people, focusing on security, job creation and regional development. The latter increased government debt (53 percent of GDP in 2015) while failing to bring down unemployment, especially among the educated youth (AFDB 2015).

So far, the Tunisian private sector has failed to create secure full-time employment for existing workforce and new labor market entrants, making the public sector a desirable source of employment. However, secure, well-paying government jobs are no longer guaranteed, resulting in increasing competition among university graduates. By January 2016, the number of unemployed had reached 700,000, 62 percent of whom were graduates and close to 37 percent of whom were among the youth (BBC 2016 a, b). By 2015, private-sector wages in Tunisia were 40 percent less than the public sector for university graduates.[6] In January 2016, after youth protests spread across the country, the Tunisian government tried to incentivize firms through tax and employment subsidies to prevent mass layoffs. It is yet to be seen if this strategy will pay off.[7]

In rural Tunisia, small farmers struggle for access to land, water, and lower irrigation costs. In recent years, the agricultural sector underwent reforms that resulted in the dispossession of small farmers through the expansion of agribusiness (Ayeb and Bush 2014). Farm workers, too, have demanded better wages, forming a Farmers' Union in 2012. Since then, there have been protests against the high costs of agricultural inputs and the low prices of crops. In March 2012, the government agreed to waive 30 percent of Tunisian farmers' irrigation costs. In urban areas, the absence of decent jobs continues to fuel public protests, especially among the educated youth of Tunisia. In February of 2016, a college graduate was electrocuted on a utility pole during a protest in the Tunisian town of Kasserine, near the Algerian border. His death ignited new protests by those who feel the promises of the revolution have not materialized. It is in towns like Kasserine where people have lost faith in the government that the rising Islamist insurgency finds fertile ground.

Various governments have done little to reform the system that Ben Ali left behind as the elite continue to benefit from privileged access to resources and institutions, leading Tunisians to wonder what has substantively changed about their society, politics and economy. Tunisia's apparently smooth political transition has come at a cost to the rest of the society whose demand to uproot corruption among the elite has been placed on the backburner for now. To patch over differences with old regime figures, the Tunisian government announced the Economic Reconciliation Law, absolving those involved in corruption under Ben Ali. Activists and civil society organizations have protested the law, arguing that policy makers need to be held accountable by the citizens through constant pressure and street presence (The Economist 2016). Some fear the return of Ben Ali-era political and economic figures after the electoral success of the Nidaa Tounes political party – a patchwork of leftists, liberals, conservatives, trade unionists and businessmen with ties to Ben Ali.

Keen to retain their hegemony in the MENA region, the IFIs have offered their own account of the uprisings followed by policy proposals to keep MENA economies firm on the neoliberal path. While the IFIs have acknowledged some of the factors that led to the uprisings, such as youth unemployment and rising inequality, they argue that the Arab revolutions took place because the economic growth generated during the neoliberal era had not been adequately redistributed among all segments of society (World Bank 2015; World Bank May 2014; Verme *et al.*, 2014, 84; El Amraoui 2015). This was not a problem of neoliberalism, but rather, with the persistence of market distortions. For example, rising unemployment was explained as a result of rigid labor legislation and the persistence of state control over certain sectors of the economy.[8]

Reflecting on Tunisia's experience with economic liberalization, the World Bank acknowledged that "inadequate economic performance" was at the root of the Tunisian revolution: "It is not the 'liberalization' of the economy that brought unemployment and low wage jobs. Tunisia was unable to advance beyond the low skills, low wage economy because it did not, in fact, open up its economy … and did not change the underlying state controlled economic model" (World Bank 2014, 5). The report goes on to argue that "Tunisia's disappointing economic performance and feeble jobs creation are the result of multiple barriers to the operation of markets and deep distortions introduced by well-intended but misguided economic policies" (World Bank May 2014, 7). The World Bank blames labor legislation for the lack of jobs and the existence of low paying jobs: "Labor market rules and institutions have exacerbated the bias toward low-value added activities in Tunisia, while failing to protect either workers or jobs" (World Bank 2014, 9). Tunisia's labor legislative framework is characterized as containing "rigid firing rules for open-ended contracts" (World Bank 2014, 9). According to the report, employer contributions to social security are another factor contributing to the lack of good jobs (World Bank 2014, 9).

IFIs claim that the main problems facing Tunisia can only be resolved if the state enhances the role of the private sector. Increased private investment, they argue, will result in job creation and economic growth. The Economist Intelligence Unit (2015), has argued that: "[w]ithout radical reform, Tunisia will be condemned to a long-term future of low growth," highlighting "an urgent need for root and branch reform in every sector of the economy", suggesting that government further deregulates sectors such as agriculture and mining, and criticizing the monopolistic practices that protect the ailing tourism sector from competition.

Proposals for Tunisian economic reforms offered by the EIU and the World Bank concur on a number of points; all three identify private investment as central to reviving economic growth and job creation. There is a consensus for liberalizing finance, strengthening competition and bankruptcy law, implementing PPPs and reforming labor law (World Bank 2014, 15–16). The gist of the proposals is captured in the following quote from the World Bank report:

> [F]or Tunisia to realize its "full potential", it must "become the 'Tiger of the Mediterranean," by creating an economic environment that facilitates a structural transformation of the economy through the removal of market distortions and the promotion of competition. In other words, to "unleash private sector growth" Tunisia needs to remove barriers to "creative destruction."
>
> (World Bank 2014, 20)

The World Bank suggests "deeper" economic integration instrumental to "locking in necessary reform" (World Bank 2014, 30).

So far, it appears that pro-investor reforms have not succeeded in attracting private investments that would generate environmentally sustainable and well-paid jobs. As Tunisia's expectation of investment flows from the GCC over the past five years were dampened, Tunisia has once again shifted its focus to the European Union (Karimeh 2015).[9] Some scholars and policymakers (Mustafa Kamel Nabli, former governor general of the Tunisian Central Bank) suspect that EU trade relations will do little to relieve the challenges of unemployment, social justice and environmental sustainability (Pfeifer 2016, 10; Middle East Monitor 2016). The uneven nature of geographic development in the face of climate change requires a radical vision to rethink Tunisia's economic policy and job creation, which requires a strong role for public investment and state regulation. This latter may be thwarted by the multi-year, multi-billion dollar loan packages that were signed by the Tunisian government and the IFIs in May 2016.

Egypt

Egypt has also faced serious economic challenges in the post-uprising period. Capital flight slowed down growth and government expenditures were increased to finance the imports, pensions and public sector salaries. Foreign exchange reserves have dwindled, while inflation and unemployment continue to rise. The insecurity of the post-uprising period has seriously affected the tourism sector. The rising cost of energy has forced various governments to explore new sites for gas and oil and increase the energy imports. The various governments that held office in the post-uprising period found it extremely challenging to reconcile the demands of citizens with the macroeconomic reality they faced. Wedded to the neoliberal economic model, policy makers neglected taking radical steps to reorient the economy, dismissing the calls of activists and workers for economic democracy. Five years on, neoliberalism remains resilient despite the larger role for the state in directing the private sector.

In the immediate post-uprising period, Egypt was ruled by the Supreme Council of the Armed Forces who promised to pave the way for civilian rule. No major economic decisions were taken by the SCAF. The first government voted into office was the one affiliated with the Muslim Brotherhood: Under the one-year rule of the FJP (2012–2013), the government promoted the manufacturing sector and established regional alliances with businessmen in Qatar and Turkey, hoping to adopt a model of Islamic finance to revive Egypt's economy. The group looked to the successful models of Islamic finance and capitalism in Turkey and Malaysia in the hope of replicating them (Ahram Online 2011). With support from Qatar, the FJP believed they could roll out their economic policy of expanding private investments, promoting medium- and small-sized businesses. Despite a belief based on sharia that the state was responsible for looking after the poor and the needy, the FJP's heavy-handed style of rule and their pursuit of neoliberal policies resulted in the deterioration of popular support for the party among some of their broader base.

By mid-2013, Egypt was back under the control of yet another transitional military government. In early 2014, former General Abdel Fatah el-Sisi was elected president and continued to implement neoliberal policies in an increasingly authoritarian environment, curtailing the rights of association and freedom of expression. Under el-Sisi's rule, the Gulf States (except for Qatar) pumped billions of dollars into the Egyptian Central Bank to stabilize the Egyptian pound (Karimeh 2015). Between 2014 and 2016, Egypt has embarked on massive infrastructure projects such as the expansion of the Suez Canal, the building of a new capital city, the expansion of ports and highways, and mining and gas exploration. These projects are mostly undertaken through Public Private Partnerships (PPPs), with the expectation of job growth. To promote the private sector, el-Sisi has introduced tax holidays, provided free land for investment projects, subsidized energy costs and reduced import restrictions to make Egypt more attractive to investors. At the same time, he has implemented austerity measures to reduce state support for public services and subsidies and has increased the cost of living by introducing a VAT.

El-Sisi's rule has also led to the rise of the military, which has restricted the space for popular dissent. As a dominant faction of the ruling class that is now in a position to dictate the terms of the economy, the military finds itself in a powerful position in both economic and political terms. Since the 1980s, the military assumed an increasingly central role in the economy, controlling between 45–60 percent of the economy and producing a variety of civilian goods such as food, housing, health services, and infrastructure, as well as cars, weapons and machinery assembly plants in partnership with transnational corporations (Transparency International 2015; Abul-Magd 2014; Nassif 2013). The military also controls vast tracts of real estate, making it an influential actor in the construction and real estate industries. With such a significant role in the economy, the military relies on its large number of conscripts – totaling a million active and reserve personnel – to absorb a large number of the unemployed.[10]

Egyptian unions are concerned with labor law reform intended to increase the role of the private sector in the economy. However, the official trade union – the Egyptian Trade Union Federation – has remained too close to governments to press for the progressive demands of workers. Newly formed independent trade unions – the Egyptian Federation of Independent Trade Unions, the Egyptian Democratic Labor Congress and the Permanent Congress of Alexandria Workers – lack the resources and institutional powers to translate numerical strength into concrete gains for its diverse membership. Labor struggles constitute an important component of a broader set of social struggles against authoritarian rule and wealth inequality. Since the uprisings, social conflict may appear to have declined, but upon closer examination, public dissatisfaction at the state of the economy persists (Beinin 2016). Despite social protests slowing down, labor protests have not ceased; the first half of 2014 witnessed 1,651 labor protests; 2015 saw 1,117 (Mada Masr 2016).

Beside labor rights, Egyptians struggle over the right to food, a right that has become ever more contentious in the face of rising levels of poverty and unemployment since the uprisings. The importance of food subsidies can be underlined by the fact that more than 80 percent of Egyptians rely on subsidized bread and that more than 50 percent of Egyptians in 2014 lived on $2 a day, a figure much higher in rural areas. That the Egyptian state spends close to $4 billion annually (or 3 percent of GDP) on subsidies does not automatically guarantee the food security of Egyptians as food prices are increasingly subjected to global fluctuations and the ability of the Egyptian state to earn sufficient foreign currency to afford wheat imports (Ayeb and Bush 2014). In rural post-uprising Egypt, small farmers have attempted to reclaim privatized land through occupations, the disruption of agricultural production and legal claims. Small farmers have also demanded rights to land, irrigation water, and lower cost of inputs. In doing so, they have established the Independent Farmers Union, which replaced the state-run General Union of Peasants and the Agricultural Cooperative Union (Ayeb and Bush 2014).

The Egyptian transition has also been complicated by political tensions. Under military rule, the Muslim Brotherhood was crushed, forcing it to go underground while the military continues to wage war in the Sinai region against Islamist forces. Increasingly, a security-oriented approach to post-revolutionary challenges has been adopted, which has shaped the response of the government not only to protestors but also to workers and their demands. Gaining legitimacy for the Egyptian state will rest not only on economic growth but also on reducing political tensions and guaranteeing the security and safety of the public.

Like in Tunisia, IFIs argue that the main problem of Egypt is not economic liberalization *per se*, but rather, the unequal distribution of the wealth generated by liberalization (IMF 2014). Regarding unemployment, they argue that protectionism in certain sectors of the economy coupled with rigid labor legislation prevents the flow of private investments that result in job creation. They recommend opening up protected economic sectors, introducing consumption taxes, and changing existing legislation such as subsidies, workers' rights, farmers' right to land and cheap credit for peasants that may discourage investors from investing in the country (IMF 2015, 16).

Keen on expanding the scope of private sector, the IMF began negotiations in 2013 with the FJP government. However, attempts to adopt more "free" market reforms led to protests forcing the government to avoid signing any agreements with the IMF. In 2011, protests prompted the government to increase the minimum wage and retain the public subsidy program. So far, deregulating the economy and dismantling labor legislation has not resulted in an increase in foreign direct investment levels; however, even if this materializes, there are no guarantees that in the absence of labor protections, investors would create decent and well-paid jobs.

The IFIs' recommendations are couched in a narrow binary framework of the state versus the market, even after the East Asian developmental experience dismantled this dichotomy. As such, the IFIs fail to understand the nature of youth grievances that are the product of two decades of neoliberal reforms which resulted in commodification of social relations manifested in displacement, disillusionment and disappointment of many. The IFIs' narrow critique of the state's role in the economy overlooks the reality of "free" market experiments and the ways that "free markets" can enhance the coercive powers of the state, while constraining the state's progressive redistributive components, i.e. subsidies, social services, social policies and other wealth equalization related policies (Mitchell 1999). In the face of these IFI pressures for maintaining neoliberalism, MENA citizens have pushed for more radical ways of imagining the economy, i.e. resource-allocation, redistribution, nature, social justice, the organization of space, labor rights, environmental rights. These latter dimensions have escaped the neoclassical framework of the IFIs, who continue to push a straitjacket model on countries without taking into account the specificities of societies around the world.

Conclusion

The post-revolutionary transitions in Tunisia and Egypt have not adequately responded to the demands of the popular classes. Instead, in a context of political instability, grassroots demands and influence of international financial institutions, both countries have re-embarked on the path of neoliberalism. The political elites of both countries are faced with serious dilemmas as they try to establish their hegemony in a post-revolutionary context and negotiate the popular demands for bread, freedom and social justice. In responding to these demands, however, the political elites often have disregarded radical proposals for reform pushed by the citizens of both countries. Instead, they have been beholden to a minority of domestic economic elites and have continued to embrace the proposals of IFIs to carry out the business of governing.

While the past five years opened the space for radical ideas such as "citizen-led democracy", and/or "democratic state-led development" (Pfeifer 2015), these ideas did not materialize in the policy realm in either Tunisia or Egypt. Despite popular uprisings and demands for democracy and social justice, it appears that in both Egypt and Tunisia "the default setting is the restoration of neoliberalism with an inclusive mask" (ibid.). The challenges ahead for Egypt and Tunisia require a serious rethinking of the policies adopted in the post-revolutionary period. It can no longer be business as usual for the elite if the two countries are to remain stable. For the citizens of both countries, the past five years have also revealed some of the limitations of public protest without equal demand for public scrutiny of state institutions and the economy (Tripp 2015, 18, 20; Bentivoglio 2014). Instead, neoliberalism has remained resilient in a context of political instability and popular discontent.

Notes

1 Trofimov (2016) suggests that disappointment with the revolution is driving many to leave Tunisia and join ISIS. He argues that fighters are ordinary citizens who are in search of relevance in society and feel that ISIS may be seeking meaningful change and thus enabling them to realize the dreams for relevance that Tunisian revolution failed to fulfill.

2 In January of 1984, under Bourguiba, the Tunisian government tried to dismantle bread subsidies, but after mass protests, which became known as the "January bread riots", the government backed down (Walton and Seddon 1984).

3 This regional disparity dates at least as far back as the 1970s, when government industrialization was concentrated in the north and coastal regions while ignoring the south, central and south-west regions (Walton and Seddon 1984).

4 Variations in Egypt and Tunisia depending on the relationship and social pacts between the official trade unions and the ruling elite.

5 Bouazizi's story however has a deeper root that is traced to a process of land dispossession in the town of Sidi Bouzid where Mohammed Bouazizi worked. Thus this act of apparently urban uprising is directly linked to rural dispossession and land grab for investors by the Tunisian government (Fautras 2015).

6 Estimates indicate that 97 percent of private sector firms are small enterprises, comprising fewer than six low-skilled workers per workplace (World Bank 2015).

7 As of May 2016, a third of workers (2 million) are found in the informal sector (according to a report by the Center for Research and Social Studies), lacking social security and facing low wages and insecure jobs, all attesting to the dismal state of the formal economy to create the needed employment (n.a. 2016).

8 What the World Bank considers state control is the product of privatization that allowed politically connected individuals to gain the support of the state to engage in oligopolistic practices.

9 The rush to invite investors to Tunisia by Essebsi's government has hampered the reconciliation process through the framework of the Truth and Dignity Commission. The Commission was tasked to investigate individuals responsible for corruption during the Ben Ali regime (Barakat 2016). A member of the Gulf Cooperation Council, the United Arab Emirates allegedly attempted to undermine the democratic transition process to get their man, Essebsi to take away power from Ennahda, hoping for a similar outcome as that of the Egyptian coup of 2013 that displaced the Muslim Brotherhood government of Morsi by the military and restored the environment for foreign investments (Donaghy and Alsaafin 2015).

10 The Tunisian military remains small in contrast to other regional militaries – numbering only 27,000 members with a budget of only 1.6 percent of GDP as of 2006 – and refrains from direct involvement in the economy. The army's primary roles are domestic security and international peacekeeping. In fact, Tunisia's military faces serious challenges of manpower, as potential conscripts engage in draft dodging. Military service seems to be disproportionately carried out by those from poorer backgrounds while the middle class manages to escape military service. This likely relates to the military lacking the resources to offer attractive salaries or benefits to retain its conscripts.

References

Abul-Magd, Zeinab. 2014. "Egypt's Adaptable Officers: Power, Business and Discontent", ISPI Online Papers 266, (Milan: Instituto per gli Studi di Politica Internazionale), Accessed: http://www.ispionline.it/sites/default/files/pubblicazioni/analysis_265__2014.pdf

Achy, Lahcen, 2011, 'Tunisia's Economic Challenges,' The Carnegie Papers, December, Washington D.C.

African Development Bank (AFDB). 2015. "Tunisia Economic Outlook", African Economic Outlook, 2015, Accessed: http://www.afdb.org/en/countries/north-africa/tunisia/tunisia-economic-outlook/

Ahram Online. 2011. "Freedom and Justice Party", December 3.

Allal, Amin. 2010. "Reformes neoliberals, clientelismes et protestations en situation autoritaire: es mouvements contestataires dans le basin minier de Gafsa en Tunisie (2008)", *Politique Africaine*, 1, 117, pp. 107–125.

Amnesty International. 2016. "Egypt: Officially You Do Not Exist: Disappeared and Tortured in the name of Counter Terrorism", 13 July, Index number: MDE.

Assaad, R. 2014. "Making Sense of Arab Labor Markets: The Enduring Legacy of Dualism" *IZA Journal of Labor & Development*, 3, 6, pp. 1–25.

Ayeb, H. and Bush R. 2014. "Small Farmer Uprisings and Rural Neglect in Egypt and Tunisia", *MER*, 272, 44, Fall.

Barakat, K. 2016. "Post-Revolution Tunisia and the Promise of Modernization", *Alaraby*, January 20.

Beinin, J. 2015. " Workers and Revolutions in Egypt and Tunisia", *Status Hour*, January 21, accessed: http://www.statushour.com/workers-and-revolutions-in-egypt-and-tunisia.html

Beinin, J. 2016. *Workers and Thieves: Labour Movements and Popular Uprisings in Egypt and Tunisia*, Stanford, CA: Stanford University Press.

Bellin, E. 2014., "Explaining Democratic Divergence: Why Tunisia Has Succeeded and Egypt has Failed", *Project on Middle East Political Science*, December 10, http://pomeps.org/2014/12/10/explaining-democratic-divergence/

Ben Rouine, Chafik (2013), "How the IMF and Global Finance Are Trying to Block a Democratic Examination of Tunisia's Debt", *Jubilee Debt Campaign*, July 17: Accessed: http://jubileedebt.org.uk/blog/imf-block-democratic-tunisia-debt
Bentivoglio, Katie (2014), "Harsh Campaign Rhetoric Deepens Tunisia's Divides", *Carnegie Endowment for International Peace*, December 5.
British Broadcasting Corporation (BBC). 2016a. "Tunisia: Curfew in Place after Unemployment Protests Spread", January 22: http://www.bbc.com/news/world-africa-35388654
British Broadcasting Corporation. 2016b. "Tunisia Protests: President Vows to End 'Ordeal' of Unemployed", January 22: http://www.bbc.com/news/world-africa-35384181
Donaghy, R. and Alsaafin, L. 2015. "UAE Conspiring to End Tunisia's Fledgling Democracy: Source", *Middle East Eye*, December 7.
Economist Intelligence Unit (EIU) (2015), "Tunisia's Economic Challenges," January 14, accessed: http://country.eiu.com/article.aspx?articleid=1342653318&Country=Tunisia &topic=Economy
El Amraoui, A. 2015. "Tunisia's Ghannouchi: Poverty Is a Root Cause of Terror", *Aljazeera*, November 14.
El-Said, H. and Harrigan, J. 2014. "Economic Reform, Social Welfare, and Instability: Jordan, Egypt, Morocco, and Tunisia, 1983–2004, " *The Middle East Journal* Vol. 68 (1), pp. 99–121.
Fautras, M. 2015. "Land Injustices, Contestations and Community Protest in the Rural Areas of Sidi Bouzid (Tunisia): The Roots of the 'Revolution'?" *Spatial Justice*, January 7.
Gamal, W. 2011. "We Will Not Pay the Debts of Tyranny", *Jadaliyya*, October 28.
Hartshorn, I.M. 2015. "Social Dialogue under the Gun in Tunisia", *Jadaliyya*, October 14.
Hoddouk, Walid (2016), "Letter from Tunis", *Carnegie Endowment for International Peace*, February 5.
International Monetary Fund. 2014. "Toward New Horizons: Arab Economic Transformations amid Political Transitions", Middle East and Central Asia Department, Washington DC.
International Monetary Fund. 2015. "Arab Republic of Egypt", IMF Country Report, No. 15/33, February.
Karimeh, A. 2015. "Tunisia Courts Foreign Investment", Al Monitor, May 1.
King, S. J. 2003. *Liberalization Against Democracy: The Local Politics of Economic Reform in Tunisia*, Bloomington, IN: Indiana University Press.
Mada M. 2016. "1117 Labour Protests across Egypt in 2015: Democracy Meter Report", January 11.
Marzouki, N. and Meddeeb, H. 2015. "Tunisia: Democratic Miracle or Mirage?", *Jadaliyya*, June 11.
Middle East Monitor. 2016. "EU-Tunisia Trade Agreements Did Not Support Development", March 4.
Mitchell, T. 1999. "Dreamland: The Neoliberalism of Your Desires", MER2010, 29, Spring.
Murphy, E. 2011. "The Tunisian Uprising and the Precarious Path to Democracy", *Mediterranean Politics*, 16, pp. 299–305.
N.A. 2016. "Third of Active Workforce Outside Formal Economy and Social Protection Programs", May 23, Tunisia-tn.com, accessed: http://tunisia-tn.com/third-of-active-workforce-outside-formal-economy-and-social-protection-programs/
Nassif, H. B. 2013. "Wedded to Mubarak: The Second Careers and Financial Rewards of Egypt's Military Elite, 1981–2011", *Middle East Journal*, 67, 4, Autumn, pp. 509–530.

Pfeifer, K. 1999. "How Tunisia, Morocco, Jordan and Even Egypt became IMF 'success stories', in the 1990s", *MER 201*, 29. Available online at: : http://www.merip.org/mer/mer210/how-tunisia-morocco-jordan-even-egypt-became-imf-success-stories-1990s (accessed December 3, 2015).

Pfeifer, K. 2015. "Rebels, Reformers and Empire: Alternative Economic Programs for Egypt and Tunisia", *MER 274*, 55, Spring. Available online at: http://www.merip.org/mer/mer274/rebels-reformers-empire (accessed January 24, 2016).

Pfeifer, K. 2016 "Neoliberal Transformation and the Uprisings in Tunisia and Egypt", in *Political and Socio-Economic Change in the Middle East and North Africa: Gender Perspectives and Survival Strategies* edited by Roksana Bahramitash and Hadi Esfahani, Basingstoke: Palgrave.

Reuters. 2016. "Tunisia Tourism Revenue Down 54 percent in Jan/Feb Follows Attacks in 2015", March 31.

Rutherford, B. K. 2008. *Egypt After Mubarak: Liberalism, Islam and Democracy in the Arab World*, Princeton, NJ: Princeton University Press.

Saghir, J. 1993. "Privatization in Tunisia", January, Report No. 11645, Private Sector Development and Privatization Group, The World Bank.

Schielke, Samuli, 2015, *Egypt in the Future Tense: Hope, Frustration and Ambivalence before and after 2011,* Indiana: Indiana University Press.

The Economist. 2015. "Tunisia Confronts Corruption, the Economy and Islamic State", November 17.

The Economist. 2016. "Truth and Reconciliation in Tunisia: Shadows from the Past", April 30.

The World Bank.2008. Tunisia's Global Integration: Second Generation of Reforms to Boost Growth and Employment, Draft Report No. 40129-TN, May. The World Bank. 2014. "MENA Quarterly Economic Brief, July 2014: Predictions, Perceptions and Economic Reality",

The World Bank. 2015 "Tunisia Overview", http://www.worldbank.org/en/country/tunisia/overview (accessed January 23, 2016).

The World Bank. 2015. "World Bank: Economic Indicators Failed to Predict Arab Uprisings", October 21: http://www.worldbank.org/en/news/press-release/2015/10/21/economic-indicators-failed-to-predict-arab-uprisings http://www.worldbank.org/en/region/mena/publication/mena-quarterly-economic-brief-july-2014_(accessed January 2, 2016).

Transparency International Defence and Security. 2015. "Egypt, Arab Rep. Country Recommendations".

Tripp, C. 2015. "Battlefields of the Republic: The Struggle for Public Space in Tunisia", *LSE Middle East Center Paper Series*, 13, December.

Trofimov, Y. 2016. "How Tunisia Became a Top Source of ISIS Recruits", *Wall Street Journal*, February 25.

Turner, R. 2015. "Travel and Tourism Economic Impact 2015: Tunisia": http://www.wttc.org/-/media/files/reports/economic%20impact%20research/countries%202015/tunisia2015.pdf

United Nations. 2015. Human Development Report 2015: Work for Human Development, http://report.hdr.undp.org/ (accessed May 2, 2016).

UNDP. 2010. "Egypt's Progress Towards Achieving The Millennium Development Goals".

Verme, Paolo 2013. "Facts vs. Perceptions: Understanding Inequality in Egypt", January 24.

Verme, Paolo, Branko Milanovic, Sherine Al-Shawarby, Sahar El Tawila, May Gadallah, and Enas Ali A. El-Majeed 2014. *Inside Inequality in the Arab Republic of Egypt: Facts and Perceptions across People, Time, and Space*, World Bank Studies. Washington, DC: World Bank.

Wahish, N. 2000. "Not so Instructable Liquidity: Recession is Dragging the Stock Market down", *Al Ahram Weekly*, no. 502, October 5–11.

Walton, J. K. and S. Seddon. 1994. *Free Market and Bread Riots*, Oxford: Wiley-Blackwell.

Index

For Product Safety Concerns and Information please contact our EU representative GPSR@taylorandfrancis.com Taylor & Francis Verlag GmbH, Kaufingerstraße 24, 80331 München, Germany